AMERICAN HISTORY IN FOCUS SERIES

Under the Editorship of
William H. Goetzmann

THE COLONIAL HORIZON:
AMERICA IN THE SIXTEENTH AND SEVENTEENTH CENTURIES
William H. Goetzmann, University of Texas

THE AMERICAN REVOLUTION:
THE ANGLO-AMERICAN RELATION, 1763–1794
Charles R. Ritcheson, Southern Methodist University

YEARS OF TURMOIL:
CIVIL WAR AND RECONSTRUCTION
John Niven, Claremont Graduate School

THE GILDED AGE: AMERICA, 1865–1900
Richard A. Bartlett, The Florida State University

THE AGE OF INSECURITY: AMERICA, 1920–1945
Robert A. Divine, University of Texas

THE AMERICAN REVOLUTION: THE ANGLO-AMERICAN RELATION, 1763–1794

Interpretive Articles and Documentary Sources

Edited by

CHARLES R. RITCHESON

Southern Methodist University

▲ ADDISON-WESLEY PUBLISHING COMPANY

Reading, Massachusetts / Menlo Park, California / London / Don Mills, Ontario

For Brendan, Mark, Philip and Steven:
The Continuum

PREFACE:
THE AMERICAN HISTORY IN FOCUS SERIES

History is the recorded deeds, ideas, and emotions of men. Living history is the re-recording of these deeds, ideas, and emotions by interpreters in each new generation. *The American History in Focus Series* seeks to provide the student with what might be called "the varieties of living historical experience," from a mid-twentieth century point of view. Each of the major historical epochs in American history is brought into focus by means of modern interpretive articles written by major scholars in the field, scholars who may be said to be on "the growing tip" of historical knowledge. Their interests span a vast range of historical methods and commitments. Collectively, they represent the multiple points of view of political, social, economic, diplomatic, military, and intellectual historians—historians who are nonetheless very much products of our own times and affected by current interests. These selections are concerned in almost every instance with answering that simple but all-important question—"so what?"—as it relates to our historical heritage. Of what relevance has past American historical experience been to the total course of human development, to the emergence of American values, achievements, problems, and predicaments? How did I, a citizen of the United States, get to be where and what I am today with all the privileges, burdens, and responsibilities that are entailed? What experiences of quality and nobility of conduct can be noted in the past against which we can measure our own aspirations and behavior—for we can the better recognize quality in our own lives for having seen it somewhere before in the recent or distant past?! By portraying realistically the complexities, relativisms, and ambiguities in the interpretations of time past, the editors and authors represented in these volumes provide new perspectives for determining our cultural identity.

Each of the volumes concentrates on a major period in American history, from colonial times to the present. Each is structured around focal, interpretive articles of modern historians with several varieties of history represented. These focal articles are supplemented by important and revealing historical documents of the particular era with which the historian is concerned. These are samples of the kinds of materials out of which he has constructed his interpretation. They are intended to serve two purposes: first, to give today's student a "feel" for the language and perspectives of the people of earlier generations; second, to provide materials with which to *test* the generalizations of the modern interpreters—to provide a laboratory situation whereby the student may critically examine some of the interpreter's answers and hopefully even some of his questions. For serious historical study requires constant criticism of historical generalizations, and it is too little recognized that such criticism might properly begin with the question, "did the historian ask the right questions of the period?"

Given the above, it should be obvious that these are experimental books especially designed as tools for learning. They are neither exercises in belletristic virtuosity, nor are they "canned" problems where the rules are clear and for the clever, the answers pat. Rather they are intended to be sophisticated, broad-based springboards to future discussion. As an added dimension we have experimented with the addition of pictorial materials which are not intended as idle embellishment but should rather serve as integral parts of the text—as further documents of the time. These, too, when examined with care, afford points of focus.

In attempting to draw a distinction between the nature of science and the nature of history, an historian of science, Derek de Solla Price, makes a striking analogy. He sees science as a "many-brained" machine into whose circuits all of the latest "growing tip" discoveries, however limited, can be wired so that advances in knowledge can result without the necessity for retracing in detail the historical steps involved in previous discoveries. History, on the other hand, is a "single-brained" enterprise in which each historian has to go back over all the sources and interpretations of the past before making his own generalization.* The *American History in Focus Series* attempts to draw upon the advantages of both. For the individual student it is clearly a "single-brained" experience. But in assembling between two covers modern interpretations, along with documents from the past, both written and pictorial, we have attempted to provide the advantages of a "many-brained" approach as well, so as to encourage the student to examine the nature of historical enquiry as a process of thought, and to address himself to the problem of cultural identity in a changing world.

William H. Goetzmann
General Editor

---

*Derek D. Price, "Two Cultures and One Historian of Science," *Teachers College Record*, **64**, 7, April 1963, pp. 528–531.

CONTENTS

INTRODUCTION

The American Revolution marked the birth of a nation and the collapse of an empire. Its central "problem" was constitutional: what was the true nature of the colonial relationship? what was sovereignty within the Empire? who possessed it? As the winds blew to storm, leaders on both sides of the Atlantic answered these questions with new concepts of imperial government; and by 1778, even in British thinking, something very like the idea of a "Commonwealth of Nations" had emerged. The American position was always one step (at least) beyond Britain's, however, and the last desperate efforts in 1778 to save the Empire by granting home rule to the colonies failed. Once Americans had made the decision for independence, the question of sovereignty had been settled to their satisfaction; there was no room for compromise.

The violent secession of the thirteen colonies was shocking and, to Britons and to many Americans—one-third of them, John Adams estimated—repugnant; but it was no bolt from the blue. True, Englishmen and Americans shared much in the eighteenth century: language; the common law; many ideas about education, religion, society, and the nature of government; and an economic system which was, on balance, mutually beneficial and profitable. These were elements of a common civilization deeply rooted in the past. Working against this and eroding it, however, was a growing body of events, conditions, and assumptions, definably "American," whose effect was to sharpen the distinction between colonials and Britons at home. The Puritan idea—a community of "visible saints"—remained a powerful and formative force in colonial (especially New England) life long after Charles II restored "Arminian and prelatical corruptions" in the mother country. This idea was the source of a strong moral certitude and, according to Professor Bernard Bailyn, a tradition of "anti-authoritarianism," which helps explain revolutionary America's extraordinary tenacity of purpose and contempt for compromise in adversity. Indian wars, too, remote to farmers of Dorset or Yorkshire, were horrors all too familiar to their colonial counterparts. Even the Great Awakening, the religious convulsion which began in the 1730's and disrupted the old ecclesiastical order, fostered a sense of common preoccupation in British America. In addition, notable technological advances—improved internal communication by road and water, a postal service, a rapidly proliferating and free press—drew Americans closer together while distance from Britain remained constant. Finally, there was colonial participation in European and "world" wars. Four times from the accession of William and Mary in 1688–1689, Americans fought for an imperial cause. While some episodes were less than glorious, there were proud, even brilliant achievements: the Bostonians' expedition against Acadia in King

William's War (1688–1697); the South Carolinians' blows at Biloxi and Mobile, and the seizure of Port Royal by Boston recruits in Queen Anne's War (1702–1713); the seige and capture of Louisburg by New Englanders in King George's War (1741–1748); and, most recently, various exploits in the French and Indian War (1754–1763). There was never a military effort involving all or even most of the colonies simultaneously, to be sure; and ministers in Whitehall, vexed by procrastinations and evasions in responding to imperial requisitions, rarely considered colonial contributions sufficient. In the American context, however, they provided precedent for and confidence in colonial military cooperation, the more meaningful for the future because they were accompanied by suspicion amounting to certainty that Britain would sacrifice Americans' gains won on the hazardous field of battle to her interests in other quarters of the globe.

Under pressures emanating from the mother country, the colonial experience hardened into the base for national existence. The terms of the process were economic and political; the issue was the imperial constitution. For a hundred years before the American Revolution, British statesmen believed that the North American colonies required a greater degree of control. Periodically, new administrative organs were created and old ones invigorated, but, in truth, little was accomplished in the way of effective centralization within the Empire. A quarrel over royal governors' salaries developed late in the seventeenth century, notably in Massachusetts and New York. The British Government insisted that colonial assemblies provide a source of funds independent of local control; the colonies held tenaciously to the power of the purse, a "right" claimed because their assemblies were "parliaments in miniature." A last attempt to impose a solution (on British terms) came in 1767 when the ill-fated Townshend taxes sought to create a colonial civil list, but, by then, the Americans were moving rapidly toward more forcible means of contesting the question.

Economically, the colonies found their roles within the British Empire prescribed by the mercantile system, the perfect means, it was believed in London (as well as in Paris and Madrid), of ensuring imperial self-sufficiency, opulence, and power. In theory, British capital and industrial production would supply the colonies who, in turn, would furnish raw materials and exotic items, like sugar, which would have to be purchased abroad if not found within the Empire. The basic assumption was the harmonious balancing of economic interests; and for much of the life of the First British Empire, the system worked to the reciprocal benefit of Britons and Americans. By 1763, however, it seemed obvious on both sides of the Atlantic that the balance had been seriously impaired. New Englanders needed more sugar and molasses (and at lower prices) than could be found in the British West Indies. Middle Atlantic colonies needed new markets for their wheat and flour. Southern colonies had more timber and victuals than customers. Acts of trade and navigation, the bastions of the mercantile system, to the contrary notwithstanding, American trade with the French and Spanish islands in the West Indies was flourishing by 1763. It was illegal, of course: under the best of conditions, smuggling; in war, trading with the enemy. British ministers, exasperated and impatient, believed that a reckoning was long overdue.

There were other problems, too, arising rather ironically from Britain's great victory over France and Spain in the French and Indian War, but bearing directly on the coming crisis in Anglo-American relations. In 1763, the Peace of Paris gave Britain an enormously expanded empire and, for the first time, a large number of civilized, non-British subjects, the French Canadians. How were new territory and people to be governed? how related to the older, seaboard colonies? how protected from Indian attack or reconquest? Further, Britain was saddled with a staggering war debt whose magnitude reflected campaigns fought for Americans, who persistently refused to bear a fair share of the cost of victory. Clearly, a new ordering of the Empire was required; but how was it to be financed? Who finally had the right to determine the matter? Upon the answers given to these deep questions turned the fate of an empire and of a nation. "You are happy in the cession of Canada," the Comte de Vergennes told an English visitor in 1763. The future first minister of France during the American Revolution continued: "We, perhaps ought to think ourselves happy that you have acquired it. Delivered from a neighbor whom they always feared, your other colonies will soon discover that they stand no longer in need of your protection. You will call on them to contribute toward supporting the burthen which they have helped to bring on you. They will answer by shaking off all dependence." The Frenchman's pronouncement was a very great simplification, and it contained more sour grapes than prescience. Yet Vergennes had clearly understood at least one aspect of Britain's imperial problem better than Britain did herself: that colonials would submit to taxation without their consent no more than Britons at home.

American historians have commonly blamed George Grenville for taking the high road to war with America. This, too, is a gross simplification. By the time he became minister in 1763, fundamental decisions about the Empire and its future had already been made: for example, the retention of Canada in preference to Britain's West Indian conquests during the French and Indian War. It had already been determined, too, to protect the vast backcountry with a force of 10,000 regular British troops. It remained to Grenville to build upon these decisions in an attempt to formulate a comprehensive imperial plan. First came the problem of defraying new expenses, some £360,000 annually for the 10,000 troops alone, and this at a time when Britons were staggering under an unprecedented national debt and tax burden. Why should not America bear at least a portion of the cost, Grenville reasoned. The colonies had benefited greatly from the recent war and now enjoyed military protection in the backcountry. Thus, Grenville sought an American revenue with the Sugar

Act of 1764, in effect, an amendment of an act passed three decades earlier. Duty on foreign molasses was reduced for American importers, but it was to be efficiently collected, a sharp break with past practice. The new measure was something more than mere regulation of trade, the traditional purpose of acts of trade and navigation. It also aimed at raising a revenue. Here was a new concept which touched upon delicate constitutional points.

At the very best, Grenville's assistants told him, anticipated revenue under the Act would not exceed £45,000 annually. More was needed if America was to contribute a respectable portion of the total required. The result was the Stamp Act passed in Spring, 1765, with virtually no opposition in Parliament. There was little question in any British mind of the justice and equity of the act; nor was there doubt in Parliament about the right to pass such legislation. At issue was the welfare of the whole Empire. Parliament alone possessed the competence to act on such a grand scale.

It was a fatal miscalculation. Action produced reaction; and the colonies took the first real steps toward union to fend off what appeared to be a calculated invasion of the first right of Englishmen: not to be taxed but by consent. The Stamp Act Congress, resolutions, combinations against British imports, a flood of pamphlets, and riots in the streets displayed the American temper. For a time, the thrust of the colonial argument went to the distinction between taxes to regulate trade (external taxes) and taxes to raise revenue (internal taxes). Whatever theoreticians might claim, it was obvious that the act would not be accepted peaceably in the colonies.

In 1766, the Rockingham Ministry (which had succeeded Grenville's in the summer of 1765) repealed the Stamp Act. The reason was not constitutional in nature, however, since a retreat from the principle of parliamentary supremacy was totally unacceptable; rather, it was because the Stamp Act was commercially "inexpedient." In fact, the power of Parliament was given its most uncompromising statement in the Declaratory Act which accompanied the repeal: Parliament possessed full power to legislate for the colonies "in all cases whatsoever."

The new legislation did not solve the pressing imperial problems, however. Indeed, the need for a colonial revenue was more urgent than ever; and Americans had added a dangerous complication by raising questions about the power of Parliament. The repeal of the Stamp Act notwithstanding, by 1765–1766, the earlier plans for a well-ordered, harmonious, expanding Anglo-American empire were giving place to the explosive and fatal constitutional issue.

Even the advent to power of William Pitt, newly created Earl of Chatham, in July, 1766, did not reverse the drift toward catastrophe. Indeed, his physical and mental collapse a few months later removed from the scene one of America's most powerful sympathizers, and opened the door to an intensification of the controversy. Without Chatham to hold him in check, the irresponsible Charles Townshend, Chancellor of the Exchequer, whose concept of Empire began and ended with the British budget, agreed to a reduction in the land tax at home and promised to make up the deficiency by taxing America for revenue. The proceeds of his taxes, he said, would provide for an American civil list. Colonial governors and other royal officials in America would thus be guaranteed salaries beyond the control of local assemblies. Americans, spurred on by a growing and vociferous radical minority, the Sons of Liberty, saw Townshend's measure as proof of a covert design in Britain to overthrow constitutional government both at home and in the colonies.

Still, the breaking point remained at some distance. In America, reaction to Townshend's measures tended to sullen resentment instead of open resistance. Despite British troops in Boston and colonial merchants' combinations against British products, there was clearly a disposition on both sides of the Atlantic to proceed cautiously. By 1770, there was an apparent relaxation of tensions, aided in no small way by Lord North, the new first minister of the King, who moved in March to repeal all of Townshend's taxes save that on tea. They were "uncommercial," he said; but tea would remain taxed as a symbol of the power of Parliament.

The exception may have saved Parliament's pride. It also saved the radical cause in America, grist to the mill for men like Sam Adams and his friends, who were already determined for many reasons, not all of them unselfish, to drive events on to a final and complete rupture with Britain. The "Boston massacre," which occurred on the very day North moved the repeal of Townshend's taxes in London, prepared the atmosphere for violence. Subsequently, Parliament's well-meant but ill-timed favor to the near-bankrupt East India Company brought tea, free of duty usually payable in Britain but still subject to the tax originally imposed by Charles Townshend, to American harbors cheaper than it could be purchased in the mother country. It was a plot, the Sons of Liberty declared, to bribe Americans to submit to an unconstitutional tax. Up and down the eastern seaboard the tea was refused. In Boston, it was destroyed, a grave sin indeed against public order and private property. "Blows," wrote King George III, "must decide."

The Coercive Acts closed the port of Boston until compensation was paid for the tea. The government of Massachusetts was reformed to give more power to the governor, particularly the right to name members of the Council. Troops were to be quartered at his order. Treason cases might (under an obsolete act of Henry VIII) be tried in England, a reflection on the impartiality of colonial courts of law. Finally, there was the Quebec Act, one of the North Ministry's few claims to statesmanship, which was unfortunately interpreted by angry Americans as an attempt to create a Roman Catholic French Canadian threat on their northern and western flanks.

The great wave of sympathy and support for Boston evident throughout the colonies should have indicated to the British Ministry that resistance was spreading far beyond Massachusetts. A Continental Congress was summoned, and in September, 1774, voted strict nonimportation and nonexportation. Thoroughly angry, Parliament responded with the harsh Restraining Act: colonies accepting the authority of Congress were forbidden to participate in the Newfoundland fisheries, a vicious blow at New England. This and certain other trade restrictions would remain in force until there was a general submission to Parliament.

Essentially a moderate and a man of peace, North, as well as a majority of his cabinet colleagues, was not content with threats and measures of force, however. In the midst of the debate on the Restraining Act, the leader of the British Government moved his "Conciliatory Proposition," the significant first glimmering of a retreat from the principle of the absolute sovereignty of Parliament. It thus marks the opening of the long road leading in the nineteenth century to a Commonwealth of Nations; but in Spring, 1775, Americans were no longer questioning Parliament's power to tax: at issue was Parliament's sovereignty in any case whatsoever. The argument espoused by many eminent Americans, among them Franklin, Jefferson, and Adams, said the colonies were bound to Britain through a common executive, the King. It was a theme which figured, too, in the Olive Branch Petition dispatched by the Second Continental Congress. However, it was a theme which ran absolutely counter to the mainstream of constitutional development in Britain since the Glorious Revolution in the seventeenth century. George III rejected American appeals to him to override Parliament and Ministry not because he was a bloody-minded tyrant, but because he was too good a Whig.

Debate became irrelevant in April, 1775, when blood flowed at Lexington and Concord. In quick sequence there came the American military thrust against Quebec, the official Proclamation of Rebellion, and the Prohibitory Act, cutting off all intercourse with colonies accepting the authority of the Continental Congress. American opinion set steadily for independence, spurred on by Thomas Paine's remarkable series, *Common Sense*, which simplified the issues for Americans by concentrating blame and hatred on the King.

Honorable men searched their hearts in agony as they considered the implications of independence; and in July, the grand pronouncement was made. For the overwhelming majority of those in positions of leadership, there was never a moment's backward glance. The Howe Peace Commission, holding out terms based on North's Conciliatory Proposition, was firmly rebuffed in September, 1776; and in 1778, the offer of "home rule" by the Carlisle Commission met a similar fate.

The success of the American Revolution turned upon seven critical points. The American thrust against Quebec late in 1775 failed; but Benedict Arnold was able to fend off the British pursuer, Sir Guy Carleton, until severe weather spoiled his opportunity to destroy the American force and to isolate New England.

Secondly, Sir William Howe's evacuation of Boston in March, 1776, was followed by retirement to Halifax. Had he gone directly to New York, where loyalists were numerous, his presence would probably have held the colony to its allegiance to the King.

Thirdly, the same general's failure to follow up his crushing victory over Washington in the New York area early in the summer of 1776 allowed the rebel chieftain and the balance of his force to escape across the Jersies and into Pennsylvania, keeping the field and rallying American morale and support.

The desperate gamble against Trenton and Princeton at the Christmas season, 1776, was critical to the American cause. Washington's most brilliant victory saved Philadelphia for a time and, even more important, American self respect.

Next, the tenacity of Washington and his small army at Valley Forge in Winter, 1777–1778, kept the rebellion alive to the south, while in other quarters important events were unfolding.

In October, 1777, John Burgoyne surrendered his army at Saratoga. At a blow, Britain lost a major portion of her army in America. More important, France dropped her policy of clandestine aid to the rebels and came into the war openly as their ally, a testimonial both to the adroit diplomacy of Benjamin Franklin and to France's desire to have revenge for the humiliation of 1763.

Finally, there was Yorktown, the result of a magnificent (and rare) coordination of forces by French and Americans. At the crucial moment, the French fleet kept the British out of the Chesapeake; and Washington and Rochambeau pushed their seige of Cornwallis to a victorious conclusion. In America, the war was over. Independence was a *fait accompli*, requiring only formal recognition in a treaty of peace.

The Peace of Paris was an unparalleled triumph for American diplomacy; and the lion's share of the credit belongs to Benjamin Franklin—a certain amount of teeth-gnashing by John Adams notwithstanding. The subtle and astute Philadelphian turned every opportunity to maximum advantage: Britain's war-weariness; her fear of a permanent Franco-American connection; desire to regain America's trade; many Britons' earnest desire for reconciliation and restoration in some form or other of an Anglo-American community; his old friendship with the Earl of Shelburne, at the head of a ministry in 1782 and the leading apostle of a new Anglo-American community; and the amiable pliancy of the British negotiator Richard Oswald, who very nearly pledged Franklin the cession of Canada. Even though the northern colony eluded Franklin and his colleagues, Adams and Jay, the terms they won were so favorable that Vergennes, the French leader, was astounded and not at all pleased. Independence was acknowledged. The "liberty" (not "right") to participate in the Newfoundland fisheries was conferred. The great expanse of backcountry east of the Mississippi and south of Canada was ceded. British forces were bound to evacuate American territory "with all convenient speed";

and they were not to carry away any Negro slaves or other property. For her part, America acknowledged that massive pre-war debts to British creditors remained binding, and that no "legal impediement" would be allowed to interfere with their recovery. Loyalists benefited from a general amnesty; and Congress, it was promised, would "earnestly recommend" to the states restoration of confiscated loyalist property. Those who chose to remove themselves from the United States would have a year to come and go freely, peaceably winding up their affairs. A secret clause, studiously withheld by American negotiators from French allies and Spanish co-belligerents, defined the southern frontier in the event of a British conquest of Florida, then held by Spain.

That the Treaty of Paris represented a defeat and humiliation for Britain cannot be denied; but, as the subsequent treaties with France and the other belligerents clearly demonstrated, it was not a case of a Britain in chains at the wheels of her enemies' chariots. Aside from the concessions to America, her losses were relatively minor, a fact which indicates to the great British imperial historian, the late Vincent Harlow, that the terms of the American treaty reflected Lord Shelburne's vision of a restored Anglo-American community. The founder of a "Second British Empire," he did not delude himself that there could be a complete restoration of the old order. Rather, he looked to "trade, not dominion"; and he saw in Britain and America a natural meshing of reciprocal interests. Let the former colonials subject the frontier, pushing ever further to the westward, settling and governing the vast inland stretches of the continent. Britain, using Canada as a base, would supply the necessary manufactured goods and capital.

The event proved Shelburne too sanguine. He underestimated war-borne bitternesses in both countries. Tensions and quarrels marked the post-war period. Britain's neo-mercantilist policy peremptorily excluded the new republic along with other foreign nations from the rich carrying trade to her West India islands in 1783. The measure greatly benefited British shippers and merchants, but Americans immediately deduced a plan to humiliate, wound, and, if possible, to destroy their country. Secondly, the peace treaty was broken by both signatories. Loyalists, returning to America to salvage what they might, met harsh and sometimes brutal treatment at "patriot" hands. Further, southerners, who owed the great balance of pre-war debts to British merchants, remained obdurate in refusing to pay. The British army had "abducted" numerous slaves after the armistice, they said; and it continued to occupy certain posts along the frontier with Canada. The sterile and frustrating controversy over "prior infraction" prolonged animosities and rendered real peace more difficult.

Under the surface of harsh words, charges, and countercharges, however, a new, complex, and powerful community of interests *was* developing between the two nations and their citizens. Intimately involved was the success of the

American Revolution, if this is understood to mean the establishment of the United States on a firm and respectable political and economic foundation. The rich pre-war commerce revived and expanded. American skippers and British factors worked together in the Far East, a fact known and countenanced by the London authorities themselves. In times of dearth, American grain sustained British North America, the West Indies, and the home islands themselves. Private capital flowed from Britain in a mighty stream to help fund the American national debt. Widespread smuggling and collusion in evading restrictions on trade and navigation furnished another kind of evidence that a new Anglo-American community of interests was emerging. Alexander Hamilton and the Federalists built a nation upon it. The era of the American Revolution ends, then, not in 1783 but with the final settlement of post-war problems in John Jay's treaty with Lord Grenville in 1794.

1 / THE DEVELOPMENT OF THE REVOLUTIONARY CRISIS

INTERPRETATION

LAWRENCE HENRY GIPSON,
Colonies Ripe for Revolt:
The Older British North American Colonies in 1763

Lawrence Henry Gipson, Research Professor of History, Emeritus, at Lehigh University, is one of the most distinguished living American historians. His masterly survey of the British Empire before the American Revolution, from which the following excerpt is taken, has just recently been brought to a conclusion with Volume XIII (Volume XIV, now in preparation, is devoted to bibliography).

The first six volumes of Professor Gipson's study were awarded the Loubat Prize in 1948 by Columbia University. Volume VII was awarded the Bancroft Prize in 1949, and Volume X was awarded the Pulitzer Prize in 1962.

A student of Charles M. Andrews, Professor Gipson has devoted the balance of his scholarly life to an examination of the First British Empire before its disruption. His massive and unique contribution has been to place the American crisis within its imperial context. He is preoccupied not merely with "politics," but with the impact on Anglo-American relations of geography, social and economic conditions, technological and scientific developments, and the emergence of cultural differences between colonies and the mother country.

The termination of the war that was waged for nine years from 1754 to 1763 between Great Britain and France and their respective allies brought many profound changes to the British Empire. Some of these were visible, such as the geopolitical revisions. Others, of equal if not greater importance, were psychological and could only be sensed. It is our purpose to examine some of the changes in both categories in order to make clear why the British Empire after 1763 was, in certain respects, quite different from the Empire that had existed for over a century before 1754, and why a crisis in the relations of Great Britain with her North American colonies soon developed after the Peace of Paris.

Lawrence Henry Gipson. *The Triumphant Empire: Thunder Clouds Gather in the West, 1763–1766,* (The British Empire before the American Revolution, Vol. X), New York, Alfred A. Knopf, 1961, Chap. I. Reprinted by permission of the publisher.

First of all, the ascertainable boundaries of the Old British Empire, or at least those that had been generally recognized, were vastly increased in 1763 over those that had existed in 1754, as has been developed in the preceding volume of this series. Indeed, new territories embraced within the limits so defined had tripled its size, at the most conservative calculation. Moreover, beyond these accepted boundaries were other areas that could now be called potential British territory—the undefined western sweep both of Canada and of the possessions of the Hudson's Bay Company. There was the expanding sphere of influence of the United East India Company with its setting up of factories in the Far East that must be included as lying within the British imperial orbit by 1763. The world, in fact, had never before witnessed so vast an accumulation of exploitable material resources by any single power as had resulted from processes of expansion which, beginning with the attempt to colonize Newfoundland by Sir Humphrey Gilbert in the days of Queen Elizabeth I, culminated in the Peace of Paris of 1763. It may properly be called in that year the great Empire—an empire with which the Spanish, Russian, and Dutch empires, extensive as they were, could in no respect be compared for dynamic quality, wide-spread enlightenment and freedom of expression, political maturity, industrial development, and accumulated wealth. Further, it possessed the ability to protect itself by means of a navy that dominated the high seas and was unchallengeable even by the combined navies of the other three great powers.

So huge an enlargement of the Empire inevitably brought with it particular problems. Among others was the difficulty involved in establishing within the new possessions a type of government that would reflect the spirit and genius of the British people and would thus be in harmony with the fundamental principles on which was based the control of the much more contracted Empire of the pre-war period. The steps taken to that end in 1763 or soon afterwards, both in North America and in the West Indies, have been given full treatment in Volume IX of this series. It is only necessary, therefore, to observe that, consistent with peculiar local conditions, the form of government decided upon was patterned roughly after that of the royal colony. The expectation was that all those things characteristic of a royal colony—for example, the setting-up of a law-making body representative of its freemen—would be realized at the earliest possible moment.

Another problem, presented by the manner in which the war was terminated in North America, had to do with the establishment of policies that would guarantee fair treatment of those western Indians, whose guardianship the British government had felt impelled to assume because of the solemn commitments made in such treaties as that concluded at Easton, Pennsylvania, in 1758. These commitments involved not only the recognition of the superior rights of the natives to trans-Appalachian lands and the safeguarding of these rights in the face of pressure by white men eager to acquire these same lands, but also the obligation to seek to protect the red men from the unfair practices of white traders and from the exclusive domination of the Indian trade by merchants of any one colony.

A third, and also a post-war, problem was the provision of adequate means for guaranteeing the security of North America, the eastern part of which, from Hudson Bay to the southern tip of Florida, was now wholly embodied within the Empire. Should or could this great responsibility be turned over to the older continental colonies, whose welfare and safety were obviously most immediately and vitally at stake? Or should this be the exclusive responsibility of the mother country? Or should it be in the nature of a joint responsibility, as had been the case in waging the New World phase of the Great War for the Empire between 1754 and 1763? If so, after what manner? One thing at least seemed to be quite clear in light of the experience of the late war: those security forces that must be employed for routine garrison duty in critical areas —such as the new Province of Quebec, the scattered forts and posts in the Indian country, and certain strategic seaboard points: Halifax in Nova Scotia, Louisbourg on Cape Breton Island, Placentia and St. John's in Newfoundland, St. Augustine in East Florida, and Pensacola and Mobile in West Florida— must be regular troops held to their duty by military discipline.

Granted this to be the case, it brings us to a fourth problem. Who should be expected to assume the burden of the very considerable expense involved in these strictly North American security measures, as well as other charges upon the tax-payers, that altered conditions in the New World seemed to require? In this connection it should be pointed out that the war had brought unprecedented prosperity to countless people and even great fortunes to many in the older colonies. This was the result of shipments of vast sums of Spanish and Portuguese specie from England to America, not only as pay for the soldiers, teamsters, army pioneers, *bateau-men*, and others, but also for the purchase at good prices of enormous quantities of food supplies and many other things needed for carrying on the war. Indeed, almost everyone, at least along the Atlantic seaboard and the interior that was tributary to its ports and chief towns, seems to have shared directly or indirectly in this lavish distribution over a period of nine years, resulting in the elevation of standards of living. But could this potential source of revenue be tapped?

A fifth problem presented itself at the termination of the war. In addition to the costs of policing all critical points in North America as well as the high seas, there was the necessity of honoring the great British public debt left by the war. From the point of view of every person responsible for making the vital decisions that brought Great Britain into a state of hostilities with France, this war debt was incurred chiefly for the protection of the most vital interests of the British North American colonies. Parliament reimbursed most of these colonies for much of their war expenditures; so that by 1763 they were rapidly and easily getting rid of the public debts resulting from the hostilities and were enjoying the progressive lightening of the burden of wartime taxation. The questions therefore inevitably arose: To what extent could the people of Great Britain, who had assumed such heavy financial obligations during the war years and who were now called upon to carry the public debt, also be expected to continue, for an indefinite period, the payment of taxes at war rates to provide for the defence of North America? And to what extent was the British government, in order to afford some relief to British taxpayers and maintain public credit, now justified in tightening up the enforcement outside the British Isles of trade and navigation regulations which, although designed to apply to all parts of the Empire, had not been at all strictly observed? This, it is obvious, would increase public revenues to service the war debt and to provide funds for the defence of North America—clearly matters of utmost importance. But, could it be done without creating great bitterness and dangerous unrest within the older colonies?

The effects of the Great War for the Empire and the remarkable manner of its termination went beyond the creation of the above-enumerated colonial problems that faced British statesmen. The war had hastened the conversion of an immature British North America into a group of mature and increasingly self-confident commonwealths. Moreover, the colonials of Massachusetts Bay, New York, Virginia, and those of the other older so-called plantations had been led to think of themselves during the war years as "American" colonials to a degree that had never previously been the case, with an outlook for the first time that was continental rather than local and with a new sense of intercolonial solidarity. Among the factors that contributed to this changed outlook were the bald facts of the war itself with its direct menace to the lives and property of all British North America. This threat served to break down much of the older isolation and exclusiveness of the colonies in relation to one another. ... While intercolonial fraternization of military units took place to some extent in connection with earlier New World conflicts, such as King George's War, the effect of it had had no such cumulative and permanent significance as of that which developed during the Great War for the Empire. In close association in this war they had fought, bled, suffered captivity—as at the surrender of Fort William Henry—and died together. All this they had done for a cause that seemed to transcend, for the moment at least, the interests of any one colony, deeply involving as it did the safety of all fellow British North Americans.

It is of equal significance that, as the result of the protracted war, for the first time British North America possessed thousands of battle-hardened veterans, men whose courage had been put to the test and who had attained some knowledge of warfare as practised among civilized peoples. But it should also be pointed out that these veterans could not, by and large, be depended upon to settle down to the dull, unambitious routine of garrison duty—they were not professional soldiers. With the end of hostilities, most of them eagerly returned to the farm, plantation, shop, fishery, or other peaceful pursuits. Nevertheless, in any future crisis that seemed to imperil them, their families, and their near neighbours, most of them could be relied upon to respond with alacrity. The importance of this fact in shaping the attitude of Americans in the post-war years, it would appear, can hardly be overestimated.

This lessening of isolation among the people of the older colonies and the creation of a certain consciousness of being fellow Americans, rather than simply subjects of the British King, was powerfully aided by the expansion of settlements and gradual development during the preceding half-century or more of improved means of intercommunication which had come with the expansion of postroads, postal service, and coastal trade along the Atlantic seaboard. This was accompanied by a steady growth in emphasis on inter-colonial business and cultural relations, all of which was intensified by the movement of thousands of people from one colony to another over well-travelled highways, such as the Valley Road of Virginia, as well as by the ties, created by religious denominations and educational institutions, that tended to forget colonial boundary lines. Nor should one ignore the contribution of the American press through the printing and circulation of newspapers, pamphlets, and books in bringing into existence an American community feeling. Indeed, so potent was the influence exerted by the press that we must stress the unique place held by the British colonial newspaper in the New World. . . .

. . . During the period from the beginning of 1763 to the end of 1774 there appeared some 4,467 distinct publications. Besides the newspapers, counting each year's issue only by title, there were many books, including those printed by authority as well as privately, pamphlets, and broadsides, making an average of 372 each year, with 239 issuing from the press in 1763, and 694 in 1774.

Although little criticism of the government of Great Britain was voiced in the American publications before, or even in 1763, since they were concerned with other and in most cases more local things, by 1774 the situation was quite reversed, with a majority of writers devoting their chief efforts to denouncing that government. Indeed, one is amply justified in raising the question as to whether there would have been an American Revolution in the course of the eighteenth century had there been no press and particularly, no free press. For is it probable that without an unleashed press, mere isolated pockets of local discontent with imperial policy could have been welded so easily into a type of colonial solidarity capable of generating a real American revolutionary movement?

If the vast power wielded by the colonial press differentiates the British America of 1763 onward to the end of the period of colonial dependence from the America of the earlier decades of the eighteenth century, factors other than those already given consideration also played a large part. For example, the inhabitants of the older colonies, instead of being hemmed in by the military forces and Indian allies of powerful and generally hostile nations, were now at last free of this brooding menace. Thus the feeling of insecurity that had hovered over them for generations, and had caused them in times of international emergency, when their very existence was threatened, to place a high value on their connections with the mother country, now tended to disappear.

It seemed in 1763 that as the result of the fortunes of war they themselves, as British colonials, would inevitably fall heir to most of a vast continent. For with France all but eliminated from North America, who now feared Spain, so disastrously defeated in the recent war and occupying, outside of Mexico, only the western part of old French Louisiana? Instead, visions began to take shape of an ever-westward expansion through what was still the seemingly endless North American western wilderness. With those visions, developed a sense of mission and high destiny that was not to be thwarted by any temporal, outside interference. Had they not already achieved greatly? Could they not point to hundreds of towns and villages and thousands of farms and plantations that they had planted along the Atlantic seaboard and well into the interior east of the Appalachians?

To understand why the feeling of self-sufficiency on the part of American colonials was so manifest in 1763 it is necessary to take into consideration the fact that they had now become a numerous, rather highly cultivated and wealthy people, who had developed to a point where they were beginning to feel themselves capable of managing their own affairs without much further guidance from the mother country. . . .

The great economic strength attained in 1763 by the people of the older colonies was due to a large extent to the high level they had reached in the development of agriculture, cattle-raising, the fisheries, and, to a lesser extent, the Indian trade in skins and furs. Of equal importance was the production of ships, iron, steel, and naval stores, and the processing on a large scale of food supplies for foreign markets, as well as the highly profitable utilization of a great merchant marine. Further, surplus wealth accumulated by such means as speculation in land had now become available for investment, and the experience acquired and the success achieved in large-scale mercantile and kindred business activities contributed significantly to these economic developments. The nature of the advantages that British North Americans enjoyed in their chief fields of commercial enterprise during the period under consideration can be made clearer by reference to the customs reports on the imports and exports of the colonies covering the year 1771. . . .

. . . British North America by 1763 was no longer in a state of infancy. In fact, it had now become a young giant as the result of the extraordinarily favourable conditions under which it had been permitted to flourish.

Along with the degree of economic maturity achieved by the older colonies at this juncture a correspondingly impressive cultural development can be noted. The period when all men had been obliged to devote their chief energies to the arduous task of gaining a mere subsistence from the land and the sea had long since passed. With the acquisition of wealth there came leisure for the cultivation of the mind. By 1763 Americans were in general a literate people, readers of newspapers and books that were readily available. Many of them had also accumulated private libraries. . . .

But many Americans did not stop with the purchase and reading of books written by others; they in turn made their own contribution to the cultural progress of America. Among these men Benjamin Franklin was an outstanding example. While dubious of the value of mere philosophical speculation, he brought to bear upon any problem that engaged his attention a remarkably clear, practical-minded type of thinking that was on occasion as profound as it was original. This is indicated by his *Experiments and Observations on Electricity* which was first published in London in 1751 and later, with additions, was reprinted in English and translated into French, German, and Italian. Franklin, who had never attended a college, was awarded degrees not only from Harvard, Yale, and William and Mary in America, but also an LL.D from St. Andrews in Scotland and a D.C.L. from Oxford, a medal by the Royal Society of London, and the rare distinction of honorary membership in that learned body.   Franklin, and a group of men closely associated with him, founded in the year 1731 the Library Company of Philadelphia. Established as America's first subscription library, with a broad interest in the literature of science or natural philosophy, as it was then called, this library by 1763 had become an important asset in the cultural life of Philadelphia. Further, Franklin promoted the establishment there of the American Philosophical Society, which, founded in 1743, had gradually languished and ceased to function until it was revived upon a broader basis in 1767 and entered upon its distinguished role as a disseminator of useful knowledge.

Nor was Franklin an isolated figure in this process of American cultural growth. With him in his efforts were many very able men, fully aware of the needs and opportunities offered in this relatively new land. For example, before 1752 there was not one general hospital in the older colonies. This lack was supplied in that year when the Pennsylvania Hospital, erected in Philadelphia, opened its doors. The preceding year had also witnessed there the founding of the College of Philadelphia which, as the successor to the Academy and Charity School, became the first non-sectarian American institution of higher education where the teaching of science, rather than philosophy, was basic in its curriculum. Moreover, in 1766 the College established its medical school, the first to be created in British North America. New York followed with the setting-up of the medical school of King's College.

These are not the only evidences of cultural progress in the older American colonies. By 1763 six colleges were engaged in the work of higher education: Harvard founded in 1636, William and Mary in 1693, Yale in 1701, the College of Philadelphia in 1740, but reorganized (as indicated above) in 1751, Princeton in 1746, and King's College in 1754. The College of Rhode Island was chartered in 1764 and 1766 saw the founding of Queen's College of New Jersey. In 1770, just before the outbreak of the War for American Independence, Dartmouth College was established with the chief purpose of educating receptive Indians. . . .

The profound interest in natural phenomena and the nature of the universe in general was also reflected by 1763, in the change of attitude on the part of many colonials toward revealed religion and especially toward the more somber aspects of Calvinistic theology. John Adams, repelled by "frigid Calvinism," turned away from plans to become a minister and began the study of law; Franklin, also reared in Calvinistic theology, reacted against it and became a deist; Colden in turn was led into a position of agnosticism. Other men of mental capacity were increasingly unwilling to accept without question tenets of seventeenth-century religious orthodoxy with its stress on predestination. . . .

Despite the drift of individuals away from the theology of Calvin, the great popular churches were strongly Calvinistic. These were the Congregationalists, the Presbyterians, the German Reformed, and the Baptists, although the latter in the seventeenth century had been influenced by Arminianism. The Congregationalists were largely concentrated in New England and their church was officially established in Massachusetts Bay, Connecticut, and New Hampshire. The Presbyterians were made up of pockets of Lowland Scots in the coastal areas, but for the most part consisted of Ulster Scots who, strongly opposed to any church establishment, gathered in congregations to the south of New England and especially in the back country of the Middle and Southern colonies. Here also dwelt most of the Baptists, although over a score of their churches were to be found in New England, with Rhode Island claiming about half this number. As for members of the German Reformed Church, they had created by the time of the outbreak of the War for American Independence the largest number of congregations of any religious denomination in Pennsylvania—over 100—and were also closely associated theologically with the members of the Calvinistic Dutch Reformed Church of New York with its seventy-five congregations.

Among the Calvinistic groups that attracted the support of the great mass of the people, the Presbyterians and the Baptists were the great proselytizing denominations, particularly in the South, stirring people to repentance through their revivals. Calvinism also stirred people in other ways.

No student who approaches the study of revolutionary movement in the older British Northern American colonies can be unmindful of the potential threat that Calvinism presented to the British system of imperial control, once a situation had arisen that inclined Americans to question the value of their continued connection with the mother country. For in its essence it called upon men to recognize no earthly superiority in the sublime presence of God, who judged all not by their temporal rank, but by their state of grace. To the sanctified Calvinist, therefore, kings, nobles, and others powerful in temporal authority, yet living outside of a state of grace, were among those destined to be judged, eternally lost, and therefore ultimately of not the slightest account. In fact, the whole concept of an earthly ruling monarch and an earthly privileged hereditary nobility was incompatible with the deepest religious convictions of a thorough-going Calvinist. . . .

Another characteristic that distinguished British North America in 1763 from the rest of the New World was the great mixture of nationalities. There were, in addition to the English, Ulster Scots by the thousands, native Irish, Highland Scots, and Quaker Welshmen—all from the British Isles. Then there were tens of thousands of people of German extraction, chiefly from the upper Rhineland, who continued to speak and read only their own language. Likewise, there were descendants of Dutchmen who had settled in the seventeenth century principally in the area of the Hudson River and its tributaries, of Swedes and Finns who had located on Delaware Bay, and of persecuted French Huguenots who had come mostly on individual initiative and had established homes in South Carolina, their chief centre, and in other colonies as far north as Massachusetts Bay. Then, too, there were the small groups of Spanish, French, and Portuguese Jews who had early come to South Carolina, Georgia, and Rhode Island. Some of these continental Europeans, such as the Huguenots, were easily assimilated by the English-speaking people among whom they settled and with whom they easily intermarried; others, particularly the German pietistic religious sects, adhered with great tenacity not only to their language but also to their individual modes of life that set them quite apart from their fellow colonials. All these groups, however, served to enrich the American cultural pattern and by 1763 had given it marked non-British characteristics. What is of equal importance is the degree to which by that date these men of varied nationalistic and religious background had come to regard themselves, not as Scots, or Ulster Scots, or Irish, or Germans, or Swiss, but simply as Americans.

Yet, it was not the presence among them of numerous peoples from European stock other than their own that most profoundly influenced and modified the mores of Englishmen in America. Rather it was the presence of the African Negro and the institution of slavery which determined his legal and social status.

While it is true that in 1763 we find many thousands of white people bound to servitude, voluntarily or otherwise, by indentures for greater or lesser periods of time, their condition was above that of slavery. In due course some of them, after obtaining their freedom of action, would become people of social and political prominence and consequence. This was not true of the African slaves. Even those who were manumitted in British North America remained without social standing during the rest of their lives. Despite whatever claim could be made for the existence of white democracy and white equalitarianism by the people of any colony, in every one the status of slavery was recognized and sanctioned by law. . . .

In consequence of the growth of slavery as an approved institution—and quite inconsistent with fundamental aspects of Calvinistic doctrine so generally accepted in the colonies—there existed in all the colonies an aristocracy of race. It went far beyond the pretensions to a superior position in life of the aristocracy of hereditary title in England in demanding respect and obedience from those in its service and in setting the conditions of this service. It is true that most white Americans were not the possessors of slaves. Many of them, leading Quakers in particular, had voiced their testimony against the institution of slavery on religious and moral grounds, and even among slave-holders the evils inherent in it were widely recognized. But economic and social demands for its perpetuation were at the time too strong to be resisted. Even the non-slave-holder tended to consider the African slave, as well as the manumitted Negro, an inferior being, inherently incapable of participating in any political activity, much less being worthy of social recognition.

Such was the aristocratic gulf that separated the white and black races in America, a gulf far wider, as suggested, than any in England that distinguished between social and economic classes. Conditions of living, especially on the frontiers and in those agricultural areas characterized by fairly small farms worked by the farmer and his family, certainly made for social equality and political democracy. But these conditions were more than counterbalanced by the fact that in 1763 the institutions of white bondage and black slavery were deeply rooted in the more politically powerful, densely settled, seaboard parts of the older colonies. These institutions were naturally identified with accumulated wealth in the cities and broad acres in the country and thus with men of large business capacity and high social standing. These same men, or at least those with whom they mingled by reason of family, social, or professional ties, likewise played a major role in almost every colony in the field of political leadership. As a result, effective political power was in 1763 centered, with few exceptions, in groups of closely associated individuals of aristocratic leanings, living either in the great seaports and other populous places or, in the case of the South, on plantations in the tidewater area—groups that may be called the British North American élite. . . .

Scores of . . . men of conservative and aristocratic inclination in America were active in political life in 1763. In the developing crisis between Great Britain and the colonies from 1763 to 1775, some of the aristocrats, such as

John Hancock, were destined to become popular revolutionary leaders; others passed from the scene, a few sought neutralism, still more became Loyalists, as was true of Thomas Hutchinson and Joseph Galloway. Nevertheless, it is important to bear in mind that in 1763 it was from the members of these powerful ruling groups that the governors of corporate colonies, lieutenant governors, and members of the provincial councils were selected. Likewise from among them judges of the superior courts, sheriffs, county lieutenants, members of the courts of general session, courts of quarter sessions, closed parish vestries, boards of aldermen, common councils, and town selectmen were usually chosen. This ruling class of Americans wanted no superiors nor any interference with their accustomed mode of life.

In addition to attaining status among the political *élite* by the force of personal leadership, past experience in public affairs, and the natural prominence that came with their wealth and social connections, the members of this privileged group possessed the property qualifications for seats in the colonial Assembly. Then, too, there was a tendency in New York, Pennsylvania, and the Carolinas, to concentrate power through weighted systems of representation and other devices in the hands of those living in or near the provincial capital or within the Tidewater. Thus the character of colonial legislation and its administration in the older American colonies was largely determined by these groups of propertied, conservative men in 1763. The combined prestige of these key American office-holders and those closely associated with their interests was much more potent in shaping government policy in each colony, as a rule, than was the influence of even the Governor of a royal province with his royal commission and instructions.

The colonial Assemblies whom the *élite* controlled present another aspect of growing American maturity by 1763. In the course of the seventeenth and the first half of the eighteenth centuries these bodies consciously patterned their procedures upon those of the English House of Commons. What is more, they tended to interpret their powers in similar terms. In so doing they demanded and secured freedom of speech, as well as freedom from arrest and molestation for their members; they decided disputed elections and claimed the right to exercise control over their membership. When a newly designated Speaker was presented to the Governor of a province for approval—something that did not apply in the corporate colonies of Connecticut and Rhode Island —he was accustomed, following the English House of Commons practice, to bring a petition in the name of the Assembly asking for the recognition of its privileges. As this was granted almost without exception, it inevitably led to the development by the assemblies of the doctrine of inherent rights; that is, rights which could not be denied to the properly elected representatives of the freeholders of a colony when duly organized as a legislative body and were comparable to the "ancient rights and privileges of the House of Commons."

Logically combined with this doctrine of legislative competence was the doctrine that colonials enjoyed, likewise by inherent right, all the liberties and privileges of Englishmen. So we find the South Carolina Commons House of Assembly, for example, resolving in 1735 (in view of the possession of these rights that had never been forfeited by the migration of Englishmen to America) that it possessed "by the laws of England and South Carolina, and ancient usage and custom, . . . all the rights and privileges pertaining to Money bills that are enjoyed by the British House of Commons." It is, nevertheless, important to observe that no claim was put forth by this Assembly or by any other, at least before the Great War for the Empire, that local legislation had an equality with that of Parliament, even with respect to money bills. Thus when in 1751 Parliament passed the statute regulating and restraining the use in New England of bills of credit, not one of the Assemblies affected by the law questioned its validity or legality although it involved an internal regulation of major importance. Yet as the North American phase of the Great War for the Empire came to a close there appeared a growing realization that a continued dependence on the mother country might no longer be an asset but rather a liability to colonial aspirations.

In 1762 the Massachusetts Bay General Court, in writing to its London agent, embodied the following highly significant declaration in its instructions to him: "The natural rights of the Colonists, we humbly concur to be the same with those of other British Subjects, and indeed of all Mankind. The principal of these Rights is to be 'freedom from any superior on Earth, and not to be under the Will or Legislative Authority of Man, but to have only the Law of Nature for his Rule.'" To what extent this extreme natural-rights position was shared by other British colonials at this period is by no means clear. But the time would come, at least in the 1770's, when the North American colonial Assemblies would be prepared to assert a perfect equality with Parliament when it came to the regulation of all domestic matters. Even in the 1760's Parliament's right to levy upon colonials was challenged.

The development of an impasse in the orderly and peaceful processes of government was destined to arise soon after 1763. It led to the shattering of the Empire by violent upheaval and may be attributed largely to a fundamental constitutional defect—that the machinery for governmental control and maintenance of the Empire could not easily be adjusted to meet the changing needs demanded by the growing maturity of the older colonies. Rather, colonial policy had followed, in the main, a pattern already fixed by the end of the seventeenth century at a time when the existing colonies were actually weak dependencies, widely separated from each other in more ways than one, and incapable of standing on their own feet vis-à-vis the world. In terms of this early pattern of control, the plantations were expected to supplement, rather than to reduce or destroy, the means available to the people of the mother country for providing themselves with a livelihood. As they prospered, the plantations were expected to contribute to the general cost of maintaining the central government as well as their own, and especially to share in supporting the royal navy, whose protection they and their ocean-born trade enjoyed. In consequence, before 1763 Parliament had passed numerous statutes regulating colonial navigation, trade, and business activities both public and private. The propriety and justice of doing so at the time was hardly questioned by members of Parliament. The fact that this system of British regulation had not prevented the phenomenal development of the American colonies that took place during the half-century or more before 1763, could only confirm the view that the system was, all in all, wisely conceived. Yet, one must not ignore the fact that much of this restrictive legislation was resented by colonials and in so far as possible was evaded.

The administration of the Empire had had as its basis from 1689 to 1763 the fundamental principle that final authority for all measures relating to its welfare must necessarily rest in Parliament, the legal custodian of all sovereign power. In its decisions, some of them most weighty, the colonials had had no direct part, despite the fact that they might have reason to feel that they were adversely affected by them. Such a situation of political inequality between the inhabitants of Great Britain, where the qualified freeman elected all members of the House of Commons, and the almost 2,000,000 inhabitants of the American colonies by 1763, who elected none, was the essence of what had now become a major anachronism in the constitution of the Empire.

While the student of today may feel that he is competent to offer what he himself considers an easy solution to the problem of political inequality as it was manifested by 1763, any proposal to that end within the constitutional framework of the British Empire which the men of that generation may have pondered, under the given circumstances, presented enormous difficulties for successful application. From time to time people of prominence such as Benjamin Franklin, Governor Bernard, and even James Otis, advanced the idea of colonial representation in the House of Commons. Assuming that there would have been no opposition on either side of the Atlantic to this idea (which one has no right to do), how could this have been accomplished in 1763 in such a manner as to have satisfied both the people of Great Britain and those of the colonies? What proportion of the total membership of the House would have had to be allotted to the British colonials to have assured them of a degree of influence in its deliberations that would have reconciled them to such an arrangement? . . .

Granted that this hurdle of the *proportion* of the seats in the House of Commons could have been surmounted in 1763, other formidable obstacles to representation would have remained. Since members were not paid for attendance, how would the necessarily heavy expenses of the British colonials holding seats have been met? Out of their own pockets? Out of appropriations by the Assemblies? Out of a general American fund to be raised by act of Parliament? Each of these possible solutions of the problem presented great difficulties. If American representatives had been paid and British members were not, would that have been a satisfactory arrangement? Again, is it likely that the type of men who had long provided leadership in the various colonial Assemblies would also serve the public in London at the potential sacrifice of their interests in America? Would these men of large business capacity as well as of political experience have been willing to contemplate either virtual exile, perhaps for years, from the center of their activities—be they counting-house or plantation or law practice—or the hazards of rather frequent crossings of the ocean? Moreover, far removed from their constituents, with months necessarily intervening between information desired and information supplied, could they have been properly instructed, if instructed at all, respecting measures that might arise in Parliament? . . .

If the feasibility of American representation in the House of Commons might have been doubted by colonials, as it came to be in 1765 with the calling of the Stamp Act Congress, what would have been their attitude toward seats in the House of Lords? In the Act of Union between England and Scotland it was provided that sixteen Scottish peers should, upon election by the peerage of Scotland, take their seats in it. What would have been the reaction of Americans, if, in the laudable desire to provide membership for them in that venerable and august body, a group of leading colonials had been made either life or hereditary peers? Assuming that the aristocrats in such provinces as New York, Virginia, and South Carolina might possibly have welcomed the elevation of some of their leading men to this status, though it is not at all clear that such would have been the case, can one easily conceive of peers being created in Rhode Island or, for that matter, in Pennsylvania? It is certain that the establishment of an American peerage was sought by no responsible colonial in 1763 and it is equally certain that if American peers had been created and provided with seats in the House of Lords and had thereupon sought to live up to their responsibilities, they would have run the risk of becoming expatriates quite out of touch, if not out of sympathy, with the aspirations of their fellow Americans. Indeed, one is almost forced to conclude that colonial representation in either of the Houses of Parliament in 1763 would not have remedied to the satisfaction of Americans the existing political inequality. Nor could it have done so without the destruction of Parliament as it then existed and the substitution in its place of something strikingly different—a procedure that few of the people of Great Britain would have contemplated with anything less than deep apprehension in view of the failure of the Cromwellian experiments in constitution-making.

If, as a possible solution of at least a phase of the problem of political inequality, one were to think of the creation within the folds of the Empire of a

North American union, endowed with administrative organs and a legislature empowered to provide for American external and internal security, one would be brought face to face with the fate of the justly celebrated Albany Plan of Union. This Plan was drawn up after due deliberations in 1754 by the Albany Congress, which was called into existence by the Board of Trade and was composed of colonials of great capacity and political experience. The Plan, as it finally evolved—certainly with respect to the fundamental principles embodied in it, if not in the language and structure—had as its chief architect that eminent American, Benjamin Franklin. Here was a moderate and states-manlike proposal, a product of American thinking, that was bitterly opposed by the Assemblies of several of the colonies, dominated as they were by what one could call today narrow provincialism. It failed to secure the approval of a single one of the Assemblies in spite of the crying need at the time for organized and unified action in the face of American involvement in hostili-ties with the French and Indians. In view of this failure, what evidence is there that the colonials themselves, once peace had been restored, could have been brought to look with the slightest favor on a movement to revive the proposed arrangement that would inevitably, as Franklin himself realized, have de-prived the various Assemblies of some of their prestige as well as some of their powers and freedom of action?

Let us assume that, without waiting for the colonies to take the initiative, the British government, realizing that the administrative machinery designed for infant dependencies was no longer suited to what had become real com-monwealths, had decided to implement the Albany Plan in 1763. This would have involved commissioning a President General under the Great Seal and sending a royal writ to each colony calling for election by the popular branch of its Assembly of members to the proposed Grand Council according to the allocation of seats laid down in the Plan itself. Is it likely that the colonials would have hailed with joy the creation, either by the use of the royal pre-rogative or by act of Parliament, of an American Union? Or, is it not more likely that, starting with New England, there would have been a chorus of outcries against it as a revival of the hated Andros Dominion of New England regime that was fastened upon the Northern colonies by James II? What is more, were the person commissioned as President General to have been a member of the Anglican communion, as would have been likely, would not the Calvinist clergy and even many Anglicans have almost certainly joined in denunciation of the whole project of union as part of a scheme whereby an American bishop would be apt to follow close after him? Under such circumstances, how many of the colonial Assemblies is it probable could have been counted on to help implement the Albany Plan by electing members to the Grand Council?

Putting aside the Albany Plan as inapplicable, is it easy to suggest any other project for an American union that in 1763 would have been given even luke-warm support by colonials? Within the framework of the growing sense of unity that bound the inhabitants of the various colonies together, were there not at the same time strong intercolonial antagonisms still alive in that year? . . . Is it not clear that the people of each colony wanted to be governed only by a law-making body and by administrators they themselves could watch and control? Were they not as deeply devoted to their respective Assemblies, as the proper instrumentality for the expression of their desires and will, as were the people of Great Britain to Parliament? Far from dreaming of an American union with effective powers, was it not their desire and aim that their respective Assemblies would grow increasingly competent to aid them in becoming less and less dependent on the world outside their boundaries? Yet, could such problems as security measures demanding the maintenance of armed forces, the relations with the western Indians, western expansion into disputed lands, as well as other issues almost equally pressing, have been dealt with successfully short of some government agency superimposed on the colonial Assemblies? What colonial Assembly or what colonial statesman was heard giving expression in 1763 to any attempted solution of this need for unified action that would lie beyond the competence of an individual colonial government?

Assuming the accuracy of this analysis of the attitude of the typical colonial, is it surprising that soon after 1763 there arose within the Empire an ominous crisis brought on by conflicting needs? On the one hand, in view of the recent embodiment within the Empire of vast American territories and a numerous alien and recently hostile people, there was need for a more efficient imperial administration. An equal need existed, on the other hand, in light of the degree of maturity attained by the older colonies, of erasing, in so far as possible, any semblance of their political inequality with the mother country. These were indeed needs that could not easily be reconciled by any feat of statesmanship in view of all the accompanying circumstances.

It is true there would doubtless have been no American Revolution had the government of Great Britain been prepared in 1763 to have made an announcement to the older colonies somewhat as follows:

"Under the general supervision of the mother country you have gradually grown in numbers, in wealth, in political experience, and in economic competence to a point where as mature offspring you have the ability to govern yourselves without outside interference in your affairs. You have been and are a free people and should now shape your own destiny. No longer need you have fear of the violation of your frontiers as in the past, for no longer are you faced by an hereditary enemy on your borders, since these areas are at last in friendly hands. Therefore, you will please us if you will indicate by whatever official instrumentality you choose to employ, the degree of connection you desire to retain with us, as we can no longer hold you in leading strings against your will. Now as adult commonwealths you are, we trust, well prepared to enter upon a new epoch in your history within the expanded British Empire. When we have heard from you, you may rest assured that such changes in the constitution and laws of the Empire as you may agree upon will be made with the least possible delay."

Such an unprecedented pronouncement could only have come from those who possessed a degree of prophetic foresight such as was vouchsafed to no British statesman of that day, not even to Pitt. One may also be sure that it would have created a degree of amazement within the thirteen colonies only equalled by that of the people of Great Britain and those of such a dependency as Ireland. Although no one is justified in affirming that such a step could possibly have been within the realm of a rational solution of the problem of political inequality within the Empire in 1763, one is at least on perfectly safe grounds in indicating that, had this solution been proposed, it would have anticipated by over a century and a half the ultimate meeting head-on of the problem as worked out in the British Imperial Conference of 1926 and given final expression in the famous Statute of Westminster in 1931.

As neither Great Britain nor colonial America was blessed in 1763 with men of either omniscience or omnipotence, the unfolding of events between the close of the Great War for the Empire and the outbreak of the War for American Independence was necessarily in the hands of mere mortals, with all their human limitations. They strove as best they could—each according to his own light—to find a way through the baffling complexities that intertwining constitutional, political, and economic problems presented to all embodied within the Old British Empire during this period.

BACKGROUND OF BRITISH POLICY

The following documents illustrate the growing annoyance in Britain at claims of the American assemblies to autonomous powers. It was presumption of a high order, for example, for Pennsylvania to undertake to "extend" an act of Parliament since in theory Parliament's actions automatically applied to all portions of the Empire. Further, the French and Indian War had broken out two years earlier; any local act undertaking a unilateral regulation of military matters was particularly irksome and, in the minds of the lords of the Privy Council, certainly unconstitutional.

Even more alarming to British leaders was the illicit trade which flourished throughout the war between the Americans and the enemy islands in the West Indies.

By the Peace of 1763, therefore, there was already a considerable backlog of irritation in London against the Americans, and a determination to reform the old imperial system at the earliest possible date. Simultaneously, the need to absorb and govern the vast new territories won during the war and to pay for the cost of defending them meant that a colonial revenue was necessary and reinforced the disposition to undertake a thorough reorganization of the Empire.

The original spelling has been preserved throughout.

Report of a Privy Council Committee

[The Privy Council* Committee reported] that the following [Pennsylvania] Act entitled

An Act for extending so much of an Act of Parliament entitled an Act for punishing Mutiny and desertion, and for the better payment of the Army and their Quarters passed in the twenty Eighth year of the present Reign, as relates to the Quartering and Billeting of Soldiers and payment of their Quarters in that part of Great Britain called England—

Appearing to them to be of an extraordinary and unusual Nature; They thought it their Duty to referr it to Your Majestys Attorney General, who hath Reported to them as his Opinion, that it is not adviseable for your Majesty to approve thereof, that the tendency of this Act must unavoidably be to Cramp the Publick Service, and obstruct the defence of the Province. That it assumes propositions true in the mother Country, and rightly asserted in the Reigns of Charles the first and Charles the Second in time of Peace, when soldiers were kept up without Consent of Parliament, but that the application of such propositions to a Colony in time of War in Case of Troops raised for their Protection by the Authority of the Parliament of Great Britain made the first time by an Assembly, many of whom plead what they call Conscience, for not making or assisting Military operations to resist the Enemy, should not be allowed to stand as Law.

Report of the Board of Trade to the Privy Council, July 7, 1756, Acts of The Privy Council, (Colonial), London, 1911, Vol. IV, pp. 337–339.
* The Privy Council generally supervised colonial affairs and reviewed colonial legislation. Its committees usually included responsible cabinet officers, however, and the "recommendatory" flavor of their reports was most often a mere literary device.

And With respect to the Act passed in November 1755 Intituled,

An Act for the better ordering and Regulating such as are willing and desirous to be united for Military purposes within this Province.

The said Lords Commissioners have Reported, that it is in every Respect the most improper and inadequate to the Service which could have been framed and passed, and seems rather calculated to exempt persons from Military Services, than to encourage and promote them. No methods are prescribed for compelling persons by proper penalties to associate in defence of their Country, or for obliging those who are conscientiously scrupulous of bearing Arms themselves, to find others in their stead, or to provide for such as might by the Executive power, be found ready and willing to enlist. The whole both in respect of enlistment, and of the Subsistence of those who may be enlisted, is voluntary; The Officers are to be elected by Ballot, and no Provision is made for that due subordination without which all Bodies of Men associated for Military purposes would be absolutely useless. But that these are not the only defective and mischievous Provisions of this Act; for it is enacted, that no person under twenty one Years of Age shall be enlisted, by which means many able Bodied Men fit for the Service of their Country as Soldiers, would be excluded; and that no Regiment, Company or Party shall be compelled or Lead more than three days March beyond the Inhabited parts of the Province, nor be detained against their Wills, longer than three weeks in any Garrison, let the necessity of the Case be what it will. A Proviso, which instead of rendering this Militia effectual to the purposes of defence, may be the means of encouraging desertion, and of Sacrificing such of Your Majestys Troops as may happen to be joined with them in the same Service, But were the Provisions of this Act never so good and proper, yet little advantage or Benefit could be hoped for from a Law, in the preamble of which it is declared, that the Majority of the Assembly, which is in effect the governing part of the Province in which it is to operate, and from whom Your Majestys Subjects ought to receive Support and protection are principled against bearing Arms; and that the making a Law to compell persons thereto would be to violate a fundamental of the Constitution, and be a direct breach of the Privileges of the People, the said Lords Commissioners were therefore of Opinion, that this Act should receive your Majestys disallowance.

Report of a Privy Council Committee

[The Committe concur with the Board of Trade, who reported on 30 March] that although it is the duty of the Assembly of New Hampshire to provide for

Report of a Privy Council Committee, April 1, 1757, *ibid.*, pp. 300–301.

the defence and Security of these and all other the Frontier Settlements of that Province, yet the Assembly have neglected or refused to make such Provision, notwithstanding it was particularly recommended to them by His Majestys Instructions to Mr. [Governor] Wentworth in August 1755; The said Lords Commissioners cannot therefore suggest any better method upon this occasion, than that Copys of the said Petitions should be transmitted to the Earl of Loudoun, Commander in Chief of His Majestys Forces in North America, with His Majestys Orders for His Lordship to take such measures for the Protection and Security of the said Settlements, as, upon examination of their respective Circumstances, shall appear to him to be requisite, and consistent with the General Good of His Majestys Service.

Report of a Privy Council Committee

(On reading the following Board of Trade representation of 31 Aug., 1759, viz:—) George Haldane Esquire Your Majesty's Governor of the Island of Jamaica, having transmitted to Us the Depositions of the Masters and other Officers of several Vessels belonging to Your Majesty's Subjects in North America which being laden with Rum, Sugars and other Produce of the French Islands, have been taken and carried into Jamaica, by Captain Edwards of Your Majesty's Ship Assistance, We beg leave humbly to lay before your Majesty the annexed Copies of the said Depositions and to represent to your Majesty Thereupon—

That it appears from these Depositions that a very considerable Trade has, during the Course of the present War, been carried on by Your Majesty's Subjects in the Northern Colonies to Monte Christi, a Spanish Port in the Island of Hispaniola: That the Cargoes of the Vessels employ'd in this Trade (of which there have been an hundred and fifty trading at one time in the Road of Monte Christi) have consisted of Provisions and Lumber, which have been sold there. And that in return for the Proceeds of these Cargoes and for Cash, which the Masters of the said Vessels have brought with them from the Northern Colonies, to a very great Amount, they have received large Quantities of Rum, Sugar and Melosses, the Produce of the French Settlements at the Cape and at Port Dauphine, in the Neighbourhood of Monte Christi, purchased for them by the Spaniards (who grow no Sugars in that part of the Island) and put on board these Vessels, without being landed at Monte Christi.

From these Facts it appears that Your Majesty's Subjects have, during the Course of the War, upon pretext of trading to a neutral Port, carried on a most

Report of a Privy Council Committee, February 16, 1760, *ibid.*, pp. 443–447.

pernicious and destructive Trade with Your Majesty's Enemies not only furnishing them with Provisions and other Necessaries for their Plantations, and taking off their Produce in return but also supplying them with that Cash which this Kingdom has been under the Necessity of remitting to the Northern Colonies for the Support of the War, and which instead of returning to the Mother Country in payment for its Produce and Manufactures, is, by this iniquitous Trade, transferr'd into the Hands of Your Majesty's Enemies.

It is evident that so much of this Trade as consists in Provisions is expressly contrary to the Act of Parliament passed in the 30th Year of Your Majesty's Reign, for prohibiting during the present War, the Exportation of all sorts of Provisions from Your Majestys Colonies to the Colony or Dominion of any foreign Prince or State. And although the trading to a Neutral Port with other Articles of British Plantation Produce, may not, in general Light of it, appear to be contrary to the Letter of the Law, Yet We beg leave humbly to submit it to Your Majesty's Consideration, whether, in the particular Circumstances of this Commerce, in which it clearly appears that the Interposition of a Neutral Port is only a Cover to direct Trade with the Enemy, is not absolutely inconsistent with the general Principles of Law and Policy which prevail in all States. From the Depositions annexed it will appear to Your Majesty that a very considerable part of this destructive Trade is carried on from the Charter Governments, and in particular from the Colony of Rhode Island, which Colony, as well as that of Connecticut, under Pretence of the Powers granted to them by their Charters assume to themselves an absolute Government, independant not only of the Sovereign Government of the Crown, but of the Legislature of the Mother Country. For they not only do not transmit any of their Acts and Proceedings, either judicial or legislative, for the Royal Approbation, but likewise do not conform to the Laws of Trade, Their Governors never being presented to the Crown for Approbation nor does it appear that they take any Oath for the due Observance of the said Laws, both which Qualifications appear to Us to be required by the Act of the 7th and 8th of King William the third, for regulating the Plantation Trade. But it is not only in this branch of illicit Trade that the Inhabitants of these Colonies are engaged; for from the various Representations which have from time to time been made to Us by the Governors of the Neighbouring Colonies that they carry on illicit Trade in other Branches of a very pernicious Nature and to a great Extent, importing into the said Colonies, directly from Holland and other foreign Parts a variety of Merchandize which, by Law, can be imported into the Plantations, only from Great Britain.

Whether the Nonconformity of the Charter Governments to the Laws of Trade, and the pernicious Commerce carried on by the Inhabitants of them arise from any Powers in their Charters inconsistent with, or from any Defects in the framing of those Laws or from the neglect and Corruption of those whose

Duty it is to watch over the Execution of them, We cannot take upon Us to say; Neither can We, doubtfull and uncertain as We are with respect to the Legality or Illegality of a great part of the Trade to Monte Christi, under the circumstances stated in the Depositions, presume to point out to Your Majesty a Remedy to the Evil, or in what manner the Persons concerned in it may be punished. We would therefore humbly submit whether it may not be proper that the whole of this Case, as well what regards the particular Circumstances of the Trade to Monte Christi, as what relates to the Nonconformity of the Charter Colonies to the Laws of Trade, and the unlawfull Commerce in general carried on by the inhabitants of them should be referr'd to Your Majestys Attorney and Sollicitor General, for their Opinion; To the End that a proper Remidy may be speedily applied to Evils of so great an extent and importance.

We would however humbly submit to Your Majesty whether in the mean time it may be not adviseable to put forth a Proclamation in Your Majestys Name, in all the Northern Colonies, stating the informations which have been received of the nature and extent of this pernicious Trade to Monte Christi, and exhorting and requiring the Legislatures of the said colonies and all the subordinate Jurisdictions of Courts, Offices and Officers to do their utmost to put a Stop to all Trade and Commerce which may be carried on from the said Colonies directly with Your Majesty's Enemies, and to punish Offenders therein to the utmost rigour of the Laws, and to take care that all the Laws for regulating the Plantation Trade be duly observed and all branches of them punished as the Laws direct. And We apprehend the doing this by Proclamation to be the more necessary, as We doubt whether any Act of Government less solemn wou'd have a due Effect on the Charter Governments of Rhode Island and Connecticut the former of which appears to have been so largely concerned in this pernicious Commerce.

THE AMERICAN RESPONSE

JONATHAN MAYHEW,
Concerning Unlimited Submission and Nonresistance to the Higher Powers

Although he died at the early age of forty-six, Jonathan Mayhew was one of the most eminent Puritan divines of eighteenth-century New England. A graduate of Harvard College and an honorary Doctor of Divinity from Aberdeen, he occupied the pulpit at influential West Church, Boston, for nearly twenty years, virtually his entire professional life. Differing from his more orthodox Calvinist colleagues, Mayhew preached a rational, optimistic, practical, and "sober-minded" Christianity, rejecting predestination and developing an essentially unitarian theology. He shared to the full, however, some basic fundamentals of the Puritan view. There was the "Puritan ethic," the assumption that God "called" all men, lay or cleric, to their temporal functions and that He would both sanctify and prosper the "sober-minded." Suspicion and dislike of the Roman and Anglican churches are also evident in Mayhew as well as in all of his colleagues, to whom "Popish idolatry" and "prelatical corruptions" were both unscriptural and unwarrantedly authoritarian. These doctrines held important implications for secular government as well. (If a congregational polity was good enough for God Almighty, it was certainly good enough for man.)

Mayhew died in 1766, but he lived long enough to see the repeal of the Stamp Act, an event which occasioned one of his most celebrated sermons, "The Snare Broken," in which he called eloquently for vigilance in the protection of liberty.

The discourse partially reprinted here Professor Bernard Bailyn describes as "the most famous sermon preached in pre-Revolutionary America," illustrating "the ultimate sources of American Revolutionary thought and the distinctive emphasis imparted to them in the process of their transmission." In his beautifully reasoned assault upon seventeenth-century Stuart absolutism,

Jonathan Mayhew, "Concerning Unlimited Submission and Resistance to the Higher Powers," in *Pamphlets of the American Revolution, 1750–1776*, ed. B. Bailyn and J. N. Garrett, Cambridge, Mass., Belknap Press of Harvard University, 1965, Vol. I, pp. 213–247, *passim*. Reprinted by permission of the editor and the publisher.

Mayhew invoked Milton, Sidney, and Locke, the great Whig apologist, as well as the natural law and the Bible, to argue not merely the right but the duty of subjects to judge their rulers and to resist tyranny. He is accordingly the connecting link between the great constitutional struggle which wracked Puritan England and the concepts informing the American Revolution and the founding of the new nation.

The sermon, occasioned by the January 30, 1750 (n.s.), anniversary of King Charles I's execution, first appeared in pamphlet form in Boston, 1750. The excerpt presented below—about one-third of the original—omits many of Mayhew's extensive footnotes and the long historical reflection upon the Puritans' resistance to Charles I.

1. Let every soul be subject unto the higher powers. For there is no power but of God: the powers that be are ordained of God.

2. Whosoever therefore resisteth the power, resisteth the ordinance of God: and they that resist shall receive to themselves damnation.

3. For rulers are not a terror to good works, but to the evil. Wilt thou then not be afraid of the power? Do that which is good, and thou shalt have praise of the same.

4. For he is the minister of God to thee for good. But if thou do that which is evil, be afraid; for he beareth not the sword in vain: for he is the minister of God, a revenger to execute wrath upon him that doth evil.

5. Wherefore ye must needs be subject, not only for wrath, but also for conscience sake.

6. For, for this cause pay you tribute also: for they are God's ministers, attending continually upon this very thing.

7. Render therefore to all their dues: tribute to whom tribute is due; custom to whom custom; fear to whom fear; honor to whom honor.*

It is evident that the affair of civil government may properly fall under a *moral* and *religious* consideration, at least so far forth as it relates to the general nature and end of magistracy and to the grounds and extent of that submission which persons of a private character ought to yield to those who are vested with authority. This must be allowed by all who acknowledge the divine original of Christianity. For although there be a sense, and a very plain and important sense, in which Christ's *kingdom is not of this world*,† his inspired apostles have, nevertheless, laid down some general principles concerning the office of civil rulers and the duty of subjects, together with the reason and obligation of that duty. And from hence it follows that it is proper for all who ac-

---

* Romans, xiii, 1–8.
† John xviii, 36.

knowledge the authority of Jesus Christ and the inspiration of his apostles to endeavor to understand what is in fact the doctrine which they have delivered concerning this matter. It is the duty of *Christian* magistrates to inform themselves what it is which their religion teaches concerning the nature and design of their office. And it is equally the duty of all *Christian* people to inform themselves what it is which their religion teaches concerning that subjection which they owe to *the higher powers*. It is for these reasons that I have attempted to examine into the Scripture account of this matter, in order to lay it before you with the same *freedom* which I constantly use with relation to other doctrines and precepts of Christianity; not doubting but you will *judge* upon everything offered to your consideration with the same spirit of *freedom* and *liberty* with which it is *spoken*.

The passage read is the most full and express of any in the New Testament relating to rulers and subjects: and therefore I thought it proper to ground upon it what I had to propose to you with reference to the authority of the civil magistrate and the subjection which is due to him. But before I enter upon an explanation of the several parts of this passage, it will be proper to observe one thing which may serve as a key to the whole of it.

It is to be observed, then, that there were some persons amongst the *Christians* of the apostolic age, and particularly those at *Rome* to whom St. *Paul* is here writing, who seditiously disclaimed *all* subjection to civil authority, refusing to pay taxes and the duties laid upon their traffic and merchandise, and who scrupled not to speak of their rulers without any due regard to their office and character. Some of these turbulent *Christians* were converts from *Judaism*, and others from *paganism*. The *Jews* in general had, long before this time, taken up a strange conceit, that being the *peculiar* and *elect* people of God they were, therefore, exempted from the jurisdiction of any *heathen* princes or governors. Upon this ground it was that some of them, during the public ministry of our blessed Saviour, came to Him with that question: *Is it lawful to give tribute unto* Caesar *or not?** And this notion many of them retained after they were proselyted to the *Christian* faith. As to the *gentile* converts, some of them grossly mistook the nature of that *liberty* which the Gospel promised, and thought that by virtue of their subjection to Christ, the *only* King and head of his church, they were wholly freed from subjection to any other prince; as though Christ's *kingdom had been of this world* in such a sense as to interfere with the civil powers of the earth, and to deliver their subjects from that allegiance and duty which they before owed to them. Of these visionary *Christians* in general who disowned subjection to the civil powers in being where they respectively lived, there is mention made in several places in the New Testament. The Apostle *Peter* in particular character-

---

* Matt. xxii, 17.

izes them in this manner: *them that . . . despise government, presumptuous are they, self-willed, they are not afraid to speak evil of dignities. . . .*

. . . The Apostle sums all up in the following words: *Render therefore to all their dues; tribute to whom tribute is due; custom to whom custom; fear to whom fear; honor to whom honor* (ver. 7), q.d.: "Let it not, therefore, be said of any of you hereafter, that you contemn government, to the reproach of yourselves and of the *Christian* religion. Neither your being *Jews* by nation nor your becoming the subjects of Christ's kingdom gives you any dispensation for making disturbances in the government under which you live. Approve yourselves, therefore, as peaceable and dutiful subjects. Be ready to pay to your rulers all that they may, in respect of their office, justly demand of you. Render tribute and custom to those of your governors to whom tribute and custom belong, and cheerfully honor and reverence all who are vested with civil authority, according to their deserts."

The Apostle's doctrine, in the passage thus explained concerning the office of civil rulers and the duty of subjects, may be summed up in the following observations, viz.:

That the end of magistracy is the good of civil society, *as such.*

That civil rulers, *as such,* are the ordinance and ministers of God, it being by his permission and providence that any bear rule, and agreeable to his will that there should be *some persons* vested with authority in society, for the well-being of it.

That which is here said concerning civil rulers extends to all of them in common: it relates indifferently to monarchical, republican, and aristocratical government, and to all other forms which truly answer the sole end of government, the happiness of society; and to all the different degrees of authority in any particular state, to inferior officers no less than to the supreme.

That disobedience to civil rulers in the due exercise of their authority is not merely a *political sin* but an heinous *offense against God and religion.*

That the true ground and reason of our obligation to be subject to the *higher powers* is the usefulness of magistracy (when properly exercised) to human society and its subserviency to the general welfare.

That obedience to civil rulers is here equally required under all forms of government which answer the sole end of all government, the good of society; and to every degree of authority in any state, whether supreme or subordinate.

(From whence it follows,

That if unlimited obedience and nonresistance be here required as a duty under any one form of government, it is also required as a duty under all other forms, and as a duty to subordinate rulers as well as to the supreme.)

And lastly, that those civil rulers to whom the Apostle enjoins subjection are the persons *in possession; the powers that be,* those who are *actually* vested with authority.

There is one very important and interesting point which remains to be inquired into; namely, the *extent* of that subjection *to the higher powers* which is here enjoined as a duty upon all Christians. Some have thought it warrantable and glorious to disobey the civil powers in certain circumstances, and, in cases of very great and general oppression when humble remonstrances fail of having any effect, and when the public welfare cannot be otherwise provided for and secured, to rise unanimously even against the sovereign himself in order to redress their grievances, to vindicate their natural and legal rights, to break the yoke of tyranny, and free themselves and posterity from inglorious servitude and ruin. ... But, in opposition to this principle, it has often been asserted that the Scripture in general (and the passage under consideration in particular) makes all resistance to princes a crime, in any case whatever.—If they turn tyrants and become the common oppressors of those whose welfare they ought to regard with a paternal affection, we must not pretend to right ourselves unless it be by prayers and tears and humble entreaties; and if these methods fail of procuring redress we must not have recourse to any other, but all suffer ourselves to be robbed and butchered at the pleasure of the Lord's *anointed*, lest we should incur the sin of rebellion and the punishment of damnation. For he has God's authority and commission to bear him out in the worst of crimes, so far that he may not be withstood or controlled. Now whether we are obliged to yield such an absolute submission to our prince, or whether disobedience and resistance may not be justifiable in some cases notwithstanding anything in the passage before us, is an inquiry in which we are all concerned; and this is the inquiry which is the main design of the present discourse.

Now there does not seem to be any necessity of supposing that an absolute, unlimited obedience, whether active or passive, is here enjoined merely for this reason, that the precept is delivered in *absolute terms*, without any exception or *limitation* expressly mentioned. We are enjoined (ver. 1) to be *subject to the higher powers*, and (ver. 5) to be *subject for conscience sake*. And because these expressions are absolute and unlimited (or, more properly, general), some have inferred that the subjection required in them must be absolute and unlimited also, at least so far forth as to make passive obedience and nonresistance a duty in all cases whatever, if not active obedience likewise. Though, by the way, there is here no distinction made betwixt active and passive obedience; and if either of them be required in an unlimited sense, the other must be required in the same sense also by virtue of the present argument, because the expressions are equally absolute with respect to both. But that unlimited obedience of any sort cannot be argued merely from the indefinite expressions in which obedience is enjoined appears from hence, that expressions of the same nature frequently occur in Scripture, upon which it is confessed on all hands that no such absolute and unlimited sense ought to be put. For example, *Love not the world; neither the things that are in the world;** *Lay not up for yourselves treasures upon earth;*† *Take therefore no thought for the morrow;*‡ are precepts expressed in at least equally absolute and unlimited terms: but it is generally allowed that they are to be understood with certain restrictions and limitations, some degree of love to the world and the things of it being allowable. . . .

It is to be observed, in the next place, that as the duty of universal obedience and nonresistance to the *higher powers* cannot be argued from the absolute unlimited expressions which the Apostle here uses, so neither can it be argued from the scope and drift of his reasoning, considered with relation to the persons he was here opposing. As was observed above, there were some professed *Christians* in the apostolic age who disclaimed all magistracy and civil authority in general, *despising government* and *speaking evil of dignities*, some under a notion that *Jews* ought not to be under the jurisdiction of *gentile* rulers, and others that they were set *free* from the temporal powers by Christ. Now it is with persons of this licentious opinion and character that the Apostle is concerned. And all that was directly to his point was to show that they were bound to submit to magistracy *in general*. . . .

. . . If we attend to the nature of the argument with which the Apostle here enforces the duty of submission to *the higher powers*, we shall find it to be such an one as concludes not in favor of submission to all who bear the *title* of rulers in common, but only to those who *actually* perform the duty of rulers by exercising a reasonable and just authority for the good of human society. This is a point which it will be proper to enlarge upon because the question before us turns very much upon the truth or falsehood of this position. It is obvious, then, in general that the civil rulers whom the Apostle here speaks of, and obedience to whom he presses upon Christians as a duty, are *good rulers*, such as are, in the exercise of their office and power, benefactors to society. Such they are described to be throughout this passage. Thus it is said that they *are not a terror to good works but to the evil; that they are God's ministers for good, revengers to execute wrath upon him that doth evil; and that they attend continually upon this very thing.* St. Peter gives the same account of rulers: *they are for a praise to them that do well, and the punishment of evildoers.* It is manifest that this character and description of rulers agrees only to such as are rulers in fact as well as in name: to such as govern well and act agreeably to their office. And the Apostle's argument for submission to rulers is wholly built and grounded upon a presumption that they do in fact answer this character, and is of no force at all upon supposition to the contrary. . . .

---

* 1 John ii, 15.

† Matt. vi, 19.

‡ Matt. vi, 34.

If it be said that the Apostle here uses another argument for submission to the higher powers besides that which is taken from the usefulness of their office to civil society when properly discharged and executed, namely, that their power is from God, that they are ordained of God, and that they are God's ministers; and if it be said that this argument for submission to them will hold good although they do not exercise their power for the benefit but for the ruin and destruction of human society—this objection was obviated, in part, before. Rulers have no authority from God to do mischief. They are not God's ordinance or God's ministers in any other sense than as it is by his permission and providence that they are exalted to bear rule, and as magistracy duly exercised and authority rightly applied in the enacting and executing good laws. . . .

Thus, upon a careful review of the Apostle's reasoning . . . it appears that his arguments to enforce submission are of such a nature as to conclude only in favor of submission *to such rulers as he himself describes;* i.e., such as rule for the good of society, which is the only end of their institution. Common tyrants and public oppressors are not entitled to obedience from their subjects by virtue of anything here laid down by the inspired Apostle.

I now add, farther, that the Apostle's argument is so far from proving it to be the duty of people to obey and submit to such rulers as act in contradiction to the public good* and so to the design of their office, that it proves *the direct contrary.* For, please to observe, that if the end of all civil government be the good of society, if this be the thing that is aimed at in constituting civil rulers, and if the motive and argument for submission to government be taken from the apparent usefulness of civil authority, it follows that when no such good end can be answered by submission there remains no argument or motive to enforce it; and if instead of this good end's being brought about by submission, a *contrary end* is brought about and the ruin and misery of society effected by it, here is a plain and positive reason against submission in all such cases, should they ever happen. And therefore, in such cases a regard to the public welfare ought to make us withhold from our rulers that obedience and subjection which it would, otherwise, be our duty to render to them. If it be our duty, for example, to obey our King merely for this reason, that he rules for the public welfare (which is the only argument the Apostle makes use of), it follows by a parity of reason that when he turns tyrant and makes his subjects his prey to devour and to destroy instead of his charge to defend and cherish, we are bound to throw off our allegiance to him and to resist, and that according to the tenor of the Apostle's argument in this passage. Not to discontinue our allegiance, in this case, would be to join with the sovereign in promoting

---

* This does not intend [mean] their acting so in *a few particular instances,* which the best of rulers may do through mistake, etc., but their acting so *habitually,* and in a manner which plainly shows that they aim at making themselves great by the ruin of their subjects.

the slavery and misery of that society the welfare of which we ourselves as well as our sovereign are indispensably obliged to secure and promote as far as in us lies. It is true the Apostle puts no case of such a tyrannical prince; but by his grounding his argument for submission wholly upon the good of civil society it is plain he implicitly authorizes and even requires us to make resistance whenever this shall be necessary to the public safety and happiness. . . .

. . . The advocates for unlimited submission and passive obedience do, if I mistake not, always speak with reference to kingly or monarchical government as distinguished from all other forms and with reference to submitting to the will of the king in distinction from all subordinate officers acting beyond their commission and the authority which they have received from the crown. It is not pretended that any persons besides kings have a divine right to do what they please so that no one may resist them without incurring the guilt of factiousness and rebellion. If any other supreme powers oppress the people it is generally allowed that the people may get redress, by resistance if other methods prove ineffectual. And if any officers in a kingly government go beyond the limits of that power which they have derived from the crown (the supposed original source of all power and authority in the state), and attempt, illegally, to take away the properties and lives of their fellow subjects, they may be *forcibly* resisted, at least till application can be made to the crown. But as to the sovereign himself, he may not be resisted in any case, nor any of his officers while they confine themselves within the bounds which he has prescribed to them. This is, I think, a true sketch of the principles of those who defend the doctrine of passive obedience and nonresistance. Now there is nothing in Scripture which supports this scheme of political principles. As to the passage under consideration, the Apostle here speaks of civil rulers in *general*, of all persons in common vested with authority for the good of society, without any particular reference to one form of government more than to another or to the supreme power in any particular state more than to subordinate powers. The Apostle does not concern himself with the different forms of government. This he supposes left entirely to human prudence and discretion. Now the consequence of this is that unlimited and passive obedience is no more enjoined in this passage under monarchical government, or to the supreme power in any state, than under all other species of government which answer the end of government, or to all the subordinate degrees of civil authority, from the highest to the lowest. Those, therefore, who would from this passage infer the guilt of resisting kings in all cases whatever, though acting ever so contrary to the design of their office, must, if they will be consistent, go much farther, and infer from it the guilt of resistance under all other forms of government and of resisting *any petty officer* in the state, though acting beyond his commission, in the most arbitrary, illegal manner possible. The argument holds equally strong in both cases. All civil rulers, as such, are the *ordinance* and *ministers of God;* and they are all, by the nature of their office and in their respective spheres and stations, bound to consult the public welfare. With the same reason, therefore, that any deny unlimited and passive obedience to be here enjoined under a republic or aristocracy or any other established form of civil government or to subordinate powers acting in an illegal and oppressive manner, with the same reason others may deny that such obedience is enjoined to a king or monarch or any civil power whatever. For the Apostle says nothing that is *peculiar to kings;* what he says extends equally to *all* other persons whatever, vested with any civil office. They are all, in exactly the same sense, the *ordinance of God* and the *ministers of God;* and obedience is equally enjoined to be paid to them all. For, as the Apostle expresses it, *there is* NO POWER *but of God:* and we are required to *render to* ALL *their* DUES, and not MORE than their DUES. And what these *dues* are, and to *whom* they are to be *rendered,* the Apostle *saith not* but leaves to the reason and consciences of men to determine. . . .

If we calmly consider the nature of the thing itself, nothing can well be imagined more directly contrary to common sense than to suppose that *millions* of people should be subjected to the arbitrary, precarious pleasure of *one single man* (who has *naturally* no superiority over them in point of authority) so that their estates, and everything that is valuable in life, and even their lives also shall be absolutely at his disposal, if he happens to be wanton and capricious enough to demand them. What unprejudiced man can think that God made ALL to be thus subservient to the lawless pleasure and frenzy of ONE so that it shall always be a sin to resist him! Nothing but the most plain and express revelation from Heaven could make a sober impartial man believe such a monstrous, unaccountable doctrine; and, indeed, the thing itself appears so shocking—so out of all *proportion,* that it may be questioned whether all the *miracles* that ever were wrought could make it credible that this doctrine *really* came from God. At present, there is not the least syllable in Scripture which gives any countenance to it. The hereditary, indefeasible, divine right of kings, and the doctrine of nonresistance, which is built upon the supposition of such a right, are altogether as fabulous and chimerical as transubstantiation or any of the most absurd reveries of ancient or modern visionaries. These notions are fetched neither from divine revelation nor human reason; and if they are derived from neither of those sources, it is not much matter from *whence they come, or whither they go.* Only it is a pity that such doctrines should be propagated in society, to raise factions and rebellions, as we see they have in fact been, both in the *last* and in the *present* REIGN.

But then, if unlimited submission and passive obedience to the *higher powers* in all possible cases be not a duty, it will be asked, "How far are we obliged to submit? If we may innocently disobey and resist in some cases, why not in all? Where shall we stop? What is the measure of our duty? This doctrine tends to the total dissolution of civil government and to introduce such scenes of wild anarchy and confusion as are more fatal to society than the worst of tyranny."

After this manner, some men object; and, indeed, this is the most plausible thing that can be said in favor of such an absolute submission as they plead for. But the worst (or rather the best) of it is that there is very little strength or solidity in it. For similar difficulties may be raised with respect to almost every duty of natural and revealed religion. ... It is indeed true that turbulent, vicious-minded men may take occasion from this principle, that their rulers may, in some cases, be lawfully resisted, to raise factions and disturbances in the state and to make resistance where resistance is needless and therefore sinful. But is it not equally true that children and servants of turbulent, vicious minds may take occasion from this principle, that parents and masters may, in some cases, be lawfully resisted, to resist when resistance is unnecessary and therefore criminal? Is the principle in either case false in itself merely because it may be abused and applied to legitimate disobedience and resistance in those instances to which it ought not to be applied? According to this way of arguing there will be no true principles in the world, for there are none but what may be wrested and perverted to serve bad purposes, either through the weakness or wickedness of men.

A PEOPLE really oppressed to a great degree by their sovereign cannot well be insensible when they are so oppressed. And such a people (if I may allude to an ancient *fable*) have, like the Hesperian fruit, a DRAGON for their *protector* and *guardian;* nor would they have any reason to mourn if some HERCULES should appear to dispatch him. For a nation thus abused to arise unanimously and to resist their prince, even to the dethroning him, is not criminal, but a reasonable way of vindicating their liberties and just rights; it is making use of the means, and the only means, which God has put into their power for mutual and self-defense. And it would be highly criminal in them not to make use of this means. It would be stupid tameness and unaccountable folly for whole nations to suffer *one* unreasonable, ambitious, and cruel man to wanton and riot in their misery. And in such a case it would, of the two, be more rational to suppose that they did NOT *resist* than that they who did would *receive to themselves damnation.* ...

Although the observation of this *anniversary* seems to have been (at least) superstitious in its *original;* and although it is often abused to very bad purposes by the established clergy, as they serve themselves of it, to perpetuate strife, a party spirit, and divisions in the Christian church; yet it is to be hoped that one good end will be answered by it quite contrary to their intention: it is to be hoped that it will prove a standing *memento* that *Britons* will not be *slaves,* and a warning to all corrupt *counselors* and *ministers* not to go too far in advising to arbitrary, despotic measures.

Exchange of Correspondence between Benjamin Franklin in London and Charles Thomson in America

Franklin's letter was published by his printer friend, William Strahan, in the London Chronicle, *November 16, 1765. Charles Thomson, teacher of Latin at a Pennsylvania academy and future secretary of the Continental Congress, was Franklin's friend and protegé of long standing.*

Depend upon it, my good Friend, every possible step was taken to prevent the passing of the Stamp Act. But the tide was too strong against us. The nation was provok'd by American claims of independence, and all parties join'd in resolving by this act to settle the point. We might as well have hindered the sun's setting. But since it is down, my Friend, and it may be long ere it rises again, let us make as good a night of it as we can. We may still light candles. Frugality and Industry will go a great way towards indemnifying us. Idleness and Pride tax with a heavier hand than Kings and Parliaments. If we can get rid of the former, we may easily bear the latter. Our country produces, or is capable of producing, all the necessaries of life, the wasting superfluities come from hence. Let us have but the wisdom to be content awhile with our own, and this country will soon feel, that its loss in point of commerce, is infinitely more than its gain in taxes.

Thomson's letter is dated Philadelphia, September 24, 1765. It too appeared in the London Chronicle *on the following November 16.*

Yes, my friend, I grant that 'Idleness and Pride tax with a heavier hand than Kings and Parliaments,' and 'that frugality and industry will go a great way towards indemnifying us.' But the misfortune is, the very thing that renders industry necessary cuts the sinews of it. With industry and frugality the subjects of eastern tyrants might be wealthier than those of England or Holland. But who will labour or save who has not a security in his property?

When people are taxed by their own representatives, though the tax is high they pay it chearfully, from a confidence that no more than enough is required, and that a due regard is had to the ability of the giver. But when taxes are laid

Exchange of Correspondence Between Benjamin Franklin and Charles Thomson, July 11, 1765, and September 24, 1765, *Benjamin Franklin's Letters to the Press,* ed. V. W. Crane, Chapel Hill, N. C., Univ. of North Carolina for the Institute of Early American History and Culture, 1950, pp. 36–68. Reprinted by permission of the publisher.

merely to "settle the point of independence, and when the quantity of the tax depends on the caprice of those who have the superiority, and who will doubtless lay it heavier in order to bring down the spirits or weaken the power of those who claim independence, what encouragement is there to labour or save? The wealth we thereby acquire will be a new motive, which fear or avarice will suggest, to tax us anew. No wonder then if people will chuse to live poor and lazy rather than labour to enrich their tax-masters or furnish matter for new oppression. There never was any mention of the colonies aiming at independence, till the ministry began to abridge them of their liberties. I will venture to affirm, and to you I can appeal for the truth of what I say, that history cannot shew a people so numerous, so far removed from the seat of Royalty, who were so loyal, so attached to their King, and who at the same time had such true sentiments of liberty, as the British American Colonies. How long this will continue God knows.

The Sun Of Liberty is indeed fast setting, if not down already, in the American colonies: But I much fear instead of the candles you mention being lighted, you will hear of the works of darkness. They are in general alarmed to the last degree. The colonies expect, and with reason expect, that some regard shall be had to their liberties and privileges, as well as trade. They cannot bring themselves to believe, nor can they see how England with reason or justice could expect, that they should have encountered the horrors of a desert, borne the attacks of barbarous savages, and, at the expence of their blood and treasure, settled this country to the great emolument of England, and after all quietly submit to be deprived of every thing an Englishman has been taught to hold dear. It is not property only we contend for. Our Liberty and most essential privileges are struck at: Arbitrary courts are set over us, and trials by juries taken away: The Press is so restricted that we cannot complain: An army of mercenaries threatened to be billeted on us: The sources of our trade stopped; and, to compleat our ruin, the little property we had acquired, taken from us, without even allowing us the merit of giving it; I really dread the consequence. The parliament insist on a power over all the liberties and privileges claimed by the colonies, and hence require a blind obedience and acquiescence in whatever they do: Should the behaviour of the colonies happen not to square with these sovereign notions, (as I much fear it will not) what remains but by violence to compel them to obedience. Violence will beget resentment, and provoke to acts never dreamt of: But I will not anticipate evil: I pray God avert it.

I congratulate you on the change in the ministry: We hope for much good from it. For such seems the state of the British constitution at present, that from them we are to look for good or ill. Heretofore we have been taught to look for redress from another quarter. . . .

JOHN ADAMS,
Instructions of the Town of Braintree to Their Representative

The instructions printed below are cast in the form of a letter dated September 24, 1765, from John Adams to Ebenezer Thayer, the local representative to the colonial Assembly. They were adopted unanimously at a Braintree town meeting.

In all the calamities which have ever befallen this country, we have never felt so great a concern, or such alarming apprehensions, as on this occasion. Such is our loyalty to the King, our veneration for both houses of Parliament, and our affection for all our fellow-subjects in Britain, that measures which discover any unkindness in that country towards us are the more sensibly and intimately felt. And we can no longer forbear complaining, that many of the measures of the late ministry, and some of the late acts of Parliament, have a tendency, in our apprehension, to divest us of our most essential rights and liberties. We shall confine ourselves, however, chiefly to the act of Parliament, commonly called the Stamp Act, by which a very burthensome, and, in our opinion, unconstitutional tax, is to be laid upon us all; and we subjected to numerous and enormous penalties, to be prosecuted, sued for, and recovered, at the option of an informer, in a court of admiralty, without a jury.

We have called this a burthensome tax, because the duties are so numerous and so high, and the embarrassments to business in this infant, sparsely-settled country so great, that it would be totally impossible for the people to subsist under it, if we had no controversy at all about the right and authority of imposing it. Considering the present scarcity of money, we have reason to think, the execution of that act for a short space of time would drain the country of its cash, strip multitudes of all their property, and reduce them to absolute beggary. And what the consequence would be to the peace of the province, from so sudden a shock and such a convulsive change in the whole course of our business and subsistence, we tremble to consider. We further apprehend this tax to be unconstitutional. We have always understood it to be a grand and fundamental principle of the constitution, that no freeman should be subject to any tax to which he has not given his own consent, in person or by proxy. And the maxims of the law, as we have constantly received them, are to the same effect, that no freeman can be separated from his property but by his own act or fault. We take it clearly, therefore, to be inconsistent with the

Works of John Adams, ed. C. F. Adams, Boston, 1851, Vol. III, pp. 465–468.

spirit of the common law, and of the essential fundamental principles of the British constitution, that we should be subject to any tax imposed by the British Parliament; because we are not represented in that assembly in any sense, unless it be by a fiction of law, as insensible in theory as it would be injurious in practice, if such a taxation should be grounded on it.

But the most grievous innovation of all, is the alarming extension of the power of courts of admiralty. In these courts, one judge presides alone! No juries have any concern there! The law and the fact are both to be decided by the same single judge, whose commission is only during pleasure, and with whom, as we are told, the most mischievous of all customs has become established, that of taking commissions on all condemnations; so that he is under a pecuniary temptation always against the subject. Now, if the wisdom of the mother country has thought the independency of the judges so essential to an impartial administration of justice, as to render them independent of every power on earth,—independent in hope and expectation of the heir-apparent, by continuing their commissions after a demise of the crown, what justice and impartiality are we, at three thousand miles distance from the fountain, to expect from such a judge of admiralty? We have all along thought the acts of trade in this respect a grievance; but the Stamp Act has opened a vast number of sources of new crimes, which may be committed by any man, and cannot be committed by multitudes, and prodigious penalties are annexed, and all these are to be tried by such a judge of such a court! What can be wanting, after this, but a weak or wicked man for a judge, to render us the most sordid and forlorn of slaves?—we mean the slaves of a slave of the servants of a minister of state. We cannot help asserting, therefore, that this part of the act will make an essential change in the constitution of juries, and it is directly repugnant to the Great Charter itself; for, by that charter, "no amerciament shall be assessed, but by the oath of honest and lawful men of the vicinage"; and, "no freeman shall be taken, or imprisoned, or disseized of his freehold, or liberties of free customs, nor passed upon, nor condemned, but by lawful judgment of his peers, or by the law of the land." So that this act will "make such a distinction, and create such a difference between" the subjects in Great Britain and those in America, as we could not have expected from the guardians of liberty in "both."

As these, sir, are our sentiments of this act, we, the freeholders and other inhabitants, legally assembled for this purpose, must enjoin it upon you, to comply with no measures or proposals for countenancing the same, or assisting in the execution of it, but by all lawful means, consistent with our allegiance to the King, and relation to Great Britain, to oppose the execution of it, till we can hear the success of the cries and petitions of America for relief.

We further recommend the most clear and explicit assertion and vindication of our rights and liberties to be entered on the public records, that the world may know, in the present and all future generations, that we have a clear knowledge and a just sense of them, and, with submission to Divine Providence, that we never can be slaves.

Nor can we think it advisable to agree to any steps for the protection of stamped papers or stamp-officers. Good and wholesome laws we have already for the preservation of the peace; and we apprehend there is no further danger of tumult and disorder, to which we have a well-grounded aversion; and that any extraordinary and expensive exertions would tend to exasperate the people and endanger the public tranquillity, rather than the contrary. Indeed, we cannot too often inculcate upon you our desires, that all extraordinary grants and expensive measures may, upon all occasions, as much as possible, be avoided. The public money of this country is the toil and labor of the people, who are under many uncommon difficulties and distresses at this time, so that all reasonable frugality ought to be observed. And we would recommend particularly, the strictest care and the utmost firmness to prevent all unconstitutional draughts upon the public treasury.

FRANCIS BERNARD, *Letter to Lord Barrington, November 23, 1765*

Bernard had been governor of New Jersey in 1758 and took office as governor of Massachusetts in 1760. He was created a baronet in 1769 as a reward for his loyal service to the crown. Viscount Barrington held the office of Secretary at War until 1778, when he resigned in the aftermath of Sir John Burgoyne's surrender at Saratoga.

It is not above a Year since I troubled your Lordship with Copies of an Essay to delineate the Principles of Law & Polity applicable to the British Colonies in America. Among these two principal Conclusions were, that the Regulation & Reformation of the American Goverments was then become a necessary Work; and that the present was the most proper time to undertake that Work. If I could have then spoke out with that earnestness with which I thought upon the Subject, I should have urged it as a Business which would admit of no Delay; a Business to which all others ought to have been postponed; as it was itself a necessary Preparative to allmost all others. But unfortunately (I speak it feelingly) the Business of the Finances took the Lead: this was undoubtedly an

Governor Bernard to Lord Barrington, November 23, 1765, *The Barrington-Bernard Correspondence,* ed. E. Channing and A. C. Coolidge, Cambridge, 1912, pp. 93–102.

Urgent & primary Concern of the Councils of Great Britain; but it did not follow that it ought to be immediately extended to America. A little Consideration would have made it at least doubtfull whether an inland Taxation of the American was practicable or equitable at that Time. If I had had the Question put to me I think I should have proved the Negative in both particulars.

It must have been supposed that such an Innovation as a Parliamentary Taxation would cause a great Alarm & meet with much Opposition in most parts of America; It was quite new to the People, & had no visible Bounds set to it; The American's declared that they would not submit to it before the Act passed; & there was the greatest probability that it would require the utmost Power of Government to carry it into Execution. Whereas at this Time the Governments were weak & impotent to a amazing Degree; The Governers & the Officers of the Crown in several of the chief Provinces intirely dependent upon the people for Subsistence; The Popular Scale so much weigtier than the Royal, that it required Address & management & frequent temporizing to preserve a tolerable ballance; The Persons of the Governors & Crown-Officers quite defenceless, & exposed to the Violence of the People without any possible Resort for Protection. Was this a Time to introduce so great a Novelty as a Parliamentary inland Taxation into America!?—Nor was the Time less favourable to the Equity of such a Taxation. I do not mean to dispute the Reasonableness of America contributing to the charges of Great Britain when she is able: nor, I believe would the Americans themselves have disputed it at a proper Time & Season. But it should be considered that the American Governments themselves have, in the prosecution of the late War, contracted very large debts, which it will take some Years to pay off, & in the mean Time occasion very burthensome Taxes for that Purpose only. For instance, this Government, which is as much before hand as any, raises every Year £37,500 sterling for sinking their Debt, & must continue it for 4 Years longer at least before it will be clear.—If therefore the parliamentary Taxation had been postponed for this Time, & the interval employed in regulating & strengthening the Governments, It probably might have been then introduced without much Difficulty. Now it seems that both one & the other are at greater distance than ever.

It were much to be wished that America could be brought to the State it was in, two Years ago; when there was a general Disposition to submit to regulations & requisitions necessary to the Reformation of the Governments & ascertaining their relation to Great Britain. But that Time is past & not to be retrieved: since the Insurrections against the Stampt-Act, The Americans have found the Governments so contemptibly weak & the People so superior to the Royal Authority, that they are not a little elated upon their Triumphs over the defenceless Officers of the Crown; & seem to be resolved that their Idea of their Relation to Great Britain, however extravagant various & inconsistent shall be the standard of it. So that it is to be feared that it will cost much time

& Treasure to bring America to that Degree of Submission which the Parliament will think necessary to require of them. The Question will not be whether there shall be a Stamp Act or not; but whether America shall or shall not be Subject to the Legislature of Great Britain.

It is my Opinion that all the Political Evils in America arise from the Want of ascertaining the Relation between Great Britain & the American Colonies. Hence it is that Ideas of that Relation are formed in Britain & America, so very repugnant & contradictory to each other. In Britain the American Governments are considered as Corporations empowered to make by-Laws, existing only during the Pleasure of Parliament, who hath never yet done any thing to confirm their Establishment, & hath at any Time a Power to dissolve them. In America they claim (I mean in publick Papers,) to be perfect States, no otherwise dependent upon Great Britain than by having the same King; which having compleat Legislatures within themselves, are no ways subject to that of Great-Britain; which in such Instances as it has heretofore exercised a legislative Power over them has usurped it. In a Difference so very wide who shall determine? The Parliament of Great Britain? No, say the Americans (I mean the violent & foolish of them); that would be to make them Judges in their own Cause. Who then? the King? He is bound by Charters & Constitutions equal to Charters; & cannot decree against his own Grants. So at this Rate there is no superior Tribunal to determine upon the Rights & Priviledges of the American Colonies.

But the general Plea of the Americans against the Stamp Act is that they are not represented in Parliament, & therefore not liable to be taxed by it. To which it has been answered in England, that they are, *virtually* represented in Parliament. Each of these Pleas tends to expose its own Cause: If the Americans rest their Defence upon their not being represented, It is in the Power of the Parliament by admitting representatives from America to take away all Pretence of their not being bound by its Acts; On the other side, if the Notion of the Americans being *virtually* represented should be falsified in fact, the Plea of the Americans will remain in its full Force. Whereas The Right of the Parliament of Great Britain to make Laws for the American Colonies is founded upon its being the Supreme Imperial Legislature, to which all Members of the Empire, whether represented or not, are subject in all Matters & Things & in Manner & Form as shall be judged most convenient for the whole.

But tho the Parliament of Great Britain does not stand in Need of a Real or Virtual Representation to ground its Authority over the Colonies, it may now be worth Consideration whether Admitting Representatives from the Colonies may not be a Proper expedient for the present Exigencies. Two Years ago a proposal of this Kind would not have bore an hearing: But so much is America altered by the late financial Acts, that a New System of Policy & of a more refined Kind than was wanted heretofore, is now become needful. The Patchwork Government of America will last no longer: The Necessity of a Parliamentary establishment of the Government of America upon fixed Constitutional Principles is brought on with a Precipitation which could not have been foreseen but a Year ago; & is become more urgent by the very Incidents which make it more difficult. The Circumstance of the Americans justifying their Disobedience by their not being represented points out a Method to inforce their Obedience upon their own Principles. Take them at their Word; let them send Representatives for the present Time & for the present Purposes: 30 for the Continent & 15 for the Islands would be sufficient. In this Parliament, the Colonies being actually represented, Let the Affair of the American Governments be canvassed to the Bottom; & let a general uniform System of American Government be formed & Established by Act of Parliament, by which the Americans according to their own Principles will be bound; and let the Relation of America to Great Britain be determined & ascertained by a Solemn Recognition; so that the Rights of the American Governments & their Subordination to that of Great Britain may no longer be a Subject of Doubt & Disputation. When this Great Work is done the American Representatives may be dismissed & left to attend their own legislatures, which will then know the Bounds of their own Authority.

Ireland affords an Example for the Usefulness of this Work & the Manner of doing it. It is owing to the wise Administration of S(ir) Edward Poynings in Henry the 7ths Time, that the Form of Government of that Island, which is as perfect for a dependent, as that of Great Britain for a supreme Power, has lasted now for 270 Years, without wanting the least Amendment of Fundamentals. Haply America has not had a Poynings to regulate here Policy & prevent the Mischeifs, which the Uncertainty of the Relative Powers of civil Government, imperial & subordinate, is now bringing on like Torrent. The Civil Policy of America is composed to temporary Expedients all derived from the Crown only; not one of the American Governments has that Sanction which none of them ought to be without, a parliamentary Establishment. And untill the parliament shall establish the American Governments upon a constitutional bottom, & ascertain the Limitation's & extension's of their Legislatures, It must be expected that the Governments will be continually subject to disturbance, whenever the Americans think fit to complain of innovations upon & infringements of their Rights; that is whenever any thing is required of them which they don't like.

Ireland also affords Instances of every Kind of Regulation which America wants; which may be brought under these Heads. 1. The Governments (especially in the Old & settled Countries) should be composed of such ample Districts, as will enable the People to keep up the State of Government without feeling the Burthen of it. 2. There should be one Form of Government as like as possible to that of Great Britain, that is the same as Ireland, with a true Middle

Legislative Power, appointed by the King for Life & separate from the Privy Council. 3. There should be a certain & sufficient civil List laid upon perpetual Funds for the Support of all his Majestys Officers, so that they may not be too dependent upon the People. 4. The Several American Governments should Maintain such standing Forces as shall be thought necessary to be kept up in America as their quota of the general Armament of the Empire, by raising the Sums requisite therefore & paying the same into the Kings Treasury in America; the Numbers of Men, & proportions of the several Governments to be settled by the Parliament of Great Britain. 5. There should be a solemn Recognition of the Supremacy of the Parliament of Great Britain over the American Governments, which should be the first Act of each Legislature after its new Establishment & be The condition of its Activity. 6. There should be a general Rivisal of the Laws of America, that they may be reduced as near as possible to the Standard of England & the Administration of Government & Law may be render'd as similar thereto as well may be.

You see here, my Lord, a Scheme for settling America; which, I doubt not, will appear to be very extravagant. It may be so; but such also is the State of the Country; extraordinary Disorders require extraordinary Means of Cure. It seems to me that the Government of Great Britain never had, in my Time, a more difficult Business, than what the Americans have now put into their Hands. If therefore any Scheme can be proposed, which by constitutional Means will probably compose the present Disorder's & prevent the like for the future, it is worth attending to. For this Purpose I have put these Thoughts into writing, in a hasty Manner; for at present I can write no otherwise: and I communicate them to your Lordship; that if you should think they deserve a deliberate Consideration you may procure it for them. I shall think myself very happy, if I can contribute to the restoring the Peace of America & establishing the Governments of it upon a Constitutional & permanent Basis, according to the foregoing or any other System. The Opportunities I have had of observing the Policy & Manners of many of the Governments of North America have afforded me a Knowledge which might be made useful, if I could freely communicate it; which cannot be done without my personal Attendance. I say this upon presumption that some effectual Alteration of the Government of America is like to be brought on the carpet: but if nothing is to be done but making Peace with the Americans, & letting them go on in their own Way & according to their own Notions, No great Consideration will be necessary.

I have extended this letter so far that I have not room to say much of myself: but Mr Pownall can inform your Lordship in that respect as well as I can. For near 3 months I have been under great difficulties & not without danger: Once my house was invested (the same night the Lieut Governors house was distroyed) but preserved by the remonstrances of the Neighbours, ourselves being at the Castle; twice have I sent away any papers plate &c; once I expected to be obliged to quit the Province for several days together; but the peremptoriness of my instructions made me desirous of trying evry experiment first, & I got over that difficulty. Even Now I am in continual expectation of fresh disturbances arising, of which I may partake more or less. But I have done my duty tho' it has been a Severe one at this time: I have waged a most unequal War, & can hardly now procure the liberty of remaining Neutral without pretending to exercise any real Authority. I send your Lordships copies of the principle papers which have passed between me & the house of representatives, from which you will see that All my Crime is vindicating the right of parliament to make Laws for the American Colonies: a conduct unavoidable by me whatever were the Consequences.

THE BRITISH DRAW THE LINE

The American Colonies Act (The Declaratory Act), 1766

The Declaratory Act accompanied the repeal of the Stamp Act. In America, public jubilation greeted the repeal of the latter; and little attention was paid to the former. In British thinking, however, the declaration of principle was much more important than the retreat from the Stamp Act.

PREAMBLE

Whereas several of the Houses of Representatives in his Majesty's colonies and plantations in America, have of late, against law, claimed to themselves, or to the general assemblies of the same, the sole and exclusive right of imposing duties and taxes upon his Majesty's subjects in the said colonies and plantations; and have, in pursuance of such claim, passed certain votes, resolutions and orders, derogatory to the legislative authority of Parliament, and incon-

The American Colonies Act (The Declaratory Act), 1766, The Complete Statutes of England, London, 1929, Vol. V, pp. 332–333.

sistent with the dependency of the said colonies and plantations upon the crown of Great Britain: May it therefore please your most excellent Majesty, that it may be declared, and be it declared by the King's most excellent Majesty, by and with the advice and consent of the lords spiritual and temporal, and commons, in this present *Parliament* assembled, and by the authority of the same, that

(1) The colonies and plantations in America declared to be subordinate unto, and dependent upon the imperial crown and Parliament of Great Britain; and the legislative authority of Great Britain declared to extend to, and bind the colonies and people of America, as subjects, in all cases whatsoever.— The said colonies and plantations in America have been, are, and of right ought to be subordinate unto, and dependent upon, the imperial crown and Parliament of Great Britain; and that the King's Majesty, by and with the advice and consent of the lords spiritual and temporal, and commons of Great Britain, in Parliament assembled, had, hath, and of right ought to have, full power and authority to make laws and statutes of sufficient force and validity to bind the colonies and people of America, subjects of the crown of Great Britain, in all cases whatsoever.

(2) All resolutions and proceedings of the said colonies denying or calling in question the said power, declared null and void.—And . . . all resolutions, votes, orders, and proceedings, in any of the said colonies or plantations, whereby the power and authority of the Parliament of Great Britain, to make laws and statutes as aforesaid, is denied, or drawn into question, are, and are hereby declared to be, utterly null and void to all intents and purposes whatsoever.

The Townshend Taxes

The obnoxious Townshend Taxes were authorized in a series of resolutions adopted by Parliament as a Committee of Supply on June 2, 1767. The grave constitutional implications of Resolution 18 should be particularly noted.

(13) That a duty of 4s. 8d. per cwt. avoirdupois, be laid upon all crown, plate, flint, and white glass, imported into the British colonies and plantations in America.

Resolutions of the Committee of Supply, June 2, 1767 (The Townshend Taxes), *Parliamentary History*, ed., W. Cobbett, London, 1814, Vol. XVI, pp. 375–376.

(14) That a duty of 1s. 2d. per cwt. avoirdupois, be laid upon all green glass imported into the said colonies and plantations.

(15) That such duties as shall be equal to a moiety of the duties granted by two acts of parliament made in the 10th and 12th of her majesty queen Anne, and now payable in pursuance thereof, or of any subsequent act of parliament, upon paper, paste-board, mill-boards, and scale-boards, respectively, be laid upon paper, paste-board, mill-boards, and scale-boards, imported into the said colonies and plantations.

(16) That a duty of 2s. per cwt. avoirdupois, be laid upon all red and white lead and painters colours, imported into the said colonies and plantations.

(17) That a duty of 3d. per pound weight, avoirdupois, be laid upon all tea imported into the said colonies and plantations.

(18) That the said duties, to be raised in the said colonies and plantations, be applied in making a more certain and adequate provision for the charge of the administration of justice, and the support of civil government in such of the said colonies and plantations where it shall be found necessary; and that the residue of such duties be paid into the receipt of his Majesty's exchequer, and there reserved to be, from time to time, disposed of by parliament, towards defraying the necessary expences of defending, protecting, and securing the said colonies and plantations.

2 / THE CONTEST FOR SOVEREIGNTY: SUPREME CENTER OR LOCAL AUTHORITY?

INTERPRETATION

RICHARD W. VAN ALSTYNE, *The Revolution Bursts*

Professor Richard W. Van Alstyne has established himself as a leading authority in Anglo-American Diplomatic History. He was educated at Harvard, University of Southern California, and Stanford University; and has taught at Chico State College, the Fletcher School of Law and Diplomacy, and the University of Southern California. From 1955 to 1960, Professor Van Alstyne edited the World Affairs Quarterly. *He was Fulbright Professor at the University of London in 1960–61; and he is presently Distinguished Professor of American History at Calliston College, University of the Pacific. The book from which the present excerpt has been taken was preceded by* Rising American Empire. *Both are marked by balanced judgment, mature scholarship, and the assumption that the struggle between Great Britain and her colonies was not a black and white affair.*

America will soon be the seat of empire—yet my fear is, they will not accept our king to rule them, but chuse one of their own; by which means we, who bought in, at a severe price too, shall lose our bread . . .—*Private Letters from an American in England to his Friends in America,* London: printed for J. Almon, 1769, p. 78

In February 1775 Alexander Hamilton, age eighteen, published a pamphlet which, for sheer candor and brilliant exposition of the forces of history, was reminiscent of the view expounded by John Adams twenty years previously. Hamilton had been reading Robinson-Morris's diagnosis of Britain's vulnerable situation. Like Robinson-Morris, he spoke out against the "unnatural quarrel," and expressed his ardent wish "for a speedy reconciliation, a perpetual and mutually beneficial union." Hamilton considered this easy to achieve: a compact had been made whereby the kings of Great Britain were also kings of America. "We hold our lands . . . by virtue of Charters from the British Monarchs; and are under no obligations to the lords or commons for them . . . ."

Richard W. Van Alstyne, *Empire and Independence*, New York, John Wiley & Sons, © 1965, Chap. III. Reprinted by permission of the publisher.

There was a difference between being subjects of his majesty and being subjects of Parliament.

Young Hamilton seemed to have no lack of confidence that Parliament would yield the point: Britain's position was so weak, America's so strong. France and Spain could not possibly pass up the opportunity, and the Dutch merchants would resort to their old practice of making profits out of war. These powers

> would undoubtedly take every clandestine method to introduce among us supplies of those things, which we stood in need of to carry on the dispute. They would not neglect any thing, in their power, to make the opposition on our part, as vigorous as our affairs would admit of . . . . And, in whatever light we view the matter, the consequence to Great Britain would be too destructive to permit her to proceed to extremities, unless she has lost all just sense of her own interest.*

Concluding his discourse, Hamilton declared himself a thorough supporter of limited monarchy and a well wisher of the royal family. The idea was by no means original with him. Franklin had said as much a few years before and in fact had based his whole conduct in London on the belief that the leaders of Parliament would be practical enough to see the necessity for altering the relationship. Parliamentary supremacy over the Colonies was a tiresome and unrealistic concept. The idea of a personal union between America and Britain under the king was much sounder historically. Edward Bancroft and Thomas Jefferson both had argued to the same end, contributing the thought that the Colonies were really independent states; and Jefferson had gone so far as to call on his majesty to veto acts of Parliament that were repugnant to the interests of the Colonies. Jefferson relied less on history to make his point than on the change of circumstances which had come about in the eighteenth century. The Colonies, he said, in effect, had come of age: they were states which had been added to the British Empire.

But the king had not invoked the veto for the better part of a century; for him to do so now was totally out of the question. It would mean a repudiation of the Revolution of 1688, an outright challenge to the authority of Parliament, whose position the Revolution had firmly secured after a century of dissension and war with the Stuart kings. No one in 1775, on either side of the water, stated this issue more accurately or more lucidly than the New York conservative, Samuel Seabury, whose writings Alexander Hamilton singled out for refutation. Seabury was exactly twice Hamilton's age; he was well established in the public life of his province; and he represented the agrarian interests of New York, who were incensed against the nonimportation and

---

* "The Farmer Refuted" in *The Papers of Alexander Hamilton*, Harold C. Syrett and Jacob E. Cooke, eds., New York, 1960–, I, pp. 159–160.

exportation agreements and distrustful of the revolutionary committees which controlled the city mobs. "To talk of subjection to the king, while we disclaim submission to Parliament is ridiculous," Seabury wrote. "It is a distinction made by the American Republicans to serve their own rebellious purposes . . . . *The king is king by act of Parliament.*"* Some alternative had to be found if the Empire was to be held together.

In Britain a number of proposals emerged, but all of them in some measure or other were anchored to the established principle of Parliamentary supremacy. Baffled by the reception the Americans had given the so-called Intolerable Acts, the government seemed unable to decide on the next step. But, thoroughly alarmed by the gravity of the crisis—a prospective civil war within the Empire, or a foreign war, with Britain exposed to a direct attack from France —Lord Chatham forced the issue. First he demanded that the government recall the troops from Boston—an idea to which others, notably Josiah Tucker, had previously given expression. Then, on the first of February, 1775, he introduced a bill into Parliament designed to heal the wounds and bind the Colonies more closely than ever to Britain. Chatham's bill began with an assertion that Parliament possessed supreme legislative and supervisory power over the Colonies. It then proposed the repeal of the Quebec Act, declared that no tax or other charge would be levied against the Americans, sanctioned the meeting of the Continental Congress scheduled to open in Philadelphia in May, and stipulated that the delegates, on assembling, recognize the supremacy of Parliament and make a free grant of a certain perpetual revenue to the king.

Chatham is revered in history as "the friend of America" in contrast to Lord North and his government who were known as "the wicked ministry" —to copy the epithet used against them by their opponents on both sides of the water. But actually the differences between the two were not very real: Chatham was groping for an avenue of escape; the government was standing firm on the abstract principle of Parliamentary supremacy but prepared to go equally far toward satisfying the Americans. Lord Mansfield, the great chief justice who the very next year was to rule Negro slavery unconstitutional in Britain, stated the government's position clearly. "We were reduced to the alternative," he declared in Parliament, "of adopting coercive measures, or of forever relinquishing our claim of sovereignty or dominion over the colonies. . . . (Either) the supremacy of the British legislature must be complete, entire, and unconditional or on the other hand, the colonies must be free and

---

* *The Congress Canvassed: or an Examination into the Conduct of the Delegates at their Grand Convention, held in Philadelphia, September 1, 1774, addressed to the Merchants of New York.* By A. W. Farmer (Samuel Seabury). I have repeated and italicized for the sake of emphasis. Seabury's writings are vital to an understanding of the constitutional issue. Since, under the Act of Settlement of 1701, Parliament controlled the throne, Seabury's position was unassailable. . . .

independent." To Mansfield, a jurist, this was the choice: either the supremacy of Parliament or an "independent American empire." The Scottish peer readily conceded that the taxes had been a mistake, but it was "utterly impossible to say a syllable on the matter of expediency, till the right was first as fully asserted on one side, as acknowledged on the other." *

We can better appreciate the predicament of the British government in 1774–1775 by comparing it with the problems of the Lincoln administration in 1861. In both cases the authority of the central government had been denied. In both cases the central government was threatened with civil war. The Americans, as Lord North correctly stated, had entered "an almost universal confederacy" to resist the will of Parliament. This meant secession and dismemberment of the Empire, from which all thinking men in Britain recoiled. . . .

With the support of the king, Lord North on February 20, 1775, offered a resolution which passed the House of Commons by a vote of 274–88. The resolution represented the utmost the government had decided it could concede. Thereafter there was no real variation in policy until 1782 when, the North ministry having lost the war, a different ministry with great reluctance admitted independence. North's resolution stated that whenever any of the Colonies made provision "for contributing their proportion to the common defence" and for the support of the governor and the courts of the Colony, Parliament would "forbear . . . to levy any duty, tax, or assessment, or to impose any farther duty, tax, or assessment, except only such duties as it may be expedient to continue to levy or to impose for the regulation of commerce; the net produce of the duties last mentioned to be carried to the account of such province or colony respectively." † In a supporting speech Lord North drew a fine line between Parliament's "right" to tax and the exercise of the right by the Colonial assemblies. He also said he favored leaving the Colonies at liberty to contribute voluntarily to the common defense, with Parliament as a matter of legal form retaining the right to reject or increase the amount of the aids offered. However, it was plain from the context that the government did not intend to exercise its "right."

Between Lord Chatham's bill of February 1 and Lord North's resolution of February 20 there were only shades of difference. Chatham was perhaps closer to the political realities then prevailing in the Colonies; he and his friends were in touch with the Americans in London, including Franklin, who were partisans of his against the government. Chatham went further than the

---

* PH, XVIII, cols. 269–271. For a full treatment of this subject see Richard W. Van Alstyne, "Parliamentary Supremacy versus Independence: Notes and Documents," Hunt. Lib. Quart., XXVI (1963), pp. 201–233.

† PH, XVIII, col. 320.

ministry in advocating the repeal of the Quebec Act and in giving Parliamentary approval to the meeting of the Continental Congress, but his bill stipulated recognition of the supremacy of Parliament, and it made an American grant of a perpetual revenue a requirement. North's resolution all but shelved this issue. Chatham was ready to recall the troops, and the followers of Lord Rockingham, including Edmund Burke, were in agreement on this. But the latter, who constituted an influential minority group in both houses of Parliament, stood firm on the Declaratory Act which Rockingham had pushed through Parliament in 1766 when the Stamp Act was repealed.

Chatham's bill failed in the House of Lords on its first reading, while North's resolution subsequently got strong support in the House of Commons. The real difference between the two lay not in these details, North's resolution being really more generous, but in the attitude with which the two men viewed the crisis. Chatham and his followers had no faith in Britain's ability to force the Colonies into submission. To block the American ports against commerce was, as Lord Camden said, to sap the life blood of Britain herself. Compared with the several powers of Europe, Britain without commerce was no more than a "bird's nest floating on a pool." Beyond that the Chathamites were terrified at the prospect of the Bourbon powers joining in a general war, with Britain in the middle and facing hopeless odds. Not only would all the gains of the previous war be lost, but also Britain herself would again become merely an island off the coast of Europe. "What can France desire more than to see her rival sinking every year, from being mistress of the world, land and sea, into the bubble of her enemies, and the scorn of nations?" So Chatham had asked in 1773.* In this state of mind he was grasping at any straw to prevent the disaster he was certain he would otherwise befall. But for the ministry the constitutional issue was overriding. It could not go beyond the North resolution. It had to have some answering gesture from the Americans. If the Americans would make a gesture of "submission," that would be enough.

Lord Camden, speaking for the Chathamites in the debates of February, ridiculed "the high sounding unintelligible phrases of legislative supremacy and parliamentary omnipotence." But it proved impossible to get past them. In March David Hartley, who belonged to the Rockingham group but who was closer to Chatham in spirit, proposed making a fresh approach through the king. His idea was that the king send to each of the provinces a letter of requisition, which Hartley himself had actually written. Stressing the importance of the Royal Navy and the need for contributing to its support, the letter proceeded to state that his majesty regretted that "needless and imprudent discussions of speculative points, from mutual misapprehensions, have been

---

* Chatham to Baron Bridport (Adm. Hood), June 6, 1773. Bridport Papers, II, British Museum Add. MSS. 35, 192.

converted into anger and animosities, which threaten the most fatal consequences." And in conclusion, it said, his majesty wished to see "unanimity restored . . . in one common obedience to the supreme legislature," so that the provinces may join "to support the dignity of his crown, the just authority of parliament, the true and combined interests of Great Britain and America. . . ."*

It was an ingenious idea: the king to assume the initiative in sending a letter written for him and approved in advance by Parliament. Parliament's ultimate position was safeguarded, at least in theory, but the hand of friendship was to come from the king. The results would be the same as those sought from the North resolution, but the stress was on voluntary action rather than on "rights." Hartley and Franklin had been friends before Franklin had taken his departure from England, and Hartley hoped to mollify the Americans through an informal approach. But unfortunately his motion received scant attention. Lord North saw it setting a dangerous precedent for a revival of the royal prerogative. He said that it suggested King Charles I's methods of imposing taxes without Parliamentary consent, and the motion was negatived without a division. A strictly constitutional monarch who implicitly accepted the principles laid down in 1688, George III at no time showed any disposition to act independently of Parliament.

Clearly the British government pinned its hopes to a belief that its efforts at conciliation would meet with a response from America. Far from any sense of playing the role of "tyrant," the government had paid meticulous attention to the requirements of the British constitution; in all its measures it consistently deferred to the will of Parliament. It could do no less, and it assumed that tempers would cool and reason prevail in the Colonies. A "little time," Lord Dartmouth had written to an American correspondent shortly after the passage of the "Intolerable Acts," would convince all who "can think with coolness and temper, that the liberties of America are not so much in danger from any thing that Parliament has done, or is likely to do here, as from the violence and misconduct of America itself."†

Nevertheless, the behavior of the First Continental Congress and its rude dismissal of the Galloway Plan did not point in this direction. Apparently the Americans felt confident that through continued resistance they could bring on the downfall of the North ministry and the restoration of Chatham to power —as Franklin had advised his Boston friends. In that case, they believed, they could get all they wanted from Britain. Thus, when the Second Continental Congress opened in May 1775, it did not act on Lord North's resolution.

---

* *PH*, XVIII, cols. 565–566.

† As quoted from the Dartmouth Papers by Jack M. Sosin, whose article, "The Massachusetts Acts of 1774: Coercive or Preventive?" *Hunt. Lib. Quart.*, XXVI (1963), pp. 235–252, shows admirably the care which the North ministry took in preparing these measures.

Before this the first battles had been fought at Lexington and Concord, and the British forces in Boston were under siege. Denouncing the "sanguinary zeal of the Ministerial Army," John Hancock, speaking for a provincial congress of Massachusetts, demanded that the Congress in Philadelphia authorize a powerful army on the side of America. With such a force, he declared, "we can hope that the authors of our miseries can be punished by the just indignation of our brethren" in Britain.*

Hancock no doubt had the zealous followers of Lord Chatham in mind; and the pages of the *London Evening Post,* if Hancock had read them, would have fully justified his optimism. John Almon who published this paper, spared no efforts to denounce the "wicked ministers" and to slant the news heavily in favor of the Americans. Almon demanded to know how the ministers were to keep Britain from becoming a province of France. Others had voiced this fear not once, but many times. Thus David Hartley, addressing Commons on May 2 when the Battle of Lexington was still not known in Britain, said:

> It is next to infatuation and madness, for one moment, to suppose that we can have an American without a French and Spanish war. I am clear that they will keep off while there is any possibility of the American dispute being made up, but when once the war is begun, and neither party can withdraw, then, Sir, in spite of all those assurances . . . gained at Paris from the French ministers, you will find them take a determined part—a part plainly pointed out by both interest and ambition. . . . Nothing but the most infantine credulity can believe the contrary; you will then find yourselves engaged in a French war, in a Spanish war, I think, in a Prussian war; and wars are so catching, Sir, when they spread, in I know not how many other wars likewise. . . .†

Nevertheless, despite these scattered protests, it was unrealistic to hope for the overthrow of the North ministry. Many Whigs, including their leader, Lord Rockingham, shared the fears of the Chathamites, but for reasons of internal politics, these two groups would not cooperate. Even so the government possessed a safe margin of support in both houses of Parliament.

Meanwhile the Second Continental Congress was moving steadily ahead toward war. Massachusetts had demanded the creation of a regular army, and New England militia captured the fort at Ticonderoga on Lake Champlain and moved its cannon south for use against the British forces in Boston. The capture of this fort cut off the British invasion route from Canada, yet the Congress

---

* Peter Force, *American Archives: Consisting of a Collection of Authentick Records, State Papers, Debates, and Letters and other Notices of Publick Affairs,* 4th series from March 4, 1774 to July 4, 1776, 5 vols., Washington, D. C., 1839, II, cols. 1826–1828. (Hereafter cited as Force.) . . .

† From the *London Morning Post and Daily Advertiser,* May 5, 1775, British Museum, Burney Collection.

voted a resolution that "indubitable evidence" existed that the British government was preparing a "cruel invasion" from that direction. Just the opposite was the case. Governor Carleton's forces in Quebec were so small as to make an offensive campaign unthinkable; and, still ignorant of the Battles of Lexington and Concord, the government in London had not even begun to formulate plans for suppressing the rebellion. Overlooking the ancient dislike that Americans harbored for the Catholic French of Quebec, and failing to appreciate that, with the Quebec Act now in force, the French Canadians would of course look to Britain as their protector, the Congress now addressed them as "oppressed inhabitants" and "fellow sufferers." The Canadians were warned of the perils of "slavery" and of the danger of enjoying their religion at the hands of a legislature in which they had no voice. A thousand copies of this message were ordered translated and printed, to be dispatched to Canada for distribution among the populace.

Next, Massachusetts got its wish for a regular army when, on June 16, George Washington was named general and commander-in-chief. If John Adams is to be taken at his word—even more than his more radical cousin Samuel, John Adams was in the forefront in pushing for vigorous measures—Washington's appointment served to silence the mutterings against New England and advance the cause of union.* Preparations, originating in New England, were undertaken shortly thereafter for an invasion and permanent subjugation of the colony on the St. Lawrence.

Early in July the Congress approved successively a declaration on the causes and necessity of taking up arms, a petition to the king, an address to "the inhabitants of Great Britain," and finally a speech to the Iroquois Indians who, as "Brothers and Friends," were exhorted to lend a hand in the defense of "liberty." Now as previously, it was important to bid for the friendship of these tribes. "Our cause is just. Our union is perfect. Our internal resources are great, and, if necessary, *foreign assistance is undoubtedly attainable*," concluded the first document, which Jefferson and John Dickinson composed together.† All of these documents studiously ignored Parliament, and gave the impression of being designed as propaganda. The strong language and the tone of defiance they adopted express a spirit of revolution rather than of conciliation. Beyond that, the Americans realized they were playing from strength and could afford to take risks: at home they were strong, abroad Britain's enemies would come to their support.

---

* John Adams to his wife Abigail, June 17, 1775. *Letters of Members of the Continental Congress*, Edmund C. Burnett, ed., 8 vols., Washington, D. C., 1921–1936, I, pp. 130–132. (Hereafter cited as Burnett.)

† Force, II, cols. 1866–1869. Italics inserted.

Dickinson, voicing the hesitancy and the last-ditch hope for peace displayed in the Middle and Southern Colonies, drafted the petition to the king. In it the ministers were made the butt of attack; they were guilty of "delusive pretences, fruitless terrors, and unavailing severities," and his majesty was entreated personally to assume the initiative in re-establishing harmony within the Empire. But the king under the constitution could take no such step, nor did the petitioners themselves propose reform beyond the repeal of the measures precipitated by the Boston Tea Party. Franklin discounted the value of this document, whereas John Adams, exasperated by the divisions of opinion in Congress, rejected it but recognized its practical necessity. An absolute refusal to petition and negotiate would spell discord and total disunion. But, he wrote Joseph Warren, "my hopes are that Ministry will be afraid of negotiation as well as we and therefore refuse it."* The procedure followed ensured that this would be the case.

The address to the British public repeated the charge that the ministry aimed at "the reduction of these Colonies to slavery and ruin," and blamed the same source for fabricating the notion that the Americans desired independence. "Have we called in the aid of those foreign powers, who are the rivals of your grandeur?" This was the proof offered that the Colonies were innocent of any such intention. And then the address noted:

> It is alleged that we contribute nothing to the common defence. To this we answer, that the advantages which Great Britain receives from the monopoly of our trade far exceed our proportion of the expense necessary for that purpose. But should these advantages be inadequate thereto, let the restrictions on our trade be removed, and we will cheerfully contribute such proportion when constitutionally required.†

Although the Americans repudiated the notion that they intended to be "independent," their attitude revealed a different purpose. Unmistakably they were prepared to insist on their de facto independence. The original controversy over taxation had become submerged in larger and more indefinite issues, and nothing short of a complete abnegation of its powers on the part of Parliament would be satisfactory. The Americans were no longer pleading their case for the redress of specific grievances, they were talking of their "rights" and framing their demands in terms of power and prestige. A personal union under the king would do, and some of the American leaders, including Jefferson, seemed to have convinced themselves that if Chatham were again at the helm in Britain, an organic change of this kind would result. But Cha-

---

* July 6, 1775, Burnett, I, pp. 151–152.
† Force, II, cols. 1872–1875.

tham, no less than Mansfield and North, accepted the principle of Parliamentary supremacy; and, although ostensibly more anxious than the ministry to accommodate the Americans, he would have faced the same cruel dilemma had he been in power. . . .

Indeed there was no disposition in America to view Lord North's resolution on its merits. Jefferson assembled a number of arguments against it, which were incorporated in the Virginia Resolutions of June 10, 1775, but these arguments seem quite unfair, especially in the context of Lord North's speech in support of his resolution. Although the resolution was really a formula for escaping from an impossible situation, Jefferson chose to attack it on legalistic grounds and ignore the spirit with which it was offered. It only changed "the form of oppression without lightening its burden," he declared. "We must saddle ourselves with a perpetual tax adequate to the expectations and subject to the disposal of Parliament alone."

Jefferson found other arguments against the resolution, including a complaint against the Quebec Act, an assertion that the British were "planning to invade us by sea and land," and a final charge that "on our agreeing to contribute our share to the common defence, they do not propose to lay open to us a free trade with all the world." Then follows an allusion to Lord Chatham, blaming the ministers for all the trouble. Under them "the component parts of the empire have . . . been falling asunder, and a total annihilation of its weight in the political scale of the World seems justly to be apprehended."*
In this spirit the Continental Congress on July 31 rejected the resolution.

At home in Monticello, Jefferson seemed more composed and anxious for a reconciliation. Still it depended, he believed, on "the returning wisdom" of Britain, and not on any concession the Americans should make. The British public, even "those in parliament who are called friends of America, seem to know nothing of our real determinations." And he was of two minds on the subject of foreign intervention:

> If indeed Great Britain, disjoined from her colonies, be a match for the most potent nations of Europe with the colonies thrown into their scale, they may go on securely. But if they are not assured of this, it would be certainly unwise, by trying the event of another campaign, to risque our accepting a foreign aid which perhaps may not be obtainable but on a condition of everlasting avulsion from Great Britain. This would be thought a hard condition to those who still wish for reunion with their parent country. . . .†

Thus Jefferson hesitated before venturing out on uncharted seas. Not possess-

---

* *The Papers of Thomas Jefferson*, Julian P. Boyd, ed., 15 vols., Princeton, N. J., 1950–1958, I, pp. 170–174. (Hereafter cited as *Jefferson Papers*.)
† To John Randolph, Aug. 25, 1775. *ibid.*, pp. 240–243.

ing Adams's cocksureness, he was aware that foreign aid would become a necessity, and he was apprehensive of its consequences. But the price for reunion, on which he held out, was that Parliament relinquish its right to legislate. Paradoxically this was what Lord North's resolution proposed to do by indirection.

Meanwhile the Congress entrusted its several communications to Richard Penn, a former lieutenant-governor of Pennsylvania, who arrived at Bristol, England, on August 13, one day behind a vessel bearing the news of the tragedy at Bunker Hill. Accompanied by Arthur Lee, who had been having secret meetings with the Frenchman, Caron de Beaumarchais, Penn formally presented the petition not to the king personally, but to Lord Dartmouth, the minister in charge of American affairs. Lee's part in this transaction can probably never be understood; only the bare facts are known, but from the scanty record his conduct seems highly equivocal. On the one hand, he was plotting with Beaumarchais to enlist the aid of the French Court; on the other hand, he was still an aspirant to membership in the House of Commons. In a speech which he published in London, but never delivered orally in Commons, he made a moving appeal for the restoration of Imperial unity, reminding his British readers of the previous war when the Americans had made common cause against the "ancient inveterate enmity" of France.*

The petition being directed against the ministry, it is hard to see how it could have borne results. However that may be, the government had already determined its course. Lord North advised the king on July 26 that the war had become such that it would have to be treated as a foreign war. And the king expressed himself simply and straightforwardly in a letter written to the minister on the same day:

> I am clear as to one point that we must persist and not be dismayed by any difficulties that may arise on either side of the Atlantick; I know I am doing my duty and therefore can never wish to retract; the Resolution proposed by the House of Commons is the utmost that can be come into; and if people will have patience this must in the end be obtained.†

These decisions led to a royal proclamation, August 23, announcing a state of rebellion in the Colonies. In retrospect this drastic step may be regarded as too hasty: also it is not clear why it was taken so soon. Sizeable French shipments of arms and gunpowder to the rebels were already being reported, but no attempt was made to stop them. The government continued to make the

---

* Arthur Lee, *A Speech intended to have been delivered in the House of Commons, in support of the Petition from the General Congress at Philadelphia*, London: J. Almon, 1775.

† *The Correspondence of King George the Third*, John Fortescue, ed., 6 vols., London, 1927–1928, No. 1683. (Hereafter cited as Fortescue.)

mistake of supposing it was dealing with an insurrection, whereas actually it was confronted with a revolution. Lord Dartmouth wrote General Gage in Boston to say that it was hoped the rebellion could be confined to New England—that the Middle Colonies would prove more reasonable and accept the conciliatory North resolution of February 20. Loyalist sentiment among the back-country settlers of the Carolinas was also taken into account; these men to be rewarded with land grants and organized into a provincial corps on equal terms with the regulars. General Gage, in the thick of things in Boston, was pessimistic, but Major General Haldimand, who had seen service in Canada, advised that with reinforcements sent to that country the insurrection could be suppressed by the following spring. On that basis it was decided to recruit a fair-sized army to be dispatched and ready for action in America when the campaigning season opened, while at the same time holding out the olive branch of Lord North's resolution.

Meanwhile awareness of the crisis produced a small flood of books and pamphlets in Britain. Both Dr. Samuel Johnson and the Methodist leader, John Wesley, took stands against the Americans. Johnson saw anarchy as the consequence of rebellion, and Wesley echoed his sentiments by deriding the American contention that the people of the Colonies were being "enslaved." "The Negroes in America are slaves, the whites enjoy liberty," declared Wesley. "Is not then all this outcry about Liberty and Slavery mere rant, and playing upon words?" And, he wanted to know: "Are women free agents?"* John Lind, a brother-in-law of Governor Hutchinson and a political writer who echoed the views of Lord Mansfield, was on a business trip to America in the summer of 1775, and published a book in New York which the next year was republished in London and went through at least five editions. The whole British people believed the Americans should be free, he declared, and that they were entitled to a hearing. Recalling the American appeals for help in past wars, he argued the case for the protection of the Colonies by British fleets and armies. But an empire with such responsibilities required a central legislature, he held; and for Americans to assume that they were not to be bound by this legislature was to invalidate their claims to the benefits of, and to destroy their title to, protection.†

Lind's book was paralleled by a tract written by the Massachusetts loyalist, Daniel Leonard, who denounced the tyranny of the revolutionary committees in America. Leonard's book is an excellent expression of conservative opinion: it warned against the exhaustion and load of debt that a war would engender,

---

* Samuel Johnson, *Taxation no Tyranny; an Answer to the Resolutions and Address of the American Congress*, London, T. Cadell, 1775; John Wesley, *A Calm Address to our American Colonies*, London: Robert Hawes, 1775.

† John Lind, *An Englishman's Answer to the Address from the Delegates to the People of Great Britain*, New York: Rivington, 1775.

and predicted that France and Spain would move in as soon as the British forces were withdrawn. In *A Friendly Address to all Reasonable Americans*, Thomas B. Chandler came to Leonard's support with a strong argument that, without the mediatory power of Great Britain, the Colonies with their competing interests would make war on one another and so tempt foreign powers to intervene. Chandler accused New England of starting the rebellion, and suggested that a new American constitution had become necessary, and could be obtained "by decent, candid and respectful application, not by threats."*

In London Arthur Young returned to the arguments of his earlier writings, publishing a two-volume work on *American Husbandry* in which he stressed the growing power and wealth of the Colonies, the likelihood that they would turn against Britain, and the opportunity the latter possessed to delay or prevent independence by stimulating settlement of the Ohio country. An agricultural country with staples to export, Young believed, would not want independence. But if commerce and manufacturing were allowed to get the upper hand, there was no doubt the Americans would assert themselves. Emphasizing even more than Arthur Young this factor of power inherent in America, Hugh Williamson, writing also from the viewpoint of an English Whig, pointed out the dangers from France and Spain. These two countries would be the real victors, if the Colonies became independent. Britain, deprived of its American trade, would cease to be formidable at sea. The French would aid the Americans and benefit accordingly. . . .

Other writers perceived the tragic position into which Britain was slipping. None shared the hopes of the ministry; all realized that the bargaining power lay with the Americans and expressed themselves as baffled when it came to offering an escape from the dilemma. As an anonymous writer who sympathized with the Americans put it, their real object was independence. If Parliament acceded to the claims asserted in the petition to the king, the era would commence when America would be the ruler of Britain. Conciliation was attractive, but not really possible. Painful as it was, there was no alternative to the recourse to arms. The sole hope, and it was a faint one, was that the Boston rebels would not get the support of the other colonies.†

Josiah Tucker returned to his earlier theme of letting the Americans fend for themselves. Parliament could not allow the king to dispense with its authority in order to please them. But to resort to arms could not bring benefits, even if Britain won. It would not mean an increase of trade; that was impossible, "for a shopkeeper will never get the more custom by beating his cus-

---

* Daniel Leonard, *The Origin of the American Contest with Great Britain* . . . New York: Rivington, 1775. In addition to the pamphlet cited above, Chandler issued a second one entitled *What think ye of Congress Now?*, in which he repeated his warning that secession would "leave us open and exposed to the avarice and ambition of every maritime power in Europe or America."

† *The Present Crisis with respect to America Considered*, London: T. Becket, 1775.

tomers: and what is true of a shopkeeper is true of a shop-keeping nation."
Tucker was well acquainted with Franklin's ambitions, and he pulled no
punches in deriding the propaganda against "the *imaginary* tyranny and the
pretended oppression of the mother country." "You want to be independent,"
he charged. "You wish to be an Empire by itself, and to be no longer the Province of another. This spirit is uppermost; and this principle is visible in all
your speeches, and all your writings, even when you take some pains to disguise it. . . ." Hence Tucker would take the Americans at their word, separate
totally from them, and offer to enter an alliance of friendship and commerce.
The Americans would pay the ultimate price, he believed; they would fall
victims to civil war.* But this medicine was too strong to be swallowed, and
Tucker's naked realism found little support.

There was another side to the problem and an anonymous author, addressing
himself directly to Dr. Johnson and to the ministers, put it most comprehen-
sively. Britain was dependent on America for its position in Europe: "It is by
the American Continent only that the balance of Europe can be any longer in
your hands." By the superiority in numbers there, he wrote, "you command
both the Americas, command Spain and Portugal, influence France and other
powers of Europe and . . . therefore instead of checking their increase by a
jealous and hostile policy, you ought to encourage it by every just and generous
institution." Britain would hazard all its American commerce and its American empire for the shadow of revenue, he asserted. Without a large army it
could levy nothing; with it the expense would overbalance the receipts. If
the army did not stay there, there would be confusion as soon as it left; if it
stayed, it would be impossible to keep its ranks filled. Further, it would be
difficult to prevent it from becoming American. And even if all these difficulties were removed, an American system could not easily be reconciled to the
principle of the British Empire, which was free and commercial. Here in a
nutshell was Britain's dilemma, one that Rome had once faced without success.†

By their deliberate onslaught on the North ministry and especially by their
ostentatious snubbing of Parliament, the Americans made a peaceful settlement practically impossible. The radicals who dominated the stage in Philadelphia did not want such a settlement. As Richard Champion, a merchant of
Bristol with many contacts in America, told his Philadelphia correspondents,
Willing, Morris & Company: "What has strengthened Administration, and

---

* Josiah Tucker, *An Humble Address and Earnest Appeal: The Respective Pleas and Arguments set
forth; and the Impossibility of a Compromise of Differences or a Mutual Concession of Rights plainly
demonstrated*, Glocester: R. Raikes, 1775.

† *An Answer to a Pamphlet entitled Taxation no Tyranny, addressed to the Author and to Persons
in Power*, London: J. Almon, 1775.

weakened the hands of the Whigs in this country more than can be conceived is this, that it is represented here, that America is adverse to every set of men among us, and [this is) urged as a proof of their aiming at independency." Champion, who kept in close contact with Burke and Lord Rockingham, had good cause for complaining that the Americans made no distinction between the Whigs and the Tories, and so tied the hands of the former in their efforts at conciliation:

> I repeat it again, and I had it from authority, that the Whig Party which is composed of men of the first rank reputation and knowledge in this country is the only reliance of America, supposing she means honestly and sincerely to be dependent on Great Britain. . . . America, instead of discrediting the Whig Party, must give them credit and support by shewing that it is of a bad system that they complain, and not of the whole country. The quarrel between a party here and all America may be decided in favour of America, without prejudice to this country; but a quarrel between the whole body of the two countries must be injurious to both, and it is hard to say to which of them in the greatest (degree).*

Replying to the Duke of Grafton, who had queried him privately on the possibility of the Colonies sending over individuals to state to Parliament their wishes and expectations, Lord North was not sanguine. His view was that:

> the leaders of the rebellion . . . manifestly aim at a total independence. Against this we propose to exert ourselves, using every species of force to reduce them, but authorizing, at the same time, either the commander-in-chief or some other commissioner, to proclaim immediate peace and pardon, and to restore all the privileges of trade to any Colony upon its submission. Authority will likewise be given to settle the question of taxation for the future . . . and to put every other matter now in dispute between them and this country in a course of accommodation. Till the Provinces have made some submission it will be in vain to hope that they will come into any reasonable terms and, I am afraid, that declaring a cessation of arms at this time would establish that independence which the leaders of the faction in America have always intended, and which they now almost openly avow.†

The king's speech, delivered at the opening of Parliament on October 26 only six days after, repeated this view more briefly and added that there was nothing to fear from France at the time. Nevertheless, lengthy and heated debates in both houses ensued. The Rockingham Whigs now came forward, pro-

---

* *The American Correspondence of a Bristol Merchant*, G. H. Guttridge, ed., Berkeley, Calif., 1934, pp. 62–65.

† The whole of this letter, from the Grafton Papers at Bury St. Edmunds, England, is printed in Van Alstyne, "Parl. Supremacy . . . ," pp. 221–222.

posing a review of the whole problem in the hope that Parliament would not commit itself to making war. But this group could not swallow the challenge to the ultimate authority of Parliament—it took its stand on the Declaratory Act—and it could find no solid basis for opposing the ministry. Only the small minority of the Chathamites were willing to go farther, proposing the repeal of all thirteen acts passed since 1763. These men had France on their minds and saw Britain facing disaster if the situation was not brought under control. Hence they were ready to negotiate with the revolutionary Continental Congress on the basis of the petition. To them events had made the dogma of Parliamentary supremacy an unreal issue; but to the king, North and the ministers, Mansfield, Rockingham, and the majority in both houses, it was everything. Lord North expressed the majority viewpoint succinctly when he said at the end of the debate that if all of the acts passed since 1763 were repealed, of course the dispute would be terminated: the Americans would be independent.*

The Chathamites now found themselves in the slough of despondency. "America is lost and the war afoot," wrote Lord Camden. "There is an end of advising preventive measures, and peace will be more difficult to make than the war was. . . . Ye claims of the Americans, if they are successful, will grow too big for concession, and no man here will venture to be responsible for such a treaty."† But the ministry felt it was equal to the occasion. On November 20 Lord North introduced a bill forbidding all trade and intercourse with the Colonies until the rebellion was over. He discounted the war spirit in America, believing reports that the rebel army was plagued with desertions and that local uprisings against it had already occurred.

---

* *PH*, XVIII, cols. 705–798, 910–936, 942–963, 963–992.

† Van Alstyne, "Parl. Supremacy . . . ," p. 230, quoting from the Grafton Papers.

THE DENIAL OF PARLIAMENTARY AUTHORITY

THOMAS JEFFERSON, *A Summary View*

Here is a lengthy extract from Thomas Jefferson's pamphlet, A Summary View
*of the Rights of British America. In 1774, Jefferson was named by the Virginia
Convention a delegate to the Continental Congress, due to meet early in September. Preparing for great events, he drafted instructions for his fellow
delegates; but delayed at home by illness, he was unable to present his proposals to Congress. Milder views prevailed there for a time. Nevertheless,
Jefferson's work was published in pamphlet form at Williamsburg, Philadelphia, and London. It is doubtless one of the most eloquent statements of the
radical view in 1774.*

Resolved that it be an instruction to the said deputies when assembled in
General Congress with the deputies from the other states of British America
to propose to the said Congress that an humble and dutiful address be presented to his majesty begging leave to lay before him as chief magistrate of
the British empire the united complaints of his majesty's subjects in America;
complaints which are excited by many unwarrantable incroachments and
usurpations, attempted to be made by the legislature of one part of the empire,
upon those rights which god and the laws have given equally and independently to all. To represent to his majesty that these his states have often indi-
vidually made humble application to his imperial throne, to obtain thro' it's
intervention some redress of their injured rights; to none of which was ever
even an answer condescended. Humbly to hope that this their joint address,
penned in the language of truth, and divested of those expressions of servility
which would persuade his majesty that we are asking favors and not rights,
shall obtain from his majesty a more respectful acceptance. And this his
majesty will think we have reason to expect when he reflects that he is no more
than the chief officer of the people, appointed by the laws, and circumscribed
with definite powers, to assist in working the great machine of government
erected for their use, and consequently subject to their superintendance. And
in order that these our rights, as well as the invasions of them, may be laid more

Thomas Jefferson, "A Summary View of the Rights of British America," July, 1774, *Papers of Thomas
Jefferson*, ed. J. P. Boyd, Princeton, N. J., Princeton Univ. Press, 1950, Vol. I, pp. 121–135.

fully before his majesty, to take a view of them from the origin and first settlement of these countries.

To remind him that our ancestors, before their emigration to America, were the free inhabitants of the British dominions in Europe, and possess a right, which nature has given to all men, of departing from the country in which chance, not choice has placed them, of going in quest of new habitations, and of there establishing new societies, under such laws and regulations as to them shall seem most likely to promote public happiness. . . .

. . . America was conquered, and her settlements made and firmly established, at the expence of individuals, and not of the British public. Their own blood was spilt in acquiring lands for their settlement, their own fortunes expended in making that settlement effectual. For themselves they fought, for themselves they conquered, and for themselves alone they have right to hold. No shilling was ever issued from the public treasures of his majesty or his ancestors for their assistance, till of very late times, after the colonies had become established on a firm and permanent footing. That then indeed, having become valuable to Great Britain for her commercial purposes, his parliament was pleased to lend them assistance against an enemy who would fain have drawn to herself the benefits of their commerce to the great aggrandisement of herself and danger of Great Britain. . . . We do not however mean to underrate those aids, which to us were doubtless valuable, on whatever principles granted: but we would shew that they cannot give a title to that authority which the British parliament would arrogate over us; and that they may amply be repaid, by our giving to the inhabitants of Great Britain such exclusive privileges in trade as may be advantageous to them, and at the same time not too restrictive to ourselves. That settlements having been thus effected in the wilds of America, the emigrants thought proper to adopt that system of laws under which they had hitherto lived in the mother country, and to continue their union with her by submitting themselves to the same common sovereign, who was thereby made the central link connecting the several parts of the empire thus newly multiplied. . . .

That the exercise of a free trade with all parts of the world, possessed by the American colonists as of natural right, and which no law of their own had taken away or abridged, was next the object of unjust incroachment. Some of the colonies having thought proper to continue the administration of their government in the name and under the authority of his majesty king Charles the first, whom notwithstanding his late deposition by the Common-wealth of England, they continued in the sovereignty of their state, the Parliament for the Common-wealth took the same in high offence, and assumed upon themselves the power of prohibiting their trade with all other parts of the world except the island of Great Britain. This arbitrary act however they soon recalled, and by solemn treaty entered into on the 12th. day of March 1651, between the said Commonwealth by their Commissioners and the colony of Virginia by their house of Burgesses, it was expressly stipulated by the 8th. article of the said treaty that they should have 'free trade as the people of England do enjoy to all places and with all nations according to the laws of that Commonwealth.' But that, upon the restoration of his majesty King Charles the second, their rights of free commerce fell once more a victim to arbitrary power: and by several acts of his reign as well as of some of his successors the trade of the colonies was laid under such restrictions as shew what hopes they might form from the justice of a British parliament were its uncontrouled power admitted over these states. History has informed us that bodies of men as well as individuals are susceptible of the spirit of tyranny. A view of these acts of parliament for regulation, as it has been affectedly called, of the American trade, if all other evidence were removed out of the case, would undeniably evince the truth of this observation. Besides the duties they impose on our articles of export and import, they prohibit our going to any Markets Northward of cape Finesterra in the kingdom of Spain for the sale of commodities which Great Britain will not take from us, and for the purchase of others with which she cannot supply us; and that for no other than the arbitrary purpose of purchasing for themselves by a sacrifice of our rights and interests, certain privileges in their commerce with an allied state. . . .

. . . That to heighten still the idea of parliamentary justice, and to shew with what moderation they are like to exercise power, where themselves are to feel no part of it's weight, we take leave to mention to his majesty certain other acts of British parliament, by which they would prohibit us from manufacturing for our own use the articles we raise on our own lands with our own labor. . . . But that we do not point out to his majesty the injustice of these acts with intent to rest on that principle the cause of their nullity, but to shew that experience confirms the propriety of those political principles which exempt us from the jurisdiction of the British parliament. The true ground on which we declare these acts void is that the British parliament has no right to exercise authority over us. . . .

That thus have we hastened thro' the reigns which preceded his majesty's, during which the violation of our rights were less alarming, because repeated at more distant intervals, than that rapid and bold succession of injuries which is likely to distinguish the present from all other periods of American story. Scarcely have our minds been able to emerge from the astonishment into which one stroke of parliamentary thunder has involved us, before another more heavy and more alarming is fallen on us. Single acts of tyranny may be ascribed to the accidental opinion of a day; but a series of oppressions, begun at a distinguished period, and pursued unalterably thro' every change of ministers, too plainly prove a deliberate, systematical plan of reducing us to slavery. . . .

Not only the principles of common sense, but the common feelings of human nature must be surrendered up, before his majesty's subjects here can be persuaded to believe that they hold their political existence at the will of a British parliament. Shall these governments be dissolved, their property annihilated, and their people reduced to a state of nature, at the imperious breath of a body of men whom they never saw, in whom they never confided, and over whom they have no powers of punishment or removal, let their crimes against the American public be ever so great? . . .

That by 'an act to discontinue in such manner and for such time as are therein mentioned the landing and discharging lading or shipping of goods wares and merchandize at the town and within the harbor of Boston in the province of Massachusett's bay in North America' which was passed at the last session of British parliament, a large and populous town, whose trade was their sole subsistence, was deprived of that trade, and involved in utter ruin. . . .

By the act for the suppression of riots and tumults in the town of Boston, passed also in the last session of parliament, a murder committed there is, if the governor pleases, to be tried in the court of King's bench in the island of Great Britain, by a jury of Middlesex. . . . A clause for a similar purpose had been introduced into an act passed in the 12th. year of his majesty's reign entitled 'an act for the better securing and preserving his majesty's dock-yards, magazines, ships, ammunition and stores,' against which as meriting the same censures the several colonies have already protested.

That these are the acts of power assumed by a body of men foreign to our constitutions, and unacknowledged by our laws; against which we do, on behalf of the inhabitants of British America, enter this our solemn and determined protest. And we do earnestly intreat his majesty, as yet the only mediatory power between the several states of the British empire, to recommend to his parliament of Great Britain the total revocation of these acts, which however nugatory they be, may yet prove the cause of further discontents and jealousies among us.

That we next proceed to consider the conduct of his majesty, as holding the executive powers of the laws of these states, and mark out his deviations from the line of duty. By the constitution of Great Britain as well as of the several American states, his majesty possesses the power of refusing to pass into a law any bill which has already passed the other two branches of legislature. His majesty however and his ancestors, conscious of the impropriety of opposing their single opinion to the united wisdom of two houses of parliament, while their proceedings were unbiassed by interested principles, for several ages past have modestly declined the exercise of this power in that part of his empire called Great Britain. But by change of circumstances, other principles than those of justice simply have obtained an influence on their determinations. The addition of new states to the British empire has produced an addition of new, and sometimes opposite interests. It is now therefore the great office of his majesty to resume the exercise of his negative power, and to prevent the passage of laws by any one legislature of the empire which might bear injuriously on the rights and interests of another. Yet this will not excuse the wanton exercise of this power which we have seen his majesty practice on the laws of the American legislatures.

One of the articles of impeachment against Tresilian and the other judges of Westminster Hall in the reign of Richard the second, for which they suffered death as traitors to their country, was that they had advised the king that he might dissolve his parliament at any time: and succeeding kings have adopted the opinion of these unjust judges. Since the establishment however of the British constitution at the glorious Revolution on it's free and ancient principles, neither his majesty nor his ancestors have exercised such a power of dissolution in the island of Great Britain. . . . But how different their language and his practice here! To declare as their duty required the known rights of their country, to oppose the usurpation of every foreign judicature, to disregard the imperious mandates of a minister or governor, have been the avowed causes of dissolving houses of representatives in America. . . .

But your majesty or your Governors have carried this power beyond every limit known or provided for by the laws. After dissolving one house of representatives, they have refused to call another, so that for a great length of time the legislature provided by the laws has been out of existence. . . .

That we shall at this time also take notice of an error in the nature of our landholdings, which crept in at a very early period of our settlement. . . .

Our ancestors . . . who migrated hither, were laborers, not lawyers. The fictitious principle that all lands belong originally to the king, they were early persuaded to believe real, and accordingly took grants of their own lands from the crown. And while the crown continued to grant for small sums and on reasonable rents, there was no inducement to arrest the error and lay it open to public view. But his majesty has lately taken on him to advance the terms of purchase and of holding to the double of what they were, by which means the acquisition of lands being rendered difficult, the population of our country is likely to be checked. It is time therefore for us to lay this matter before his majesty, and to declare that he has no right to grant lands of himself. From the nature and purpose of civil institutions, all the lands within the limits which any particular society has circumscribed around itself, are assumed by that society, and subject to their allotment only. . . .

That, in order to inforce the arbitrary measures before complained of, his majesty has from time to time sent among us large bodies of armed forces, not made up of the people here, nor raised by the authority of our laws. Did his majesty possess such a right as this, it might swallow up all our other rights whenever he should think proper. But his majesty has no right to land a single armed man on our shores. . . . In like manner is his majesty restrained in every part of the empire. He possesses indeed the executive power of the laws in every state; but they are the laws of the particular state which he is to administer within that state, and not those of any one within the limits of another.

That these are our grievances which we have thus laid before his majesty with that freedom of language and sentiment which becomes a free people, claiming their rights as derived from the laws of nature, and not as the gift of their chief magistrate. Let those flatter, who fear: it is not an American art. To give praise where it is not due, might be well from the venal, but would ill beseem those who are asserting the rights of human nature. They know, and will therefore say, that kings are the servants, not the proprietors of the people. Open your breast Sire, to liberal and expanded thought. Let not the name of George the third be a blot in the page of history. You are surrounded by British counsellors, but remember that they are parties. You have no ministers for American affairs, because you have none taken from among us, nor amenable to the laws on which they are to give you advice. It behoves you therefore to think and to act for yourself and your people.

. . . This, Sire, is the advice of your great American council, on the observance of which may perhaps depend your felicity and future fame, and the preservation of that harmony which alone can continue both to Great Britain and America the reciprocal advantages of their connection. It is neither our wish nor our interest to separate from her. We are willing on our part to sacrifice every thing which reason can ask to the restoration of that tranquility for which all must wish. On their part let them be ready to establish union on a generous plan. Let them name their terms, but let them be just. Accept of every commercial preference it is in our power to give for such things as we can raise for their use, or they make for ours. But let them not think to exclude us from going to other markets, to dispose of those commodities which they cannot use, nor to supply those wants which they cannot supply. Still less let it be proposed that our properties within our own territories shall be taxed or regulated by any power on earth but our own. The god who gave us life, gave us liberty at the same time: the hand of force may destroy, but cannot disjoin them. This, Sire, is our last, our determined resolution: and that you will be pleased to interpose with that efficacy which your earnest endeavors may insure to procure redress of these our great grievances, to quiet the minds of your subjects in British America against any apprehensions of future incroachment, to establish fraternal love and harmony thro' the whole empire, and that that may continue to the latest ages of time, is the fervent prayer of all British America.

The Petition of Congress to the King

The tone of the petition printed below should be compared with that of the preceding document. It becomes obvious that Congress was still in the hands of the moderates, who wished a peaceful settlement of differences with Great Britain, but who rather unrealistically looked to the King to save them from the measures of Parliament.

To the Kings most excellent majesty

Most gracious Sovereign

We your majestys faithful subjects of the colonies of Newhampshire, Massachusetts-bay, Rhode-island and Providence Plantations, Connecticut, New-York, New-Jersey, Pennsylvania, the counties of New-Castle Kent and Sussex on Delaware, Maryland, Virginia, North-Carolina, and South Carolina, in behalf of ourselves and the inhabitants of these colonies who have deputed us to represent them in General Congress, by this our humble petition, beg leave to lay our grievances before the throne.

A standing army has been kept in these colonies, ever since the conclusion of the late war, without the consent of our assemblies; and this army with a considerable naval armament has been employed to enforce the collection of taxes.

The Authority of the commander in chief, and, under him, of the brigadiers general has in time of peace, been rendered supreme in all the civil governments in America.

The commander in chief of all your majesty's forces in North-America has, in time of peace, been appointed governor of a colony.

The charges of usual offices have been greatly increased; and, now, expensive and oppressive offices have been multiplied.

The judges of admiralty and vice-admiralty courts are empowered to receive their salaries and fees from the effects condemned by themselves. The officers of the customs are empowered to break open and enter houses without the authority of any civil magistrate founded on legal information.

The Petition of Congress to the King, October 26, 1774, *Journals of the Continental Congress*, Vol. I, Washington, D. C., 1904, pp. 115–121.

The judges of courts of common law have been made entirely dependant on one part of the legislature for their salaries, as well as for the duration of their commissions.

Councellors holding their commissions, during pleasure, exercise legislative authority.

Humble and reasonable petitions from the representatives of the people have been fruitless.

The agents of the people have been discountenanced and governors have been instructed to prevent the payment of their salaries.

Assemblies have been repeatedly and injuriously dissolved.

Commerce has been burthened with many useless and oppressive restrictions.

By several acts of parliament made in the fourth, fifth, sixth, seventh, and eighth years of your majestys reign, duties are imposed on us, for the purpose of raising a revenue, and the powers of admiralty and vice-admiralty courts are extended beyond their ancient limits, whereby our property is taken from us without our consent, the trial by jury in many civil cases is abolished, enormous forfeitures are incurred for slight offences, vexatious informers are exempted from paying damages, to which they are justly liable, and oppressive security is required from owners before they are allowed to defend their right.

Both houses of parliament have resolved that colonists may be tried in England, for offences alledged to have been committed in America, by virtue of a statute passed in the thirty fifth year of Henry the eighth; and in consequence thereof, attempts have been made to enforce that statute. A statute was passed in the twelfth year of your majesty's reign, directing, that persons charged with committing any offence therein described, in any place out of the realm, may be indicted and tried for the same, in any shire or county within the realm, whereby inhabitants of these colonies may, in sundry cases by that statute made capital, be deprived of a trial by their peers of the vicinage.

In the last sessions of parliament, an act was passed for blocking up the harbour of Boston; another, empowering the governor of the Massachusetts-bay to send persons indicted for murder in that province to another colony or even to Great Britain for trial whereby such offenders may escape legal punishment; a third, for altering the chartered constitution of government in that province; and a fourth for extending the limits of Quebec, abolishing the English and restoring the French laws, whereby great numbers of British freemen are subjected to the latter, and establishing an absolute government and the Roman Catholick religion throughout those vast regions, that border on the westerly and northerly boundaries of the free protestant English settlements; and a fifth for the better providing suitable quarters for officers and soldiers in his majesty's service in North-America.

To a sovereign, who "glories in the name of Briton" the bare recital of these acts must we presume, justify the loyal subjects, who fly to the foot of his throne and implore his clemency for protection against them.

From this destructive system of colony administration adopted since the conclusion of the last war, have flowed those distresses, dangers, fears and jealousies, that overwhelm your majesty's dutiful colonists with affliction; and we defy our most subtle and inveterate enemies, to trace the unhappy differences between Great-Britain and these colonies, from an earlier period or from other causes than we have assigned. Had they proceeded on our part from a restless levity of temper, unjust impulses of ambition, or artful suggestions of seditious persons, we should merit the opprobrious terms frequently bestowed upon us, by those we revere. But so far from promoting innovations, we have only opposed them; and can be charged with no offence, unless it be one, to receive injuries and be sensible of them.

Had our creator been pleased to give us existence in a land of slavery, the sense of our condition might have been mitigated by ignorance and habit. But thanks be to his adoreable goodness, we were born the heirs of freedom, and ever enjoyed our right under the auspices of your royal ancestors, whose family was seated on the British throne, to rescue and secure a pious and gallant nation from the popery and despotism of a superstitious and inexorable tyrant. Your majesty, we are confident, justly rejoices, that your title to the crown is thus founded on the title of your people to liberty; and therefore we doubt not, but your royal wisdom must approve the sensibility, that teaches your subjects anxiously to guard the blessings they received from divine providence, and thereby to prove the performance of that compact, which elevated the illustrious house of Brunswick to the imperial dignity it now possesses.

The apprehension of being degraded into a state of servitude from the pre-eminent rank of English freemen, while our minds retain the strongest love of liberty, and clearly foresee the miseries preparing for us and our posterity, excites emotions in our breasts, which though we cannot describe, we should not wish to conceal. Feeling as men, and thinking as subjects, in the manner we do, silence would be disloyalty. By giving this faithful information, we do all in our power, to promote the great objects of your royal cares, the tranquility of your government, and the welfare of your people.

Duty to your majesty and regard for the preservation of ourselves and our posterity, the primary obligations of nature and society command us to entreat your royal attention; and as your majesty enjoys the signal distinction of reigning over freemen, we apprehend the language of freemen can not be displeasing. Your royal indignation, we hope, will rather fall on those designing and dangerous men, who daringly interposing themselves between your royal

person and your faithful subjects, and for several years past incessantly
employed to dissolve the bonds of society, by abusing your majesty's authority,
misrepresenting your American subjects and prosecuting the most desperate
and irritating projects of oppression, have at length compelled us, by the
force of accumulated injuries too severe to be any longer tolerable, to disturb
your majesty's repose by our complaints.

BRITAIN BEGINS THE RETREAT
FROM PARLIAMENTARY SUPREMACY

LORD NORTH, *Conciliatory Proposition*

*This resolution, duly adopted by the House of Commons, was forwarded to
the colonial governors in a circular letter dated March 3, 1775. There was no
attempt made to draw the colonies into serious negotiations until the Howe
Commission began to function more than a year later. The Proposition was too
little and too late.*

That it is the opinion of this Committee (of the whole house) that when the
governor, council, and assembly, or general court, of any of his Majesty's
provinces or colonies in America, shall propose to make provision, according
to the condition, circumstances, and situation, of such province or colony,
for contributing their proportion to the common defence (such proportion to
be raised under the authority of the general court, or general assembly, of such
province or colony, and disposable by parliament) and shall engage to make
provision also for the support of the civil government, and the administration
of justice, in such province or colony, it will be proper if such proposal shall
be approved by his Majesty and the two Houses of Parliament, and for so long
as such provision shall be made accordingly, to forbear, in respect of such
province or colony, to levy any duty, tax, or assessment, or to impose any
farther duty, tax, or assessment, except only such duties as it may be expedient

Lord North's "Conciliatory Proposition," February 20, 1775, *Parliamentary History*, ed. W. Cobbett,
Vol. XVIII, p. 320.

to continue to levy or to impose for the regulation of commerce; the nett produce of the duties last mentioned to be carried to the account of such province or colony respectively.

WILLIAM JOHNSTONE, *Speech to the House of Commons*

At the time of the speech, William Johnstone, former colonial governor, was an independent member of the opposition to the North Government. Johnstone presents here the first clear statement yet heard in Parliament of the idea that two independent legislatures could coexist within the same political community. His pronouncement indicated that a new principle was at work in imperial thinking, one which Britain was eventually to accept under the harsh necessity of military defeat. Johnstone was in fact far ahead of his colleagues, even those in opposition.

Subsequently, Johnstone became a member of the ill-fated Carlisle Peace Commission dispatched to America in 1778. Unfortunately, his usefulness was destroyed when he became discredited in an attempt to communicate privately and, perhaps, to bribe two members of Congress. He thereupon withdrew from the Commission.

The speech from which this excerpt is taken had as its immediate purpose refutation of the explanation and defense of North's American policy made by one of the ministry's supporters, "the hon. gentleman," in the House of Commons.

The hon. gentleman says, "the Americans had some reasons for their conduct in the first of those disputes; but now they have refused their just proportion of taxes, by rejecting lord North's conciliatory proposition of last year, and resisting the constitutional authority of parliament, he is ready to devote them to destruction." Who does not see that the whole question, even according to this hon. gentleman, turns upon just proportion and constitutional authority? Now I deny that the people of America have ever refused to contribute their just proportion, when called upon in a constitutional way, and those who assert the contrary ought to prove it. If the hon. gentleman vindicates the severity of his conduct against his fellow subjects in America, for rejecting the proposition of last year, I think he rests on as feeble ground as any man ever stood. How does he vindicate the severities in which he concurred before

---

Governor Johnstone's speech to the House of Commons, November, 1775, *ibid*, pp. 740–757.

it could be known whether the subjects in America Would accede to this marvellous indulgence or not? His mind must have been strangely biassed to the noble lord if this could turn the scale of his reason. I really thought this foolish piece of paper had been so universally condemned, that I should never again have heard any arguments founded on so flimsy a foundation. The purpose was clearly to amuse the people on this side of the Atlantic, and to divide the people on that. Having failed in its effect, I understood from many friends of government, that every rational argument in support of the proposition had been reprobated; for what, indeed, can be more truly ridiculous, than in a dispute concerning the power of taxation, seriously to say to a sensible people, We admit there are many unanswerable reasons why this assembly are unfit to impose taxes upon you, and therefore if you will only tax yourselves to our satisfaction, we will forbear the exercise of a right to which we declare by the proposition we are incompetent. But some men will say the parliament can judge sufficiently well of the gross sum, though unfit and incapable of determining on the manner in which it is to be raised. Who that is accustomed to reason accurately, does not perceive that the estimate of supply must be regulated from a thorough knowledge of the ways and means, and that they are united in common sense, as well as by the English constitution, to reside in the same persons. But the hon. baronet forgets that the main argument which drew the concession of the conciliatory proposition turns on this: the Americans have no representatives in the British parliament, they have not the security of other subjects residing in Britain, who may not be represented, namely, that the members in taxing them must tax themselves; on the contrary, it is the interest of every member to lay as much as possible on America to ease himself. This was the consideration which "drew iron tears from Pluto's cheek," and has affected so many members not remarkably tender towards the feeding of their fellow creature. But let us consider if this irresistible objection, as it has been called by one of the friends of administration, against taxing America by the British parliament, does not equally apply, when we approve of the sum offered, and tax them in the lump, as when we tax them by detail.

However, Sir, absurd as this appears, it is not my capital objection to that mode of raising money, nor is it the objection of the Americans; they maintain the power of giving and granting their own money by their own free and voluntary consent, is the only security they can retain for the just administration of government, at so great a distance from the seat of empire. That it is the main spring in their several establishments upon which the meeting and power of their several assemblies depend, from whence the singular prosperity of the British colonies, above all others on the face of the earth, have flowed. They admit you have the power of limiting the means by which they may acquire property, but they deny you the power of disposing of this property,

after it is so acquired. Thus in his Majesty's speech the same general undefined axioms prevail. "To be a subject of Great Britain, with all its consequences, is to be the freest member of any society in the known world." All
Americans, with one voice, agree in this truth; their writings and their actions
proclaim their belief: but they maintain, as I assert in their behalf, that one of
the unalienable consequences of that situation, is the giving and granting
of aids for the support of government, according to the exigency that shall
appear to their own understanding: and that to tax them in an assembly where
they have no representatives, and by men who have no interest in the subsidy
they impose, is contrary to the spirit of the British constitution, and in its
consequences must deprive them of all the essential rights of a British subject.
Another essential right of a British subject is trial by jury, has not this been
abrogated in many cases by the late acts of parliament, and totally destroyed
in all civil causes in the extensive province of Quebec? The writ of Habeas
Corpus is another essential right of a British subject; has not this also been
done away? I forbear to enumerate the other oppressive proceedings, contrary
to the whole tenor of our government, dissolving of charters without evidence,
trial, or forfeiture; laws to deny the natural gifts of the elements, confounding
the innocent with the guilty: because when once three great pillars of the
British constitution are removed, taxing without representatives, trial without
jury, imprisonment without relief by writ of Habeas Corpus, the whole must
neccesarily fall into confusion, and the rest is not worth contending for. The
people in America wisely foresee the suppression of all their rights, in the train
of those iniquitous innovations. They perceive that every thing which is dear
to a freeman is at stake, and they are willing as becomes the children of their
ancestors, to put all to the risk, and sacrifice their lives and fortunes, rather
than give up the liberty of a subject of Great Britain, with all its consequences.
The hon. baronet has concluded his speech with another reason for inducing us
to join in the coercive measures proposed by the Address, which is still more
extraordinary, saying, "Whether we succeed or not may be uncertain; but if
we fail we shall even then be no worse than we were." . . . If America is forced
to invite foreign powers to share in her commerce; if she is drove to the necessity of following the example of Holland and Switzerland; if our armies are
destroyed, our fleets wrecked, our treasures wasted, our reputation for justice
and humanity lost, our senates corrupted by the emoluments which must fall
to individuals, in the prosecution of so expensive a war, and 4s. land tax
entailed on us forever, will the hon. gentleman say we are only where we were?
What objects can call the attention of the House in a stronger degree than those
I have enumerated? And yet they are all involved in the question now before
you. . . .

I know there are many men high in favour who are for abridging the liberties of the people in the colonies. My system, on the contrary, is for preserving

these sacred and inviolate, according to their several and ancient institutions, the variety of which forms the beauty and harmony of the whole. There is no middle institution, as in this country, to balance between the people and the crown: the assemblies are their only barrier; they are, therefore, the favorite institution of the people; to them they look for protection against the exactions, oppressions, and extortions of governors, and are, on that account, cautious and jealous of any infringement that shall diminish their power. . . .

. . . I say again, the whole of our blunders, oppressions and mistakes in these unfortunate disputes, have arisen from ignorance in the first principles of government; gross ignorance in the several constitutions of the colonies; ignorance in the power we could apply to subdue them, and still greater ignorance of the end to be obtained by such an attempt. To each of those I will severally speak. I say it demonstrates a perfect ignorance of the history of civil society to assert (which is the captivating argument used in this House, for breaking down all the barriers of liberty in America) that two independent legislatures cannot exist in the same community, and therefore we are to destroy the whole fabric of those governments which have subsisted for so many years. Mankind are constently quoting some trite maxim; and appealing to their limited theory in politics, while they reject established facts. I say, a free government necessarily involves many clashing jurisdictions, if pushed to the extreme. I maintain this species of government must ever depend more on the spirit of freedom that first established it, than on all the parchment you can cover with words. . . .

. . . I should not be surprized if half the people in England should at first join against the Americans; national prejudice, pride, false glory, and false arithmetic, all contribute to deceive them; but that any man assuming the character of a statesman, should proceed in this mad career, to destroy in a few years that beautiful system of empire our ancestors have been raising with so much pains and glory; first under the false pretence of raising a revenue, and next under a more false pretence that America wishes to throw off her just dependence on Great Britain. This, I confess, does surprize me. For this reason my indignation chiefly rises against the noble lord on the floor; I am willing to acquit all his colleagues and most of his followers, even if they had not the interested motives of places and pensions to bias their judgment; but that the noble lord, who yearly considers the riches that come into the public treasury, who knows and can trace all the circuitous channels by which riches flow into this country, that he should place no more to the credit of America than the paltry sum collected by his insignifigant commissioners, and endeavour to mislead others by such assertions. This, indeed, is beyond belief. When the noble lord is pleased to take the other side of the argument, what abundance of wealth does he sometimes pour forth in the most copious flow of eloquence. When he supports this rugged coercive system, how he labours and flags nothing but sounding words and unmeaning phrases. The dignity of parliament! now to say this is the best supported by humanity and justice, and maintaining the freedom of the subject. The supremacy of the legislative authority of Great Britain! this I call unintelligible jargon; instead of running the different priviledges belonging to the various parts of the empire into one common mass of power, gentlemen should consider that the very first principles of good government in this wide-extended dominion consist in subdividing the empire into many parts, and giving to each individual an immediate interest, that the community to which he belongs should be well regulated. This is the principle upon which our ancestors established those different colonies or communities; this is the principle on which they have flourished so long and so prosperously; this is the principle on which alone they can be well-governed at such a distance from the rest of the empire. Yet we are breaking through all those sacred maxims of our forfathers, and giving the alarm to every wise man on the continent of America. That all his rights depend on the will of men whose corruptions are notorious, who regard him as an enemy, and who have no interest in his prosperity, and feel no control from him as a constituent. The most learned writer on government has defined civil and political liberty to consist in a perfect security as to a man's rights; after the acts of parliament of last year, can any man on the great continent of America say that he feels that security? Could any thing less than an entire want of policy, a species of political phrenzy here, have produced this wonderful effect? You blame the Americans but do not consider the next step which your conduct necessarily drives them on to. You assert they aim at independence; I assert they wish for nothing more than a constitutional dependence on Great-Britain, according as they have subsisted from their first establishments, and according as Ireland depends on the British legislature at this moment. . . .

. . . The nature of government will not allow us to define what are the precise points where resistence may be made to the governing powers; but will any man conclude from thence that acts of King, Lords and Commons ought not to be resisted, if they should sap the fundamentals of the constitution? Nothing but the general feeling of the community can determine the point; and was ever this sense of a people so unanimous on any subject? I declare, upon my honour, I have not conversed with one man from America (and I have chiefly sought out the friends of administration) who have not universally agreed, that all America is unanimous in resisting the power of taxing them by the British parliament where they have no representatives; that they will never yield in this point; that in case they were made easy on this point, and secure as to their charters, on which their property depends, they would immediately return to their duty and obedience. This I aver to be the universal report and opinion of all men with whom I have conversed from America. If any one disputes the truth of my assertions, I now defy him to bring any evidence to contradict me, and I now undertake to bring men of the best characters in support of what I aver. But respecting general opinion, I still go further; I maintain that the sense of the best and wisest men in this country, are on the side of the Americans; that three to one in Ireland are on their side; that the soldiers and sailors feel an unwillingness to the service; that you never will find the same exertions of spirit in this as in other wars. . . . The conduct of the people of New England for wisdom, courage, temperance, fortitude, and all those qualities that can command the admiration of noble minds, is not surpassed in the history of any nation under the sun. Instead of wreaking our vengeance against that colony, that heroism alone should plead their forgiveness. . . .

I come now to consider the consequences of all those measures, supposing we should succeed. If national strength is to be calculated from the fitness of every part to preserve and improve the advantages of their constitution and to support their country in pursuit of its objects. If institutions that secure property and prevent oppression, encourage the settlement of families, and facilitate the rearing of children, are the most favorable to mankind, and therefore to be protected and prefered, as the best writer on government has asserted, surely the establishments of the English colonies, as excelling all others which have appeared in the history of the world, deserve to be revered in this respect. But a success in the present war, after destroying all the principles which have produced those glorious effects in civil society, must leave the country desolate, must spread through that wide dominion, forfeitures, executions, change of property, military oppression, and every misery that can engender hatred and distract mankind. But these are but temporary evils, in comparison to the last dreadful catastrophe. It must establish a military despotism in the colonies, which the revenues of an oppressed people never can pay. An army that the men of this country can never supply, which therefore foreign mercenaries must fill, and all this with additional powers in the crown, that must end in the subversion of the constitution. I make no doubt many men labour in the support of this business, purposely to effect that end. The contentions in a free government do not accord with their feeble, corrupt, luxurious dispositions. That the spirit of the people should so long lie deceived by their arts and management is to me astonishing. I shall wait patiently some further calamity, for no reasoning on the certain progress of things in a growing empire can affect their narrow minds. That this may soon happen in a small degree, as the only means of saving the dissolution of the whole, I sincerely wish, for the good of the public; misfortunes if duly watched are oftentimes as profitable to an unfeeling multitude as they are useful to private individuals. But let those who now encourage measures that must inevitably end in such dreadful calamities, beware of the turn of the tide. Let them look into history and remember the fate of cruel oppression and arrogant statesmen. Let even kings attend to the examples which history presents on this subject—but I blame not them; it is unnatural for beings, with human passions, placed in such high situations, mixing little with men, and generally deceived, to bear contradiction to their will, and opposition even to their arms, with any degree of patience: irritation and resentment must be the consequences: encroachments on their part often proceed from a conscious rectitude of their own intentions; but the people I do blame are the members of this House, placed as the guardians of the people's rights and priviledges, daily sacrificing them to some interested motive. Let any one consider all the national advantages that can be drawn from colonies, and ask his own heart, if we have not hitherto drawn, and may not in time to come draw all these from the ancient constitution. To what motive, then, can these innovations be imputed? I have showed you the bad consequences in proceeding; show me the good you propose from slaughter and devastation. . . .

THE LAST APPEAL

Resolutions of Congress

The resolutions adopted by Congress on May 26, 1775, clearly portray the state of mind of that body following the outbreak of hostilities at Lexington and Concord the preceding month. In reality they constituted a declaration of war despite the import of Resolutions 3 and 4. Colonial leaders already knew the British view and could have been under no illusion about the efficacy of their "dutiful" petition.

Resolved, that it be recommended to the congress afores^d. to persevere the more vigourously in preparing for their defence, as it is very uncertain whether the earnest endeavours of the Congress to accommodate the unhappy differences between G. Britain and the colonies by conciliatory Measures will be successful. . . .

The Congress then resolved themselves into a committee of the whole, to take into consideration the state of America; after some time spent therein,

---

Resolutions of Congress, May 26, 1775, *Journals of the Continental Congress*, Vol. II, Washington, D. C., 1905 pp. 64–66.

the president resumed the chair, and Mr. (Samuel) Ward reported from the committee, that they had come to certain resolutions respecting the state of America, which he was desired to report, but not having finished the business referred to them desired him to move for leave to sit again.

The report from the committee being read, the Congress came into the following Resolutions:

Resolved unanimously, 1, That his Majesty's most faithful subjects, in these colonies, are reduced to a dangerous and critical situation, by the attempts of the british Ministry to carry into execution, by force of arms, several unconstitutional and oppressive acts of the british parliament for laying taxes in America; to enforce the collection of those taxes, and for altering and changing the constitution and internal police of some of these colonies, in violation of the natural and civil rights of the colonists.

Unanimously 2. Hostilities being actually commenced in the Massachusetts bay, by the British troops, under the command of General Gage, and the lives of a number of the inhabitants of that colony destroyed, the town of Boston having not only been long occupied as a garrisoned town in an enemy's country, but the inhabitants thereof treated with a severity and cruelty not to be justifyed even towards declared enemies; large re-inforcements too being ordered and soon expected, for the declared purpose of compelling these colonies to submit to the operation of the s^d acts; *Resolved*, therefore, that for purpose of securing and defending these colonies, and preserving them in safety against all attempts to carry the s^d acts into execution by force of arms, these colonies be immediately put into a state of defence.

Unanimously 3. But, as we most ardently wish for a restoration of the harmony formerly subsisting between our Mother country and these colonies, the interruption of which must, at all events, be exceedingly injurious to both countries, *Resolved*, that with a sincere design of contributing by all the means in our power, not incompatible with a just regard for the undoubted rights and true interests of these colonies, to the promotion of this most desireable reconciliation, an humble and dutiful petition be presented to his Majesty.

Resolved, 4, That measures be entered into for opening a Negotiation, in order to accommodate the unhappy disputes subsisting between Great Britain and these colonies, and that this be made a part of the petition to the King.

BRITAIN SURRENDERS THE RIGHT TO TAX

The Taxation of Colonies Act

The Taxation Act was part of North's over-all plan to conciliate the colonies with the offer of home rule. Ironically, it was drafted in early February, 1778, at the very same time that the Franco-American Treaty of Alliance was being negotiated in Paris. Again, it was too little too late. Even so, the Act remains important in the development of British imperial thinking, renouncing as it does Parliament's right to tax for revenue—the more remarkable when placed against the assumption explicit in the Declaratory Act of 1766.

An Act for removing all doubts and Apprehensions concerning Taxation, by the Parliament of Great Britain in any of the Colonies, Provinces and Plantations in North America and the West Indies . . .

PREAMBLE

Whereas taxation by the Parliament of Great Britain for the purpose of raising a revenue in his Majesty's colonies, provinces and plantations in North America has been found by experience to occasion great uneasiness and disorders among his Majesty's faithful subjects who may nevertheless be disposed to acknowledge the justice of contributing to the common defence of the empire, provided such contribution should be raised under the authority of the general court or general assembly of each respective colony, province or plantation: And whereas, in order as well to remove the said uneasiness, and to quiet the minds of his Majesty's subjects who may be disposed to return to their allegiance, as to restore the peace and welfare of all his Majesty's dominions, it is expedient to declare that the King and Parliament of Great Britain will not impose any duty, tax or assessment for the purpose of raising a revenue in any of the colonies, provinces or plantations: May it please your Majesty that it may be declared and enacted, and it is hereby declared and enacted by the King's most excellent Majesty, by and with the advice and consent of the lords spiritual and temporal, and commons, in this present Parliament assembled, and by the authority of the same that

(1/ No tax to be hereafter imposed by the King and Parliament of Great Britain on any of the colonies in North America or the West Indies, except certain duties for regulation of commerce.—From and after the passing of this Act the King and Parliament of Great Britain will not impose any duty, tax or assessment whatever, payable in any of his Majesty's colonies, provinces and plantations in North America or the West Indies, except only such duties as it may be expedient to impose for the regulation of commerce, the net produce of such duties to be always paid and applied to and for the use of the colony, province or plantation in which the same shall be respectively levied, in such manner as other duties collected by the authority of the respective general courts or general assemblies of such colonies, provinces or plantations are ordinarily paid and applied.

THE AMERICAN REBUFF

Proceeding of the Congress Relative to the Carlisle Peace Commission

The Carlisle Peace Commissioners, Undersecretary of State William Eden and Governor Johnstone, in addition to the young Earl of Carlisle, drafted their initial communication to the Congress during their voyage to America in late Spring, 1778. They wished, they wrote to the Americans, "to reestablish on the Basis of equal Freedom and mutual Safety the tranquility of this once happy Empire." They would concur in every just arrangement, looking to an end of hostilities as well as the restoration and freedom of trade. They would agree to the prohibition of any military forces in the states of North America without the consent of Congress or of the individual assemblies. They would even accept a reciprocal deputation of representatives, colonials sitting in Parliament and Britons in the assemblies. They would confer upon the American states "the Irrevocable Enjoyment of every Privilege, that is short of a Total separation of Interests."

Proceeding of the Congress Relative to the Carlisle Peace Commission, *Journals of the Continental Congress,* Vol. XI, Washington, D. C., 1908, pp. 605–606; 609–611; 614–616.

Then, the tone of the letter changed as the Commissioners addressed themselves to France's part in the struggle, an "insidious interposition." The
traditional Bourbon enemy, they charged, had made her treaty with America
only after Britain's plan for conciliation had become known; and they
appealed to ties of language, blood, and religion in an effort to draw America
away from the French alliance.

Saturday, June 13, 1778

During the debate, an express arrived with a letter of the 11th, from General
Washington, which was read; and, a packet, in which was enclosed, together
with other papers, a letter signed "Carlisle, William Eden, George Johnstone,"
dated at Philadelphia, 9 June, 1778, and directed "to his excellency Henry
Laurens, the president, and others, the members of Congress"; which letter
was read to the words, "insidious interposition of a power which has, from the
first settlement of these colonies, been actuated with enmity to us both; and,
notwithstanding the pretended date or present form of the French offers,"
inclusive; whereupon the reading was interrupted, and a motion was made
not to proceed farther, because of the offensive language against his most
Christian majesty: debates arising thereon.

Ordered, that the farther consideration of the motion be postponed.

Tuesday, June 16, 1778

Congress resumed the consideration of the motion respecting the letter from
the commissioners of the king of Great Britain, which was amended, and is
as follows:

"That this Congress cannot hear any language reflecting upon the honor of
his most Christian majesty, the good and faithful ally of these states:"

On motion, that the consideration thereof be postponed, Mr. William Henry
Drayton required the yeas and nays: . . .

So it was resolved in the affirmative.

A motion was then made, that the letter from the commissioners of the king
of Great Britain lie on the table: passed in the negative.

On motion, Resolved, That the letter and papers accompanying it, be read:
Whereupon,

The letter, of the 9th, and one dated June 1778, both signed Carlisle, William
Eden, and George Johnstone; a paper endorsed copy of the commission for
restoring peace, &c. To the earl of Carlisle, lord viscount Howe, Sir William
Howe, or in his absence Sir Henry Clinton, William Eden, and George

Johnstone, were read; and also three acts of the parliament of Great Britain:

Ordered, That they be referred to a committee of five;

The members chosen, Mr. [Richard Henry] Lee, Mr. S[amuel] Adams, Mr. [William Henry] Drayton, Mr. [Gouverneur] Morris, and Mr. [John] Witherspoon. . . .

The committee to whom were referred the letters and papers from the Earl of Carlisle, &c. commissioners from the king of Great Britain, reported the draught of a letter, which was read: and after debate,

Resolved, That the farther consideration thereof be postponed until to morrow.

Wednesday, June 17, 1778

Congress resumed the consideration of the draught of a letter in answer to the letter and papers received from the Earl of Carlisle, &c. commissioners from the king of Great Britain:

On motion to agree to the letter, Mr. [Francis] Dana required the ays and noes. . . .

So it was unanimously agreed to, and is as follows:

I have received the letter from your excellencies of the 9th instant, with the enclosures, and laid them before Congress. Nothing but an earnest desire to spare the further effusion of human blood could have induced them to read a paper containing expressions so disrespectful to his most Christian majesty, the good and great ally of these states, or to consider propositions so derogatory to the honor of an independent nation.

The acts of the British parliament, the commission from your sovereign, and your letter, suppose the people of these states to be subjects of the crown of Great Britain, and are founded on the idea of dependence, which is utterly inadmissable.

I am further directed to inform your excellencies, that Congress are inclined to peace, notwithstanding the unjust claims from which this war originated, and the savage manner in which it hath been conducted. They will, therefore, be ready to enter upon the consideration of a treaty of peace and commerce not inconsistent with treaties already subsisting, when the king of Great Britain shall demonstrate a sincere disposition for that purpose. The only solid proof of this disposition, will be, an explicit acknowledgment of the independence of these states, or the withdrawing his fleets and armies. I have the honor to be,

Your excellencies most obedient and humble servant.

Resolved, That a committee of three be appointed to make proper extracts from the journals and files relative to the letters received from the British commissioners, and report to Congress previous to a publication:

The members chosen, Mr. [Gouverneur] Morris, Mr. [Richard Henry] Lee, and Mr. [William Henry] Drayton. . . .

The committee appointed to report upon the means of preventing a correspondence with the enemy, brought in a report; Whereupon, Congress came to the following resolution:

Whereas, many letters, addressed to individuals of these United States, have been lately received from England, through the conveyance of the enemy, and some of them, which have been under the inspection of members of Congress, are found to contain ideas insidiously calculated to divide and delude the good people of these states:

Resolved, That it be, and it is hereby earnestly recommended to the legislative and executive authorities of the several states, to exercise the utmost care and vigilance, and take the most effectual measures to put a stop to so dangerous and criminal a correspondence.

Resolved, That the Commander in Chief and the commanders in each and every military department be, and he and they are hereby directed to carry the measures recommended in the above resolution into the most effectual execution.

Ordered, That the foregoing resolutions be forthwith published, and it is recommended to the several printers in the United States to re-publish the same.

3 / MONARCHY OR REPUBLIC: THE NEW RELATION

INTERPRETATION

VINCENT T. HARLOW,
Shelburne's Imperial Policy at the Peace Settlement:
The American Negotiations

Vincent T. Harlow, late Beit Professor of the History of the British Empire and Fellow, Balliol College, Oxford, has made a monumental contribution not only to British Imperial History in general, but also to American Revolutionary History in particular. He, like Gipson, sees the problem within the broad context of Britain's worldwide concerns and he avoids assigning personal blame for the disruption of the First British Empire.

In his interpretation of Lord Shelburne's policies toward America, he has been influenced by the American historian, Clarence V. Alvord, particularly by the latter's brilliant essay on Shelburne and Anglo-American reconciliation.

Despite the worldwide scope of Professor Harlow's work, his treatment of the negotiations leading to the Peace of 1783 is detailed and objective.

. . . In political matters he [Lord Shelburne] had been deeply influenced by Chatham. The State was in jeopardy because the constitution was being distorted: the equipoise between Crown, Lords and Commons must be restored. 'A high-toned prerogative prince,' he declared, 'and a servile corrupt parliament, was the strongest symptom of despotism and tyranny.' But that did not imply that the Sovereign ought to be like the King of the Mahrattas, 'a mere nominal monarch,' subjected to a group of magnates who to all intents and purposes held the reins of government, 'while they kept the King locked up in pretty nearly a state of ideotism.' His Majesty ought to be treated with the profound respect due to his person and the reverence due to his situation. It was better that the King should have a mind of his own and take an active part in the management of the realm than that he should be a puppet; and a puppet he must necessarily become if those had their way who aimed at government by a single faction, who wished to inhibit the King from appointing his own Ministers, and who tried to insist that the Cabinet must have the right of appointing to all vacancies. The remedy for the present discontents

Vincent T. Harlow, *The Founding of the Second British Empire,* London, Longmans, Green & Co., Ltd., Chap. VI. Reprinted by permission of the publisher.

was a free and reformed parliament and the exercise by the House of Lords of its 'latent powers' to correct any abuses of the prerogative. As already noted, this was the genesis of a new Toryism of which the younger Pitt was to be the leader.

Like Chatham, too, he combined an ardent advocacy of American rights with a feeling of horror at the thought of the approaching disruption of the Empire. It had ever been his opinion, he declared, that American independence would be a dreadful blow to the greatness of Britain, and that when it took place, 'the sun of England might be said to have set.' Later he expressed his conviction that the sun would rise again in different circumstances, but his enemies put the phrase to effective use against him when the opportunity offered. Confronted with an American and an Irish revolution, he was passionately opposed to a negative surrender and in both cases strove to achieve a working partnership on a basis of equality and reciprocal concession. In that respect Shelburne's ideas were beyond Chatham's range, and indeed beyond that of most of his countrymen.

No form of effective association with either an independent North America or a self-governing Ireland was practicable without a substantial abandonment of mercantilist principles. Partly, perhaps, for this reason he had become by 1782 a convinced free trader. He came to regard the two revolts as an opportunity for taking an important initial step towards the establishment of a more enlightened system of international commerce. He had great hopes, too, that the France which had produced Quesnay and the school of economists known as the Physiocrats would be prepared to negotiate a comprehensive reciprocity treaty.

Shelburne's ideas for the future were not, however, confined to considerations of immediate expediency. He was deeply convinced that the British Constitution (purged and reformed) was the surest guarantee of liberty and had, moreover, a universal validity: a proposition which on the second count still awaits final determination. Conscious of the gigantic potentialities of the North American continent, he considered that the abandonment by the Thirteen Colonies of a balanced monarchical system of government and their consequent decline into 'democratical' republicanism and probable anarchy would be a major catastrophe. On the other hand, the colonization of a continent under free ordered government, and directed by a completely autonomous American authority, linked to Britain by allegiance to a common Crown, would mean the growth of a great trans-Atlantic society, practising and guaranteeing for all its parts political and economic freedom. Such a society, in Shelburne's belief, could find common ground with the European country which had given birth to the ideas of Voltaire, Montesquieu, Diderot and Rousseau. While the Anglo-American association was maturing, Britain in Europe should return to the foreign policy of Elizabeth and Cromwell by working in alliance with

France. By this means, the predatory Powers, Russia, Prussia and Austria, could be effectively restrained by the West and the security of the civilized world be maintained. This was a policy directly opposed to the views of Fox and most of the Whigs, who relied on a resumption of good relations with the Northern Powers to check the ambition of the Bourbon Family Compact.

On the American side of his comprehensive design, Shelburne was planning as if he could pick up the threads again and find them essentially the same as in 1768. He had been out of office for fourteen years and without access to confidential information, and he underestimated the psychological revolution which the brutalities and counter-brutalities of a long war had effected. South of the St. Lawrence the Crown and the English social and political system had become foreign. On the European side Shelburne could not foresee the French Revolution and the Napoleonic dictatorship, but more modern developments have not invalidated his hopes of a British-American-French accord in defence of freedom.

In this broad conception of the peace settlement Shelburne was following the prevailing trend in favor of the development of commercial intercourse instead of dissipating valuable manpower in trying to create markets by colonization. But Shelburne added to this his own views about free trade. His opponents, therefore, were not only triumphant enemies abroad, but included the representatives of vested interests and traditional opinions at home.

The Genesis of Shelburne's North American Policy

For the sake of a clear appreciation of British aims during the negotiations with the American Commissioners in Paris it is important to note the gradual shaping of Shelburne's thought on the future character of Anglo-American relations. From the Stamp Act onwards he had shared the views of his leader, Chatham, the champion alike of colonial rights and of the supremacy of the metropolitan Parliament. In the early stages of the conflict Shelburne had insisted again and again that, although the war was monstrous, political separation must never be accepted; and when Burgoyne's surrender at Saratoga made the intervention of France a certainty and most of Shelburne's friends began to urge acceptance of American independence, he clung to the belief that separation could still be avoided.

Speaking in the Lords on 11 December, 1777, he stated that in treating with the Colonies for peace and reconciliation, the question of independence, 'like the preamble to a statute,' should not be mentioned until 'the body of conditions' had been agreed. There was still, he added, a faint glimmer of hope: America had been so successful in the war that she had not been entirely thrown into the arms of France. He did not specify the conditions which he contemplated, and at this stage he was probably still groping.

Three months later he made a speech repeating his previous ideas. He would never assent to the severance of the Colonies from the Mother Country. He had always held that the connection between the two countries should be that they had 'one purse and one sword,' and that Britain should superintend the interests of the whole. Both countries should have but one will, though the means of expressing that will might be 'different, distinct and varied.' He still retained strong hopes that it could be effected. If the war was stopped at once and a beginning made in restoring the confidence of the Americans in British intentions, much might be hoped for from the natural inclinations of a people having the same religion, the same language, similar institutions and interwoven interests. At that stage he was opposed to the suggestion of separation followed by a commercial alliance. The political interests of two independent States would, almost certainly, diverge, and experience had shown that, when this happened, any commercial agreement between them dwindled to nothing. What was needed was a solemn and binding compact, based on the reciprocal interests of the two parties; and he cited the Navigation Act of 1660 as the great measure which had 'united the commercial interests of the whole British Empire.' There were, he concluded, many cool and able men in Congress who, when they came to contemplate the future, would almost certainly perceive that a connection with Britain would be the best means of advancing the interest of their own.

During the famous debate of 8 April, 1778 on the state of the nation, when the dying Chatham uttered his final warning and protest, Shelburne followed with an eloquent oration. America was not yet finally lost; but there was no hope that the Commissioners who were about to cross the Atlantic could achieve a reconciliation, for the colonists had lost all faith in an Administration, 'totally immersed in the deepest and dirtiest ways of corruption.' The constitution must first be cleansed and reformed, and the initial step must be the expulsion from power of a combination of men who for dark and crooked purposes had vested an unnatural power in the Crown, giving it an interest distinct from that of the people. The Ministers, having failed to enslave America, now hoped to save their sinister system at home by a formal surrender to the colonists.

The true way was a reformation, permeating the structure of the whole Empire. Once that process had begun at the center, there would be hope that the Americans would become convinced that England was sincere and in earnest and would co-operate in effecting a reunion on the most comprehensive and solid foundations. Such a plan, he declared, should extend its influence throughout the Empire, to the East and West Indies, and to Ireland. Thus would London become, what it ought to be, 'the metropolis of Ireland, Asia and America.'

What was the plan that was taking shape in his mind? Not imperial federa-
tion: he derided the idea of deputies from Congress sitting at Westminster
with their constituencies entirely disconnected from 'every species of British
taxation.' Equally he condemned the conception of coordinate sovereignties:
to cut off the executive and legislative powers of the British Parliament from
'all real communication' with the internal legislation of the several colonies
would form such a system of polity as had never before entered into the mind
of man to conceive. The powers of the Imperial Government could be dele-
gated, but not divided. 'To the great purposes of government there must,
according to the spirit and letter of the constitution, be but one will.'

Normally the superintending power of the Parliament at Westminster would
be confined to matters of trade, defence and foreign relations, and it was to be
superintendence by consent. Between Britain and a self-governing Ireland and
a self-governing America he hoped to see a commercial union, freely negotiated
on a basis of mutual interests, and then implemented by imperial legislation.
Similarly, the maritime power of the Empire as a whole would be 'cemented'
by an agreed Navigation Act. Like Adam Smith, he justified this exception to
the free trade rule on the ground that defence (in the words of the economist)
was 'more important than opulence.'

In Shelburne's mind the American and the Irish problems were both 'imperial' and were closely associated. His handling of the Irish demand for independence in 1782 was on parallel lines to his approach to the American
Commissioners in Paris. Shelburne did not, of course, anticipate the 19th
Century device of Colonial 'responsible' government: the system of collective
ministerial responsibility had yet to be developed at home. But the self-govern-
ment for America and Ireland within the Empire which he strove to establish
would have approximated in degree, if not in form, to that enjoyed by the
British Dominions in 1914—with the addition of an imperial *Zollverein* and
a 'free-trade' connection between the British group and one or more foreign
Powers.

As the negotiations with Franklin, Jay and Adams in Paris followed their
tortuous course during the summer and autumn of 1782, Shelburne began to
realize that he had greatly overestimated the extent to which American
friendship for Britain had survived the corrosion of war and the intolerable
arrogance of a Germain or a Stormont. He accordingly abandoned, though with
great reluctance, the hope of a speedy reunion and set himself to fashion a
peace settlement which would as far as possible wipe the slate clean and
provide a sound basis for the revival of Anglo-American goodwill. At some
future time and in one form or another, he [Shelburne] hoped and believed
[that] the two branches of the English-speaking race would come together
again.

In July, 1782, when the Paris negotiations were making little progress, he
expressed that conviction in the following terms:

I have never made a Secret of the deep Concern I feel in the Separation of Countries united by Blood, by Principles, Habits, and every Tie short of Territorial Proximity. But you very well know that I have long since given it up *decidedly* tho' *reluctantly*: and the same motives which made me perhaps the last to give up all Hope of Re-union, make me most anxious, if it is given up, that it should be done *decidedly*, so as to avoid all future Risque of Enmity, and the Foundation of a new Connection better adapted to the present Temper and Interest of both Countries.

In that view, he continued, he went further with Dr. Franklin than perhaps he was aware of and further perhaps than those who were urging him to concede American independence without regard to conditions were prepared to admit.

My private Opinion would lead me to go a great way for Federal Union. But is either Country ripe for it? If not, means must be left to advance it.

Shelburne did not specify what he meant by the term 'Federal Union.' Judging from his attitude prior to American independence, it seems almost certain that he did not contemplate an Anglo-American federal parliament. Something more than alliance: possibly an intimate association for purposes of trade and joint defence, formulated and operated by concurrent legislation. If so, he was contemplating an arrangement in this final stage of his thinking not incomparable with the intention of the Anglo-Irish Treaty of 1921. In the instructions which he sent to the British plenipotentiary in Paris there occurs an intriguing clause: 'to propose an unreserved system of naturalization as the foundation of a future amicable connection.'

If neither country was ripe for any form of reunion (and they were not), then at least the peace settlement must be shaped so as to facilitate a subsequent getting-together. Some three months later, when the American negotiations were at an advanced stage, Shelburne wrote a private letter to Oswald, the British delegate, giving him a friendly but urgent warning that he was not serving the cause of future Anglo-American friendship by actually 'going before' the American Commissioners on every point where a concession might be demanded.

If we are to look to regain the Affections of America, to Re-union in any shape, or even to Commerce and Friendship, is it not to the last Degree of consequence to retain every Means possible to gratify America at a future, [and] I hope not very distant day, when the Negotiation will not be carried on at a Foreign Capital, nor under the Eye, if not Controul, of inveterate

Enemies, nor under the reputed Impulse of absolute Necessity. . . . And if there is the Disposition you mention in the Commissioners towards Great Britain, and it is stated to them with Address, I should think they might be brought to enter into it, as they must feel it perfectly consistent with the Language hitherto held to them.

The final form of Shelburne's policy in making peace with America was to offer generous terms to a completely independent United States, without however yielding to demands (with regard to Canada, for example, and American debts to British merchants) which would be likely to cause or revive dissension. The peace treaty could thus be a first step leading to a *rapprochement*: at the least, to friendship and commercial alliance, and perhaps in the end to some form of political association. . . .

The American Commissioners and the Diplomatic Background

We have now seen something of Shelburne's hopes and plans with regard to America as well as the political *milieu* in which he was working. It is also important to appreciate the background of the American Commissioners, particularly as Shelburne was seriously misled about their attitude. On receiving Franklin's letter, he assumed that his old friend shared his conviction that a trans-Atlantic partnership was a *desideratum* for all concerned. This was not in fact the case. Franklin did not believe that a connection with Britain, however defined, could in practice be other than political and economic subordination. His one object was to ensure the future greatness of an independent America by extracting the maximum of concession. In that cause and to that end he manipulated the European Powers, ally and enemy alike. His tactics during the peace negotiations were accordingly complicated and at times equivocal. It has often been said that he was a cosmopolitan; but he was also one of the first 'Americans.'

Shelburne's design of a free America and a free Ireland, voluntarily associated with Britain, evoked in Franklin a 'sales resistance.' 'We have pretty good information,' he wrote in June to Robert Livingston, the American Secretary for Foreign Affairs, 'that some of the Ministers still flatter the King with the hope of recovering his sovereignty over us on the same terms as are now making with Ireland. However willing we might have been at the commencement of this contest to have accepted such conditions, be assured we can have no safety in them at present. The King hates us most cordially. If he is once admitted to any degree of power and government among us, however limited, it will soon be extended by corruption, artifice and force until we are reduced to absolute subjection, and that the more easily as by receiving him again for our King we shall draw upon us the contempt of all Europe.' So deeply is the present moulded by the iron hand of the past.

Franklin's use of the qualifying words 'at present' is possibly significant. At some future time, presumably when George III was dead, the two countries might agree to march together. Some such distant prospect may account for the encouragement which he gave to the idea of reconciliation ('a sweet word'), as he walked and talked with Oswald or Grenville in his garden at Passy. But the emotion dominant in his mind was rancour, which derived partly from remembered insults and even more from a humanism, outraged by the devastation inflicted in the course of an unjust war.

Englishmen in 1782 found it difficult to believe that Americans had become 'foreigners' to the extent of preferring to remain in the Bourbon camp and so running the risk of being dragged into a new war about extraneous objects such as Gibraltar and the Coromandel coast. They had won their own war and England was prepared to recognize the fact: surely that was enough. Franklin, aware of the emptiness of the Congress treasury and its dependence on French loans, was very anxious for peace; but he was determined to retain the French alliance (on his own terms) as a primary weapon in dealing with England. When, therefore, English friends and diplomats from London calmly assumed that he and his fellow Commissioners were prepared to leave France to shift for herself and conclude a separate peace, his response was one of contemptuous anger. Few things are more irritating to an American than to be assessed as an Englishman at heart.

And so the shrewd Benjamin decided that the British desire to exchange the kiss of peace and be friends could be exploited to the advantage of the future America. Much could be asked—the surrender of Canada, for example—as a contribution towards the reestablishment of goodwill. The idea of reconciliation was therefore discretely encouraged, but with no specific commitment. The British were to invest in redeemable though undated stock; but when they suggested an interim dividend in the form of a separate peace treaty, the proposition (until Jay decided otherwise) was rejected with scorn. Shelburne thought that Franklin was with him in trying to found an Anglo-American Commonwealth; on his side the Philadelphian assessed the situation from the point of view of international diplomacy and played it accordingly. . . .

Aspects of British Policy

(i) *Canada and the Back Lands.* In examining the policy of the Shelburne Ministry as they began the task of adjusting British aims in North America to the consequences of revolution three specific issues have been left for separate treatment. These are: the question of Canada and the American 'Middle West,' the plan to retain West Florida as a British trade corridor into the Mississippi Basin, and thirdly, the project of an Anglo-American commercial union.

Shelburne's attitude in 1782 to the question of the shape and future of the United States was based in part on the ideas which he had evolved in 1767 for promoting westward expansion as a joint Anglo-American enterprise. Since then, fourteen years of opposition to a disastrous policy of coercion and his own acceptance of free-trade principles had developed in him a conviction that the economic interdependence of Britain and America offered vast possibilities which could be implemented on no other basis but that of voluntary co-operation. When he finally realized that the Thirteen States would reject any form of political association with Great Britain, he accepted the fact and resolved that American independence should be acknowledged 'decidedly' and without territorial restriction. It was for the Americans to people the fertile wilderness between the Appalachians and the Mississippi. That such was his intention is abundantly clear from his successive instructions to the British negotiators.

With regard to the future of Canada it is quite certain that the heir of Chatham had no intention at any time of giving away the fruits of Wolfe's victory on the Heights of Abraham. Franklin's initial suggestion to that effect was flatly rejected and his 'advisable' Articles, which included the cession of Canada, were never even considered. At the Cabinet meeting of 29th August, when Shelburne persuaded his colleagues to accept startling concessions, it was decided that the enlarged Canada of 1774 should be contracted, but to limits not less than those laid down by the Proclamation of October, 1763.

Shelburne's instructions to Carleton were as explicit about the retention and defence of Canada as about the intention to cede the 'Back Lands' to the Thirteen States. In July Carleton was told that disquieting rumors had reached London of a projected French-American invasion of Canada by land and sea. 'I must very particularly desire you,' wrote Shelburne, 'to pay every possible attention to the security of the Province of Nova Scotia and to that of Canada.' It was of the utmost consequence that he should send sufficient reinforcements and supplies thither to overawe any internal disaffection and throw back the enemy. 'You will therefore, I trust, look out for every possible information, and contribute every assistance in your power to the protection of our possessions to the Northward.'

Closely related to the territorial adjustments between the Ohio and the St. Lawrence was the question of the future participation of Americans in the British Atlantic fisheries. The point on which Strachey and Fitzherbert fought so strenuously, under orders from London, was about the drying and curing of fish in the Newfoundland creeks, which would have given rise to endless friction; but the basic claim (and a very substantial one), that Americans should be as free to fish the Newfoundland Banks and the St. Lawrence estuary as the British themselves, was accepted in London from the outset of the negotiation.

In short, all the fundamental provisions of the Treaty—acknowledgment of independence, cession of the Back Lands, preservation of a contracted Canada, and a sharing of the British Atlantic fisheries—had been present in Shelburne's mind as proper and reasonable conditions for a lasting settlement when he took office in the previous April. All the diplomatic wrangles that followed, delaying and bedevilling the negotiation, did not alter that essential framework of the peace. It could, of course, be argued that Shelburne made these sweeping concessions, not as a measure of constructive statesmanship, but because circumstances obliged him to pay virtually any price demanded in order to buy America out of the Bourbon camp. The test in that regard is to be found in his reaction to the persistent offers of the French to assist in reducing the American demands. During his confidential talks with Shelburne in September Rayneval advanced the argument that in the negotiations immediately preceding the outbreak of the Seven Years' War Britain had admitted French claims as far south as the Ohio. The obvious implication was that Britain as the heir of France under the Treaty of Paris, had every right to retain that territory in 1782. As Shelburne observed to the King, France appeared to be jealous of American claims rather than partial to them. . . .

The . . . circumstances would appear to demand some modification of the generally accepted thesis that Britain, having announced to the world that the American war must cease forthwith, was forced to accept a peace which exceeded the worst fears of her own people and the most optimistic expectations of America. The timid ineptitude of Oswald, it is maintained, was overwhelmed by the brilliant diplomacy of Jay and Adams and the urbane subtleties of Franklin. Even Canada, according to some historians, was almost in the American bag when Jay in September reduced his terms in his anxiety to conclude a deal with Britain before being double-crossed by France.

The courage and tenacity of Jay and Adams in their fight contra mundum for the future greatness of America has deservedly won the admiration of their countrymen. Moreover, it is very understandable that from the Canadian point of view the loss of an important fur-trading region, which was also the natural hinterland for modern Canada, should be attributed to a British surrender, dictated by force of circumstances and the inferior skill of her negotiators. Such interpretations, however, pay insufficient attention to the conception of an eventual Anglo-American reunion which (however impracticable) inspired the British Prime Minister and filled his mind with a determination to frame the sort of peace that would allay present bitterness and promote future co-operation.

Accordingly, there was never any question from the British side of a surrender of Canada; and it does not appear that Jay or Adams thought that there was. Nor was there any question in Shelburne's mind but that the Americans must be free to expand to the Mississippi under their own flag. His attempt to secure territory or alternatively the proceeds of land sales in the back areas for the benefit of Loyalist refugees was no more than a bargaining counter; indeed, a revival of a suggestion originally made by Franklin and then withdrawn. Similarly, there was never any question about the broad principle of American participation in the British Atlantic fisheries. How could there be, when Shelburne hoped and intended to give that principle general application by removing all artificial barriers between the economies of Britain, Ireland and the United States? . . .

(iii) *Commercial Reciprocity.* The project of an economic union between Britain and the United States is the third and last issue affecting the subsequent course of British policy which emerges from these peace negotiations. It will be recalled that the plan of a treaty which Jay handed to Oswald on 5th October had included commercial arrangements of a far-reaching character. Britain and America were to share in perpetuity a free and open navigation of the Mississippi; and the goods and ships of the two nations were to enjoy equal commercial privileges and be liable to the same duties throughout each other's domains in all parts of the world, but saving the exclusive rights of the chartered trading companies of Great Britain. In the amended draft, as returned from London, the only part of the commercial Article that remained was the provision for a free navigation of the Mississippi. The rest had been struck out, because the Crown had no power to conclude a treaty which would alter the operation of the Navigation Acts.

But that was not the end of the matter. Shelburne's purpose coincided with that of Jay; and in order to achieve it, he intended to carry through the hazardous enterprise of introducing a revolutionary change in British commercial policy. Jay, as a patriotic American, naturally desired that emancipation from economic restraints should not, if possible, deprive the American States of the privileges in the British market which they had enjoyed as colonies. On his side, Shelburne hoped to rebuild British prosperity by replacing cramping monopolies with a widening system of commercial reciprocity. With that end in view he followed, both in the American and in the French negotiations, a similar plan of action. First, a peace settlement which each side could accept as just and equitable, and then the negotiation of a commercial treaty. That with France was not concluded until 1786—by the Pitt Administration; but the ground had been well prepared during the long talks between Shelburne and Rayneval four years before, and the French saw to it that the project was not abandoned.

On 5 December, 1782, five days after the signing of the Provisional Articles of peace with America, the King opened a new session of Parliament, and in the Speech from the Throne Shelburne indicated the policy which he was pursuing. The main objective was 'an entire and cordial reconciliation' with the American Colonies; and since it had been found that political separation was an indispensable condition, it had been agreed that they should be recognized in the Treaty as 'free and independent states.' But the hope that this would be a transitory stage, leading eventually to a positive *rapprochement*, was explicitly stated. 'Religion—language—interest—affections may, and I hope will, yet prove a bond of permanent union between the two countries.' In a subsequent passage, after a reference to the commercial concessions recently granted to Ireland, the proposal to effect a fundamental change in economic policy was announced in challenging terms. 'I would recommend to you a revision of our whole trading system, upon the same comprehensive principles, with a view to its utmost possible extension.' Shelburne was totally deficient in the gifts of great political leadership, without which there could be no such triumph over ancient tradition; but it would be difficult to withhold acknowledgment of his vision and courage.

The practical implications of the intended change in commercial policy were revealed when Grantham and Townshend presented the Preliminary Treaties with France, Spain and America to Parliament on 27 January, 1783. In the French Treaty it was provided that Commissioners should be appointed to inquire into the state of Anglo-French commerce, 'in order to agree upon new arrangements of trade on the footing of reciprocity and mutual convenience.' And in the preamble to the American Treaty it was agreed that the guiding principle of the settlement was to establish perpetual harmony and 'a beneficial and satisfactory intercourse between the two countries' by applying the principles of 'liberal equity and reciprocity.' The rapidly increasing forces of the Opposition poured scorn on this verbiage. Where was the principle of reciprocal advantage to be found in a treaty by which Britain made every conceivable concession and received nothing in return?

The answer to that derisive challenge was intended to be an Anglo-American commercial agreement of such an intimate character that statutory authority had first to be obtained. For two months after the signing of the American Peace Treaty, Shelburne and Grantham struggled to reach agreement with France and Spain. During that hectic period, when a breakdown and a renewal of the war again and again seemed almost unavoidable, there was little opportunity for considering the future adjustment of Anglo-American trade. Nevertheless the intended legislation was prepared and under Shelburne's direction. Towards the end of February, when the Ministry was already doomed, William Pitt, as Chancellor of the Exchequer, introduced in the Commons 'A Bill for the Provisional Establishment and Regulation of Trade and Intercourse between the Subjects of Great Britain and those of the United States of North America.' Had this measure passed into law, its effect would have exempted the United States from all but a few of the restraints imposed by the Navigation Acts. Americans would have been in many important respects on the same footing as citizens of Great Britain and would have enjoyed greater privileges than the remaining Colonies.

In the preamble it was stated that a considerable time must inevitably elapse before a commercial treaty could be completed for the regulation of Anglo-American intercourse on a permanent footing, and it was therefore highly expedient to establish that intercourse in the meantime 'on the most enlarged principles of reciprocal benefit to both countries.' The first article provided that American ships and their cargoes were to be admitted to British ports in the same manner as ships belonging to other sovereign states, but that American products or manufactured goods carried in American ships were to be liable to the same duties and charges as if the cargo had been British-owned and had been conveyed in a ship, British-owned and British-manned. Secondly, American vessels were to be at liberty to carry American commodities to British colonies and plantations in the Western Hemisphere, with liberty to export therefrom into the United States, 'any merchandise or goods whatsoever.' Moreover, goods so imported into, or exported from, British colonies were to be liable only to the same duties and charges as British-owned goods carried in British ships. Thirdly, during the interval before the conclusion of a permanent arrangement, commodities exported from Great Britain to the United States were to enjoy the same exemptions, drawbacks and bounties as were allowed in the case of exports to British American Colonies.

It will be observed that the only restraints were in connection with certain branches of the carrying trade. American vessels would rank as 'foreign' on arriving at a port in Great Britain with a foreign or British-colonial cargo, and they were barred from carrying non-American products to the Canadian and West Indian Colonies. In all other respects they were to be accorded a position of unique privilege. It is not surprising, therefore, that the American Commissioners in Paris noted the introduction in the House of Commons of such a far-reaching measure with pleasure and approval. The story of Lord Sheffield's publicity 'campaign' against it and of its gradual demise in Parliament properly falls into the scope of a later chapter in this work. The character and purpose of the Bill is outlined here because it indicates the close association between the British Empire and the United States in terms of trade which was envisaged for the future.

Shelburne hated the idea of separation. For him it was something vicious and unnatural, a failure that would gravely injure both societies. They came of the same stock; they represented the same culture; and their destinies were inexorably interwoven. As he saw it, America could not deny her heritage of Anglo-Saxon institutions without disaster to herself. The prospect of a new continent being opened up by a jarring group of little republics appalled him. Along that road lay anarchy. And unless the gates of the Mississippi Basin were kept open, the trade and seapower by which Britain maintained her place in the world would be truncated. Britain and America alike needed the institution of limited monarchy, as he had insisted in his talk with Henry

Laurens; and the prosperity of the two countries required the abolition of commercial barriers. By means of parliamentary, administrative and fiscal reforms, he set himself to provide the Anglo-American association of the future with a 'new deal.' Meantime, he reluctantly accepted separation as unavoidable and endeavoured to establish interim conditions that would facilitate and not impede the process of reconciliation.

In all this there was a large element of wishful thinking. The privileged orders in the Britain of 1782 had no intention whatever of surrendering, even in part, to middle-class democracy; and emergent nationalism in America was no less determined to preserve the New World from the consequences of European entanglements, British or other. I have found no evidence that Shelburne thought out in clear practical terms what would be involved in a form of 'federal union.' He clung to the idea that a reformed monarchical system could win acceptance on the other side of the Atlantic, regardless of the fact that the Crown as the bond of association had become impossible because the person of George III had become anathema.

And yet the visionary is sometimes nearer the truth than the so-called realist. Neither reunion nor alliance was practicable, nor perhaps even desirable: but friendship was both desirable and attainable. Britain and the United States in the 19th Century did business together on an enormous scale; but in their political relations cordiality was notably absent. The peace treaty which Shelburne framed in collaboration with Jay and Adams and, to a lesser degree, with Franklin, cost him his career. It was execrated by political rivals and viewed with gloom by a British public sore with humiliation. But it was ratified unaltered by the Fox-North Administration which supplanted him: and as one reflects in this mid-20th Century upon the intimacy of the United States and the member nations of the British Commonwealth and the importance of that relationship for the survival of Western civilization, the greatness of Shelburne's conception impresses itself upon the mind.

BRITAIN GIVES UP THE WAR

General Conway's Motion in the Commons

General Henry S. Conway, nephew of Sir Robert Walpole and somewhat fickle political ally of the Rockingham Whigs, served as Secretary of State under the Chatham Administration until 1768. He was a steady opponent of the American war, and upon the fall of North from power in 1782, served briefly as Commander-in-Chief.

His motion was made on February 22, 1782. Failing by a single vote, it was brought up again on the 27th; and on March 4th, an address to the King incorporating the substance of Conway's motion passed without a division.

. . . General Conway rose to make the motion of which he had given notice. He began with stating, that the words which had fallen from him some time ago, had been the means of inducing gentlemen to request him to move the question, which they all considered to be essentially necessary in the present moment, when they saw, notwithstanding all the assurances which the nation had received, that measures were apparently taking for the further prosecution of the American war. At this day it would be surely idle and impertinent in him to try to interest the passions of the House, by a description of this unhappy and miserable struggle. Its progress had been marked in the best blood of the empire. It was to be traced by havoc and desolation; by the ravaging of towns and the murder of families; by outrages in every corner of America, and by ruin at home. It came home to the feelings of every individual in the House, and he doubted not but they had so much of it, as to wish sincerely for that thing, which could alone put a stop to the further calamities, called peace. In the present moment, when there were certain indications of a design to continue that war; when a new general was appointed, and when, as he had been credibly informed, there were preparations making for the next active, offensive campaign; in this moment he thought it necessary to ask of the new secretary, what was the design of government, not with regard to particular operations, but to the general system? We were at present entering, as it were, into a new era; we had got a new Secretary of State, who, though not a young

General Conway's Motion in the Commons, Feb. 22, 1782, *Parliamentary History,* ed. W. Cobbett, Vol. XXII, pp. 1028–1047.

man, was nevertheless a young minister; if he was not young in body, he was still possessed of youthful vigour of mind; and therefore he wished to know what were the principles, what the sentiments of this new minister respecting the American war? . . . Were we with a new conductor to have a new plan, or were we to go on in the same manner as we had begun and continued so long, in the obstinate rejection of all advice which we could derive either from experience or disaster? The desire of our gracious and well-inclined sovereign must be for peace. He had expressed it in his speech from the throne; and it would therefore, in the present moment, become that House to approach the throne with an humble, earnest, and dutiful solicitation that he would be graciously pleased to follow the benevolent wishes which he had expressed, to put an end to that calamitous war with our fellow brethren in America. He desired to put a question or two to his Majesty's ministers, which he hoped they would have no objection to answer. He was given to understand, and he had it from good authority, that there were now, or had been lately, persons very near at hand, disposed and authorized to treat of peace with America. It was a question which he had desired them to answer openly and seriously. He was pretty well informed, both from the correspondence that he had himself, and from the enquiries that he had made, that there was a disposition at this time in America to treat of peace; and that it was not unknown to ministers that persons, such as he had hinted, properly instructed and authorized, were now, or lately had been, not far distant. He desired to know another thing, whether they had lent an ear to those proposals, and had treated them as they had deserved. The right hon. general made some very strong and pressing observations on the urgent necessity of bringing about this desirable end; and he wished exceedingly to know, what this new and young minister was to do in this situation into which he was introduced. We paid for 73,000 men, now said to be employed in America. This force was only upon paper, though we paid for them: in fact, by the last returns it appeared, that the force under sir Henry Clinton was 9,500, and that captured in Virginia only 5,400; so that, in reality, every soldier, actually employed in America, cost us 100£ a year. Having exhorted the House to consider the necessity of the moment, and to bend all their anxiety to the accomplishment of peace; for the man who, in the present distress, did not wish for peace in preference to war, not only had not a heart, but he had not a soul in his bosom, he concluded with moving, "That an humble Address be presented to his Majesty, that, taking into his royal consideration the many and great calamities which have attended the present unfortunate war, and the heavy burthens thereby brought on his loyal and affectionate people, he will be pleased graciously to listen to the humble prayer and advice of his faithful Commons, that the war on the continent of North America may no longer be pursued for the impracticable purpose of reducing the inhabitants of that country to obedience by force; and expressing their hope, that the earnest desire and diligent exertion to restore the public tranquility, of which we have received his Majesty's gracious assurance, may, by a happy reconciliation with the revolted colonies, be forwarded and made effectual, to which great end his Majesty's faithful Commons will be ready most cheerfully to give their utmost assistance."

AMERICAN GOALS

Letter from Secretary Robert R. Livingston to Benjamin Franklin

Following the allied victory at Yorktown, it became obvious that Britain was abandoning the war in America. Robert R. Livingston, appointed Secretary of Foreign Affairs by Congress in 1781, immediately opened correspondence with Benjamin Franklin, minister to Paris, looking to the coming peace negotiations. In the letter presented here, he gives a clear and succinct statement of American ambitions. The reader will find it instructive to compare his expectations with the terms of the provisional treaty, which is reproduced later.

As it does not appear improbable that the humiliation and misfortunes of Great Britain may produce the same sentiments which a spirit of moderation dictates to the other belligerent powers, and lead her to concur with them in their wishes for peace, it can not be improper to acquaint you with the objects America most wishes to attain, and to furnish you with the arguments on which they found their claim to them. . . .

The first point of discussion will be the limits of the United States. The instructions given to Mr. Adams . . . explain the wishes of Congress on that subject, nor can they admit of many doubts, except so far as they relate to our southern extent, the boundary between us and Canada being very well ascertained by grants, charters, proclamations, and other acts of government, and more particularly by the settlements of people who are engaged in the same

Secretary Livingston to Benjamin Franklin, Philadelphia, January 7, 1782, *The Diplomatic Correspondence of the American Revolution*, ed. Francis Wharton, Washington, D. C., 1889, Vol. V, pp. 87–93.

cause with us, and who have the same rights with the rest of the subjects of the United States.

Our western and northwestern extent will be contested with some warmth, and the reasoning on that subject be deduced from general principles and from proclamations and treaties with the Indians.

The subject is undoubtedly intricate and delicate, yet upon candid investigation I believe it will appear that our extension to the Mississippi is founded in justice, and that our claims are at least such as the events of the war give us the right to insist upon. . . .

From hence, then, it follows that if the King of Great Britain has any right over the back lands in America it must be as king of the people of America; ceasing to be king of those people, his right also ceases. If he has no right over the back lands but merely as protector of the savage nations that inhabit them, that connexion and duty also devolve upon us, since they evidently claimed that protection from him as a king of the Colonies, and through the governors of those Colonies, and not as sovereign of a country three thousand miles from them. This country having chosen a new sovereign, they may rightfully claim its protection. . . .

They already possess Canada and Nova Scotia; should that immense territory, which lies upon the rear of the States from the Gulf of St. Lawrence to the Gulf of Mexico, be acknowledged to be vested in Great Britain, it will render our situation truly hazardous. The lands, as you know, are infinitely better than those on the coast; they have an open communication with the sea by the rivers St. Lawrence and the Mississippi, and with each other by those extensive inland seas with which America abounds. They will be settled with the utmost rapidity from Europe, but more particularly from these States. Attachment to the government, freedom from taxes, a prospect of bettering their fortunes, and the fertility of the soil will invite numbers to leave us. This co-operating with the leaven of dissatisfaction, which will continue to work here for many years, may produce the most dangerous effects, especially upon the southern States, which will, from the nature of their soil and husbandry, be thinly settled for many years, while the lands which lie near them, beyond the mountains, will soon be filled with a hardy race of people inimical to them, who to their own strength will be enabled to join that of the savages subject to their command.

If it is an object with the maritime powers to lessen the powers, and by that means diminish the dangerous dominion that Great Britain has in some measure usurped over the ocean, they must prevent her possessing herself of the country in question, since, besides the whole fur and peltry trade that she will thereby engross, the demands of this great country will give a new spring to her manufactures, which, though the Floridas should be ceded to Spain, will find their way into it by the river St. Lawrence and through the numerous lakes and rivers which communicate with it. Add to this that settlements are already formed beyond the Appalachian Mountains by people who acknowledge the United States, which not only give force to our claims, but render a relinquishment of their interest highly impolitic and unjust. These, and a variety of other reasons, which will suggest themselves to you and the gentlemen joined in the commission with you, will doubtless be urged in such terms as to convince the court of France that our mutual interests conspire to keep Great Britain from any territory on this continent beyond the bounds of Canada. Should the Floridas be ceded to Spain, she will certainly unite with you on this point, as the security of that cession will depend upon its success.

The *fisheries* will probably be another source of litigation, not because our rights are doubtful, but because Great Britain has never paid much attention to rights which interfere with her views.

The argument on which the people of America found their claim to fish on the banks of Newfoundland arises, first, from their having once formed a part of the British empire, in which state they always enjoyed, as fully as the people of Britain themselves, the right of fishing on those banks. . . . If we were tenants in common with Great Britain while united with her, we still continue so, unless by our own act we have relinquished our title. . . . Our rights, then, are not invalidated by this separation, more particularly as we have kept up our claim from the commencement of the war, and assigned the attempt of Great Britain to exclude us from the fisheries as one of the causes of our recurring to arms.

The second ground upon which we place our right to fish on the banks of Newfoundland, provided we do not come within such distance of the coasts of other powers as the law of nations allows them to appropriate, is the right which nature gives to all mankind to use its common benefit so far as not to exclude others. . . .

An idea has also gone forth, and it is fomented by the disaffected, that France wishes, from interested views, to monopolise the fisheries, or at least to exclude all other competitors but Great Britain. Those who have attended to the disinterested conduct of France during the war oppose to this sentiment the honor and good faith of their ally, the little interest that he can have in excluding a people from a right which would not interfere with his, since France does little more than supply itself; and the New England fishery, for the most part, only supplies the continent and islands of America. . . .

It is not improbable that Great Britain will endeavor to make some stipulations in favor of their American partizans who have been banished the country or whose property has been forfeited. You will doubtless be sensible of the inconvenience and danger to which their return will subject us and the injustice of restoring to them what they had so justly forfeited, while no compensation is made to us for the loss of property and the calamities they have occasioned.

There can be little doubt that every society may rightfully banish from among them those who aim at its subversion and forfeit the property which they can only be entitled to by the laws and under the protection of the society which they attempt to destroy. Without troubling you, therefore, on the point of right, I will just mention a few of the consequences that would result from a stipulation in their favor.

In the first place, it will excite general dissatisfaction and tumults. They are considered here as the authors of the war. Those who have lost relations and friends by it, those who have been insulted by them while starving in prisons and prison ships, those who have been robbed and plundered, or who have had their houses burned and their families ill treated by them, will, in despite of all law or treaties, avenge themselves if the real or supposed authors of these calamities ever put themselves in their power; nor will the government be able to prevent what the feeling of the body of the people will justify.

Should they be permitted to reside among us, they will neglect no means to injure and subvert our constitution and government and to sow divisions among us, in order to pave the way for the introduction of the old system. They will be dangerous partizans of the enemy, equally unfriendly to France and to us, and will show themselves such upon every occasion. To restore their property in many instances is now become impossible. It has been sold from hand to hand; the money arising from it has been sunk by depreciation in the public treasury. To raise the value by taxes or to wrest the lands from the hands of the proprietors is equally unjust and impossible. Many of the very people who would demand the restitution have grown rich by the spoil and plunder of this country. Many others, who were beggars at the beginning of this war, owe their present affluence to the same cause.

So that at least the account between the two nations should be liquidated before any claim can be set up by the aggressors. How far it will be possible to obtain a compensation for the injuries wantonly done by the enemy you will be best able to judge; be assured that it is anxiously desired. . . .

NEGOTIATIONS

Letter from Lord Shelburne to Franklin

Franklin's contact, albeit indirect, with Shelburne, began as early as February, 1782, when a copy of his letter to his former friend, David Hartley, a Member of Parliament, was forwarded by the recipient to the British minister. In an important letter ostensibly to Hartley, of March 22, 1782, Franklin invited Shelburne to begin negotiations. The Briton's response is printed below.

Shelburne was castigated both by contemporaries and by subsequent writers as being sly and hypocritical. There is no reason, however, to doubt his sincerity in his letter to Franklin.

I have been favored with your letter, and am much obliged by your remembrance. I find myself returned nearly to the same situation, which you remember me to have occupied nineteen years ago, and I should be very glad to talk to you as I did then, and afterwards in 1767, upon the means of promoting the happiness of mankind, a subject much more agreeable to my nature than the best concerted plans for spreading misery and devastation. I have had a high opinion of the compass of your mind and of your foresight. I have often been beholden to both, and shall be glad to be so again, as far as is compatible with your situation. Your letter discovering the same disposition, has made me send to you Mr. Oswald. I have had a longer acquaintance with him than even I have had the pleasure to have with you. I believe him an honest man, and, after consulting some of our common friends, I have thought him the fittest for the purpose. He is a pacifical man, and conversant in those negociations which are most interesting to mankind. This has made me prefer him to any of our speculative friends, or to any person of higher rank. He is fully apprized of my mind, and you may give full credit to everything he assures you of. At the same time, if any other channel occurs to you, I am ready to embrace it. I wish to retain the same simplicity and good faith which subsisted between us in transactions of less importance. . . .

Lord Shelburne to Franklin, London, April 6, 1782, *ibid*, p. 536.

Richard Oswald's First and Second Commissions

Shelburne's chief diplomatic agent in negotiating the treaty of peace was Richard Oswald, a Scottish merchant of liberal economic views. Sincerely desiring reconciliation with the former colonies, he favored generosity to the Americans. His first commission for negotiating peace was dated July 25, 1782. It was subsequently amended in a significant way in a new commission dated September 21. In the interim period, Oswald had approached the American commissioners, Franklin now joined by John Jay and John Adams, in Paris. Jay, suspicious of French policy, quickly decided to forward separate negotiations between England and America even at the expense of violating— in spirit if not in letter—the stipulations of the treaty between his country and France forbidding a separate peace with the enemy. Using a mixture of blandishments and threats, he persuaded Oswald and, through him, Shelburne and the ministry, to grant what was in effect acknowledgment of American independence prior to negotiations. The maneuver was in fact a brilliant success for both parties, the Americans recognized as independent by London and separated from France for purposes of negotiation. The commission printed below is that of July 25, 1782. Portions changed by the new commission, dated September 21, have been italicized; and the changes set forth in the later instrument are printed in the footnotes.

July 25, 1782

George the Third, by the grace of God king of Great Britain, France, and Ireland, defender of the faith, and so forth. To our trusty and well-beloved Richard Oswald, of our city of London, esquire, greeting. Whereas, by virtue of an act passed in the last session of parliament, entitled "An act to enable his majesty to conclude a peace or truce with certain colonies in North America therein mentioned," it is recited "that it is essential to the interest, welfare and prosperity of Great Britain and the colonies or plantations of New Hampshire, Massachusetts Bay, Rhode Island, Connecticut, New York, New Jersey, Pennsylvania, the lower counties on Delaware, Maryland, Virginia, North Carolina, South Carolina, and Georgia, in North America, that peace, inter-

---

Oswald's First and Second Commissions, July 25 and September 21, 1782, *ibid*, pp. 613–614, 748–750; Franklin to Livingston, Passy, Oct. 14, 1782, *ibid*, p. 811.

course, trade, and commerce should be restored between them." Therefore, and for a full manifestation of our most earnest wish and desire, and that of our Parliament, to put an end to the calamities of war, it is enacted that it should and might be lawful for us to treat, consult of, agree, and conclude, with any commissioner or commissioners named or to be named by the said colonies or plantations, or with any body or bodies, corporate or politic, or any assembly or assemblies, or description of men, or any person or persons whatsoever, a peace or truce with the said colonies or plantations, or any of them, or any part or parts thereof, any law, act or acts of Parliament, matter or thing, to the contrary in any wise notwithstanding.

Now know ye that we, reposing special trust in your wisdom, loyalty, diligence, and circumspection in the management of the affairs to be hereby committed to your charge, have nominated and appointed, constituted and assigned, and by these presents do nominate and appoint, constitute and assign, you, the said Richard Oswald, to be our commissioner in that behalf, to use and exercise all and every the powers and authorities hereby entrusted and committed to you, the said Richard Oswald, and to do, perform, and execute all other matters and things hereby enjoined and committed to your care, during our will and pleasure, and no longer, according to the tenor of these our letters patent. And it is our royal will and pleasure, and we hereby authorise, empower, and require you, the said Richard Oswald, to treat, consult, and conclude, with any *commissioner or commissioners, named or to be named by the said colonies or plantations, and any body or bodies, corporate or politic, assembly or assemblies, or descriptions of men, or person or persons whatsoever, a peace or truce with the said colonies or plantations, or any of them, or any part or parts thereof;*[1] any law, act, or acts of Parliament, matter or thing, to the contrary notwithstanding.

And it is our further will and pleasure that every regulation, provision, matter or thing, which shall have been agreed upon between you, the said Richard Oswald, and such *commissioner or commissioners, body or bodies, corporate or politic, assembly or assemblies, descriptions of men, person or persons as aforesaid,*[2] with whom you shall have judged meet and sufficient to enter into such agreement, shall be fully and distinctly set forth in writing, and authenticated by your hand and seal on one side, and *by such seal or other signatures on the other as the occasion may require, and as may be suitable*

---

[1] *. . . commissioners or persons vested with equal powers, by and on the part of the thirteen United States of America, viz, New Hampshire, Massachusetts Bay, Rhode Island, Connecticut, New Jersey, Pennsylvania, the three lower counties on Delaware, Maryland, Virginia, North Carolina, South Carolina, and Georgia, in North America, a peace or a truce with the said thirteen United States. . . .*

[2] *. . . commissioners or persons as aforesaid. . . .*

to the character and authority of the commissioner or commissioners, &c., as aforesaid so agreeing,[3] and such instruments so authenticated shall be by you transmitted to us through one of our principal secretaries of State. . . .[4]

[3] . . . and by the hands and seals of such commissioners or persons on the other. . . .

[4] At this point the following addition was made:

And whereas in and by our commission and letters patent, under our great seal of Great Britain, bearing date the seventh day of August last, we nominated and appointed, constituted and assigned, you, the said Richard Oswald, to be our commissioner to treat, consult of, agree, and to conclude, with any commissioner or commissioners named or to be named by certain colonies or plantations in America therein specified, a peace or a truce with the said colonies or plantations, now know ye, that we have revoked and determined, and by these presents do revoke and determine, our said commission and letters patent, and all and every power, article, and thing therein contained.

JOHN ADAMS, *Diary and Autobiography*

Despite his testiness, vanity, jealousy of Dr. Franklin, and excessive preoccupation with New England fishing interests, John Adams gives a full, convenient, and delightful account of the negotiations leading to the treaty of peace. During the fateful month of November, 1782, Franklin, Adams, and Jay confronted the British emissaries, Oswald and Strachey, in a classic diplomatic battle. The "sticky" issues were boundaries, pre-war debts, American access to the Newfoundland fisheries and, especially, the treatment of the American loyalists. There is also interesting evidence of Adams's deep suspicions of France (fully shared by Jay) and his growing conviction that America should stand aloof from European affairs.

1782. November 3. Sunday

In my first Conversation with Franklin on Tuesday Evening last, he told me of Mr. Oswalds Demand of the Payment of Debts and Compensation to the Tories. He said their Answer had been, that We had not Power, nor had Congress. I told him I had no Notion of cheating any Body. The Question of paying Debts, and that of compensating Tories were two.—I had made the same Ob-

Excerpted by permission from pages 43–82 of *Diary and Autobiography of John Adams*, Volume III, edited by L. H. Butterfield, Cambridge, Mass.: The Belknap Press of Harvard University Press. Copyright 1961 by the Massachusetts Historical Society.

servation, that forenoon to Mr. Oswald and Mr. Stretchy, in Company with
Mr. Jay at his House. . . . I saw it struck Mr. Stretchy with peculiar Pleasure,
I saw it instantly smiling in every Line of his Face. Mr. O. was apparently
pleased with it too.

In a subsequent Conversation with my Colleagues, I proposed to them that
We should agree that Congress should recommend it to the States to open their
Courts of Justice for the Recovery of all just Debts. They gradually fell in to
this Opinion, and We all expressed these Sentiments to the English Gentlemen, who were much pleased with it, and with Reason, because it silences
the Clamours of all the British Creditors, against the Peace, and prevents them
from making common Cause with the Refugees.

November 4. Monday

Called on J. and went to Oswalds and spent with him and Stretchy from 11. to
3. in drawing up the Articles respecting Debts and Tories and Fishery. . . .

Stretchy is as artfull and insinuating a Man as they could send. He pushes
and presses every Point as far as it can possibly go. He is the most eager,
earnest, pointed Spirit.

We agreed last night to this.

Whereas certain of the united States, excited thereto by the unnecessary
Destruction of private Property, have confiscated all Debts due from their
Citizens to British Subjects and also in certain Instances Lands belonging to
the latter. And Whereas it is *just* that private Contracts made between Individuals of the two Countries before the War, should be faithfully executed,
and as the Confiscation of the said Lands may have a Latitude not justifiable
by the Law of Nations, it is agreed that british Creditors shall notwithstanding,
meet with no lawfull Impediment, to recovering the full value, or Sterling
Amount of such bonâ fide Debts as were contracted before the Year 1775, and
also that Congress will recommend to the said States, so to correct, if necessary,
their said Acts respecting the Confiscation of Lands in America belonging to
real british Subjects as to render their said Acts consistent with perfect Justice
and Equity.

November 5. Tuesday

Mr. Jay likes Frenchmen as little as Mr. Lee and Mr. Izard did. He says they
are not a Moral People. They know not what it is. He dont like any Frenchman.—The Marquis de la Fayette is clever, but he is a Frenchman—Our

Allies dont play fair, he told me. They were endeavouring to deprive Us of the Fishery, the Western Lands, and the Navigation of the Mississippi. They would even bargain with the English to deprive us of them. They want to play the Western Lands, Mississippi and whole Gulph of Mexico into the Hands of Spain.

Oswald talks of Pultney, and a Plott to divide America between France and England. France to have N. England. They tell a Story about Vergennes and his agreeing that the English might propose such a division, but reserving a Right to deny it all. These Whispers ought not to be credited by Us.

1782. November 11. Monday

Mr. Whitefoord* the Secretary of Mr. Oswald came . . . with a Copy of Mr. Oswalds Commission attested by himself (Mr. Oswald). He delivered the Copy and said Mr. Oswald was ready [to] compare it to the original with me. I said Mr. Oswalds Attestation was sufficient as he had already shewn me his original. He sat down and We fell into Conversation, about the Weather and the Vapours and Exhalations from Tartary which had been brought here last Spring by the Winds and given Us all the Influenza. Thence to french Fashions and the Punctuality with which they insist upon Peoples wearing thin Cloaths in Spring and fall, tho the Weather is ever so cold, &c. I said it was often carried to ridiculous Lengths, but that it was at Bottom an admirable Policy, as it rendered all Europe tributary to the City of Paris, for its Manufactures.

We fell soon into Politicks. I told him, that there was something in the Minds of the English and French, which impelled them irresistably to War every Ten or fifteen Years. He said the ensuing Peace would he believed be a long one. I said it would provided it was well made, and nothing left in it to give future Discontents. But if any Thing was done which the Americans should think hard and unjust, both the English and French would be continually blowing it up and inflaming the American Minds with it, in order to make them join one Side or the other in a future War. He might well think, that the French would be very glad to have the Americans join them in future War. Suppose for Example they should think the Tories Men of monarchical Principles, or Men of more Ambition than Principle, or Men corrupted and of no Principle, and should therefore think them more easily seduced to their Purposes than virtuous Republicans, is it not easy to see the Policy of a French Minister in wishing them Amnesty and Compensation? Suppose, a french Minister foresees that the Presence of the Tories in America will keep up

---

* [Caleb Whitefoord was Secretary to the British Commission.]

perpetually two Parties, a French Party and an English Party, and that this will compell the patriotic and independant Party to join the French Party is it not natural for him to wish them restored? Is it not easy to see, that a French Minister cannot wish to have the English and Americans perfectly agreed upon all Points before they themselves, the Spaniards and Dutch, are agreed too. Can they be sorry then to see us split upon such a Point as the Tories? What can be their Motives to become the Advocates of the Tories? The french Minister at Philadelphia has made some Representations to Congress in favour of a Compensation to the Royalists, and the C. de Vergennes no longer than Yesterday, said much to Me in their favour. The Comte probably knows, that We are instructed against it, that Congress are instructed against it, or rather have not constitutional Authority to do it. That We can only write about it to Congress, and they to the States, who may and probably will deliberate upon it 18 Months, before they all decide and then every one of them will determine against it.—In this Way, there is an insuperable Obstacle to any Agreement between the English and Americans, even upon Terms to be inserted in the general Peace, before all are ready.—It was the constant Practice of The French to have some of their Subjects in London during the Conferences for Peace, in order to propagate such Sentiments there as they wished to prevail. . . . They can easily perswade the Tories to set up their Demands, and tell them and the Ministers that the Kings Dignity and Nations honour are compromised in it.

For my own Part I thought America had been long enough involved in the Wars of Europe. She had been a Football between contending Nations from the Beginning, and it was easy to foresee that France and England both would endeavour to involve Us in their future Wars. I thought [it] our Interest and Duty to avoid [them] as much as possible and to be compleatly independent and have nothing to do but in Commerce with either of them. That my Thoughts had been from the Beginning constantly employed to arrange all our European Connections to this End, and that they would be continued to be so employed and I thought it so important to Us, that if my poor labours, my little Estate or (smiling) sizy blood could effect it, it should be done. But I had many fears.

I said the King of France might think it consistent with his Station to favour People who had contended for a Crown, tho it was the Crown of his Ennemy. Whitefoord said, they seem to be, through the whole of this, fighting for Reputation. I said they had acquired it and more. They had raised themselves high from a low Estate by it, and they were our good Friends and Allies, and had conducted generously and nobly and We should be just and gratefull, but they might have political Wishes, which We were not bound by Treaty nor in Justice or Gratitude to favour, and these We ought to be cautious of. He agreed that they had raised themselves very suddenly and surprisingly by it. . . .

November 17. Sunday

On Fryday the 15, Mr. Oswald came to Visit me, and entered with some Freedom into Conversation. I said many Things to him to convince him that it was the Policy of my Lord Shelburne and the Interest of the Nation to agree with Us upon the advantageous Terms which Mr. Stratchey carried away on the 5th. Shewed him the Advantages of the Boundary, the vast Extent of Land, and the equitable Provision for the Payment of Debts and even the great Benefits stipulated for the Tories.

He said he had been reading Mr. Paines Answer to the Abby Raynal, and had found there an excellent Argument in favour of the Tories. Mr. Paine says that before the Battle of Lexington We were so blindly prejudiced in favour of the English and so closely attached to them, that We went to war at any time and for any Object, when they bid Us. Now this being habitual to the Americans, it was excuseable in the Tories to behave upon this Occasion as all of Us had ever done upon all the others. He said if he were a Member of Congress he would shew a Magnanimity upon this Occasion, and would say to the Refugees, take your Property. We scorn to make any Use of it, in building up our System.

I replied, that We had no Power and Congress had no Power, and therefore We must consider how it would be reasoned upon in the several Legislatures of the separate States, if, after being sent by Us to Congress and by them to the several States in the Course of twelve or fifteen Months, it should be there, debated. You must carry on the War, Six or Nine months certainly, for this Compensation, and consequently spend in the Prosecution of it, Six or Nine times the Sum necessary to make the Compensation for I presume, this War costs every Month to Great Britain, a larger Sum than would be necessary to pay for the forfeited Estates.

How says I will an independant Man in one of our Assemblies consider this. We will take a Man, who is no Partisan of England or France, one who wishes to do Justice to both and to all Nations, but is the Partisan only of his own.

Have you seen says he, a certain Letter written to the C. de V. wherein Mr. S. A.* is treated pretty freely.—Yes says I and several other Papers in which Mr. J. Adams has been treated so too. I dont know, what you may of heard in England of Mr. S. A. You may have been taught to believe, for what I know, that he eats little Children. But I assure you he is a Man of Humanity and Candour as well [as] Integrity, and further that he is devoted to the Interest of his Country and I believe wishes never to be, after a Peace, the Partisan to France or England, but to do Justice and all the good he can to both. I thank you for mentioning him for I will make him my orator. What will he say, when the Question of Amnesty and Compensation to the Tories, comes before the Senate

---

* [Samuel Adams]

of Massachusetts. And when he is informed that England makes a Point of it and that France favours her. He will say here are two old, sagacious Courts, both endeavouring to sow the Seeds of Discord among Us, each endeavouring to keep Us in hot Water, to keep up continual Broils between an English Party and a french Party, in hopes of obliging the Independent and patriotic Party, to lean to its Side. England wishes them here and compensated, not merely to get rid of them and to save them selves the Money, but to plant among Us Instruments of their own, to make divisions among Us and between Us and France, to be continually crying down the Religion, the Government, the Manners of France, and crying up the Language, the Fashions, the Blood &c, of England. England also means by insisting on our compensating these worst of Ennemies to obtain from Us, a tacit Acknowledgment of the Right of the War—an implicit Acknowledgment, that the Tories have been justifiable or at least excuseable, and that We, only by a fortunate Coincidence of Events, have carried a wicked Rebellion into a compleat Revolution.

At the very Time when Britain professes to desire Peace, Reconciliation, perpetual Oblivion of all past Unkindnesses, can She wish to send in among Us, a Number of Persons, whose very Countenances will bring fresh to our Remembrance the whole History of the Rise, and Progress of the War, and of all its Atrocitys? Can she think it conciliatory, to oblige Us, to lay Taxes upon those whose Habitations have been consumed, to reward those who have burn'd them? upon those whose Property has been stolen, to reward the Thieves? upon those whose Relations have been cruelly destroyed, to compensate the Murtherers?

What can be the design of France on the other hand, by espousing the Cause of these Men? Indeed her Motives may be guessed at. She may wish to keep up in our Minds a Terror of England, and a fresh Remembrance of all We have suffered. Or She may wish to prevent our Ministers in Europe from agreeing with the British Ministers, untill She shall say that She and Spain are satisfyed in all Points.

I entered largely with Mr. Oswald, into the Consideration of the Influence this Question would have upon the Councils of the British Cabinet and the Debates in Parliament. The King and the old Ministry might think their personal Reputations concerned, in supporting Men who had gone such Lengths, and suffered so much in their Attachment to them.—The K. may say I have other dominions abroad, Canada, Nova Scotia, Florida, the West India Islands, the East Indies, Ireland. It will be a bad Example to abandon these Men. Others will loose their Encouragement to adhere to my Government. But the shortest Answer to this is the best, let the King by a Message recommend it to Parliament to compensate them.

But how will My Lord Shelburne sustain the shock of Opposition? When Mr. Fox and Mr. Burke shall demand a Reason why the Essential Interests of the Nation, are sacrificed to the unreasonable demands of those very Men, who have done this great Mischief to the Empire. Should these Orators indulge themselves in Philippicks against the Refugees, shew their false Representations, their outragious Cruelties, their innumerable demerits against the Nation, and then attack the first Lord of the Treasury for continuing to spend the Blood and Treasure of the Nation for their Sakes.

Mr. Vaughan came to me Yesterday, and said that Mr. Oswald had that morning called upon Mr. Jay, and told him, if he had known as much the day before as he had since learned, he would have written to go home. Mr. V. said Mr. Fitzherbert* had received a Letter from Ld. Townsend, that the Compensation would be insisted on. Mr. Oswald wanted Mr. Jay to go to England. Thought he could convince the Ministry. Mr. Jay said he must go, with or without the Knowledge and Advice of this Court, and in either Case it would give rise to jealousies. He could not go. Mr. Vaughan said he had determined to go, on Account of the critical State of his Family, his Wife being probably abed. He should be glad to converse freely with me, and obtain from me, all the Lights and arguments against the Tories, even the History of their worst Actions, that in Case it should be necessary to run them down it might be done or at least expose them, for their true History was little known in England.— I told him that I must be excused. It was a subject that I had never been desirous of obtaining Information upon. That I pitied those People too much to be willing to aggravate their Sorrows and Sufferings, even of those who had deserved the Worst. It might not be amiss to reprint the Letters of G[overnor] Bernard, Hutchinson and Oliver, to shew the rise. It might not be amiss to read the History of Wyoming in the Annual Register for 1778 or 9, to recollect the Prison Ships, and the Churches at New York, where the Garrisons of Fort Washington were starved in order to make them inlist into Refugee Corps. It might not be amiss to recollect the Burning of Cities, and The Thefts of Plate, Negroes and Tobacco.

I entered into the same Arguments with him that I had used with Mr. Oswald, to shew that We could do nothing, Congress nothing. The Time it would take to consult the States, and the Reasons to believe that all of them would at last decide against it. I shewed him that it would be a Religious Question with some, a moral one with others, and a political one with more, an Economical one with very few. I shewed him the ill Effect which would be produced upon the American Mind, by this Measure, how much it would contribute to perpetuate Alienation against England, and how french Emmissaries might by means of these Men blow up the flames of Animosity and War. I shewed him how the Whig Interest and the Opposition might avail

---

* [Alleyne Fitzherbert, the future Lord St. Helens, in charge of negotiating preliminaries of peace with France and Spain.]

themselves of this Subject in Parliament, and how they might embarrass the Minister.

He went out to Passy, for a Passport, and in the Evening called upon me again. Said he found Dr. Franklins Sentiments to be the same with Mr. Jays and mine, and hoped he should be able to convince Lord Shelburne. He was pretty confident that it would work right.—The Ministry and Nation were not informed upon the Subject. Ld. Shelburne had told him that no Part of his office gave him so much Paine as the Levy he held for these People, and hearing their Stories of their Families and Estates, their Losses, Sufferings and Distresses. Mr. V. said he had picked up here, a good deal of Information, about those People, from Mr. Allen and other Americans. . . .

November 18. Monday

Returned Mr. Oswalds Visit. . . .

We went over the old ground, concerning the Tories. He began to use Arguments with me to relax. I told him he must not think of that, but must bend all his Thoughts to convince and perswade his Court to give it up. That if the Terms now before his Court, were not accepted, the whole negotiation would be broken off, and this Court would probably be so angry with Mr. Jay and me, that they would set their Engines to work upon Congress, get us recalled and some others sent, who would do exactly as this Court would have them. He said, he thought that very probable. . . .

I said to him that England would always be a Country which would deserve much of the Attention of America, independently of all Considerations of Blood, Origin, Language, Morals &c. Merely as a commercial Country, She would forever claim the Respect of America, because a great Part of our Commerce would be with her provided She came to her Senses and made Peace with Us without any Points in the Treaty that should ferment in the Minds of the People. If the People should think themselves unjustly treated, they would never be easy, and they were so situated as to be able to hurt any Power. The Fisheries, the Mississippi, the Tories were points that would rankle. And that Nation that should offend our People in any of them, would sooner or later feel the Consequences. . . .

You are afraid says Mr. Oswald to day of being made the Tools of the Powers of Europe.—Indeed I am says I.—What Powers says he.—All of them says I. It is obvious that all the Powers of Europe will be continually maneuvring with Us, to work us into their real or imaginary Ballances of Power. They will all wish to make of Us a Make Weight Candle, when they are weighing out their Pounds. Indeed it is not surprizing for We shall very often if not always be able to turn the Scale. But I think it ought to be our Rule not to meddle, and that of all the Powers of Europe not to desire Us, or perhaps even to permit Us to interfere, if they can help it.

I beg of you, says he, to get out of your head the Idea that We shall disturb you.—What says I do you yourself believe that your Ministers, Governors and even Nation will not wish to get Us of your Side in any future War?—Damn the Governors says he. No. We will take off their Heads if they do an improper thing towards you.

Thank you for your good Will says I, which I feel to be sincere. But Nations dont feel as you and I do, and your nation when it gets a little refreshed from the fatigues of the War, when Men and Money are become plenty and Allies at hand, will not feel as it does now.—We never can be such damned Sots says he as to think of differing again with you.—Why says I, in truth I have never been able to comprehend the Reason why you ever thought of differing with Us.

Nov. 20. Wednesday

Dr. Franklin came in, and We fell into Conversation. From one Thing to another, We came to Politicks. I told him, that it seemed uncertain whether Shelburne could hold his Ground without leaning Upon Ld. North on one hand or Fox on the other. That if he joined North, or North & Co. should come in, they would go upon a contracted System, and would join People at this Court to deprive Us of the Missisippi and the Fisheries &c. If Fox came in or joined Shelburne they would go upon a liberal and manly System, and this was the only Choice they had. No Nation had ever brought itself into such a Labyrinth perplexed with the demands of Holland, Spain, France and America. Their Funds were failing and the Money undertaken to be furnished was not found. Franklin said, that the Bank came in Aid, and he learned that large Sums of Scrip were lodged there.—In this Situation says I they have no Chance but to set up America very high—and if I were King of G.B. I would take that Tone. I would send the first Duke of the Kingdom Ambassador to Congress, and would negotiate in their favour at all the Neutral Courts &c. I would give the strongest Assurances to Congress of Support in the Fisheries, the Missisippi &c. and would compensate the Tories myself.

I asked what could be the Policy of this Court in wishing to deprive Us of the Fisheries? and Missisippi? I could see no possible Motive for it, but to plant Seeds of Contention for a future War. If they pursued this Policy they would be as fatally blinded to their true Interests as ever the English were.

Franklin said, they would be every bit as blind. That the Fisheries and Missisippi could not be given up. That nothing was clearer to him than that the Fisheries were essential to the northern States, and the Missisippi to the

Southern and indeed both to all. I told him that Mr. Gerard had certainly appeared to America, to negotiate to these Ends, vizt. to perswade Congress to give up both. This was the Reason of his being so unpopular in America, and this was the Cause of their dislike to Sam Adams, who had spoken very freely both to Gerard and [in?] Congress on these heads. That Marbois appeared now to be pursuing the same Objects. Franklin said he had seen his Letter. I said I was the more surprized at this, as Mr. Marbois, on our Passage to America, had often said to me, that he thought the Fisheries our natural Right and our essential Interest, and that We ought to maintain it and be supported in it. Yet that he appeared now to be maneuvring against it. . . .

Nov. 22. Fryday

Mr. Jay says that Oswald received a Courier from London last Evening. That his Letters were brought in while he was there. That Oswald read one of them and said, that "the Tories stick." That Stratchey is coming again, and may be expected today. Oswald call'd upon him this morning, but young Franklin was there: so he said nothing, as he would not speak before him. Jay says We had now to consider, whether We should state the question in writing to the Comte de Vergennes, and ask his Answer.

I said to him We must be more dry and reserved and short with him (Oswald) than We had been. He said We must endeavour to discover, whether they agree to all the other Points. I asked what he thought of agreeing to some Compensation to the Tories, if this Court advised to it. He said they would be very mad if We did. He said that a Tract of Land, with a Pompous Preamble, would satisfy the English. But he would call upon Oswald this Afternoon, and endeavour to know more, and call upon me in the Evening. . . .

1782. November 25. Monday

Dr. F., Mr. J. and myself at 11. met at Mr. Oswalds Lodgings.

Mr. Stratchey told Us, he had been to London and waited personally on every one of the Kings Cabinet Council, and had communicated the last Propositions to them. They every one of them, unanimously condemned that respecting the Tories, so that that unhappy Affair stuck as he foresaw and foretold that it would.

The Affair of the Fishery too was somewhat altered. They could not admit Us to dry, on the Shores of Nova Scotia, nor to fish within three Leagues of the Coast, nor within fifteen Leagues of the Coast of Cape Breton.

The Boundary they did not approve. They thought it too extended, too vast a Country, but they would not make a difficulty.

That if these Terms were not admitted, the whole Affair must be thrown into Parliament, where every Man would be for insisting on Restitution, to the Refugees.

He talked about excepting a few by Name of the most obnoxious of the Refugees.

I could not help observing that the Ideas respecting the Fishery appeared to me to come piping hot from Versailles. I quoted to them the Words of our Treaty with France, in which the indefinite and exclusive Right, to the Fishery on the Western Side of Newfoundland, was secured against Us, According to the true Construction of the Treaties of Utrecht and Paris. I shewed them the 12 and 13 Articles of the Treaty of Utrecht, by which the French were admitted to Fish from Cape Bona Vista to Cape Rich.

I related to them the manner in which the Cod and Haddock come into the Rivers, Harbours, Creeks, and up to the very Wharfs on all the northern Coast of America, in the Spring in the month of April, so that you have nothing to do, but step into a Boat, and bring in a parcel of Fish in a few Hours. But that in May, they begin to withdraw. We have a saying at Boston that when the Blossoms fall the Haddock begin to crawl, i.e. to move out into deep Water, so that in Summer you must go out some distance to fish. At Newfoundland it was the same. The fish in March or April, were inshore, in all the Creeks, Bays, and Harbours, i.e. within 3 Leagues of the Coasts or Shores of Newfoundland and Nova Scotia. That neither French nor English could go from Europe and arrive early enough for the first Fare. That our Vessells could, being so much nearer, an Advantage which God and Nature had put into our hands. But that this Advantage of ours, had ever been an Advantage to England, because our fish had been sold in Spain and Portugal for Gold and Silver, and that Gold and Silver sent to London for Manufactures. That this would be the Course again. That France foresaw it, and wished to deprive England of it, by perswading her, to deprive Us of it. That it would be a Master Stroke of Policy, if She could succeed, but England must be compleatly the Dupe, before She could succeed.

There were 3 Lights in which it might be viewed. 1. as a Nursery of Seamen. 2 as a Source of Profit. 3. as a Source of Contention. As a Nursery of Seamen, did England consider Us as worse Ennemies than France. Had She rather France should have the Seamen than America. The French Marine was nearer and more menacing than ours. As a Source of Profit, had England rather France should supply the Marketts of Lisbon and Cadiz, with Fish and take the Gold And Silver than We. France would never spend any of that Money in London, We should spend it all very nearly. As a Source of Contention, how could We restrain our Fishermen, the boldest Men alive, from fishing in prohibited Places. How could our Men see the French admitted to fish and themselves excluded by the English; it would then be a Cause of Disputes, and such Seeds France might wish to sow.

Mr. Jay desired to know, whether Mr. Oswald had now Power to conclude and sign with Us?

Stratchey said he had absolutely.

Mr. Jay desired to know if the Propositions now delivered Us were their Ultimatum. Stratchey seemed loth to answer, but at last said No.—We agreed these were good Signs of Sincerity. . . .

Nov. 26. Tuesday

Breakfasted at Mr. Jays, with Dr. Franklin, in Consultation upon the Propositions made to Us Yesterday by Mr. Oswald. We agreed unanimously, to answer him, that We could not consent to the Article, respecting the Refugees as it now stands. Dr. F. read a Letter upon the Subject which he had prepared to Mr. Oswald, upon the Subject of the Tories, which We had agreed with him that he should read as containing his private Sentiments. . . .

Before Dinner Mr. Fitsherbert came in, whom I had never seen before. A Gentleman of about 33, seems pretty discreet and judicious, and did not discover those Airs of Vanity which are imputed to him.

He came in Consequence of the desire, which I expressed Yesterday of knowing the State of the Negotiation between him and the C. de Vergennes, respecting the Fishery. He told Us that the C. was for fixing the Boundaries, where each Nation should fish. He must confess he thought the Idea plausible, for that there had been great dissentions between the Fishermen of the two nations. That the french Marine Office had an whole Appartment full of Complaints and Representations of disputes. That the French pretended that Cape Ray was the Point Riche.

I asked him if the French demanded of him an exclusive [Right] to fish and dry between Cape Bona Vista and the Point riche. He said they had not expressly, and he intended to follow the Words of the Treaty of Utrecht and Paris without stirring the Point. . . .

The rest of the Day, was spent in endless Discussions about the Tories. Dr. F. is very staunch against the Tories, more decided a great deal on this Point than Mr. Jay or my self.

1782. Nov. 27. Wednesday

Mr. Benjamin Vaughan came in, returned from London where he had seen Lord Shelburne.

He says he finds the Ministry much embarrassed with the Tories, and exceedingly desirous of saving their Honour and Reputation in this Point. That it is Reputation more than Money &c. . . .

1782. November 29. Fryday

Met Mr. Fitsherbert, Mr. Oswald, Mr. Franklin, Mr. Jay, Mr. Laurens and Mr. Stratchey at Mr. Jays, Hotel D'Orleans, and spent the whole Day in Discussions about the Fishery and the Tories. I proposed a new Article concerning the Fishery. It was discussed and turned in every Light, and multitudes of Amendments proposed on each Side, and at last the Article drawn as it was finally agreed to. . . .

. . . Mr. Stratchey proposed to leave out the Word Right of Fishing and make it Liberty. Mr. Fitsherbert said the Word Right was an obnoxious Expression.

Upon this I rose up and said, Gentlemen, is there or can there be a clearer Right? In former Treaties, that of Utrecht and that of Paris, France and England have claimed the Right and used the Word. When God Almighty made the Banks of Newfoundland at 300 Leagues Distance from the People of America and at 600 Leagues distance from those of France and England, did he not give as good a Right to the former as to the latter. If Heaven in the Creation gave a Right, it is ours at least as much as yours. If Occupation, Use, and Possession give a Right, We have it as clearly as you. If War and Blood and Treasure give a Right, ours is as good as yours. We have been constantly fighting in Canada, Cape Breton and Nova Scotia for the Defense of this Fishery, and have expended beyond all Proportion more than you. If then the Right cannot be denied, Why should it not be acknowledged? and put out of Dispute? Why should We leave Room for illiterate Fishermen to wrangle and chicane?

Mr. Fitsherbert said, the Argument is in your Favour. I must confess your Reasons appear to be good, but Mr. Oswalds Instructions were such that he did not see how he could agree with Us. And for my Part, I have not the Honour and Felicity, to be a Man of that Weight and Authority, in my Country, that you Gentlemen are in yours . . . and Mr. Oswalds Instructions are so particular.

I replied to this, The Time is not so pressing upon Us, but that We can wait, till a Courier goes to London, with your Representations upon this Subject and others that remain between Us, and I think the Ministers must be convinced.

Mr. Fitsherbert said, to send again to London and have all laid loose before Parliament was so uncertain a Measure—it was going to Sea again.

Upon this Dr. Franklin said, that if another Messenger was to be sent to London, he ought to carry Something more respecting a Compensation to the Sufferers in America. He produced a Paper from his Pocket, in which he had

drawn up a Claim, and He said the first Principle of the Treaty was Equality
and Reciprocity. Now they demanded of Us Payment of Debts and Restitution
or Compensation to the Refugees. If a Draper had sold a Piece of Cloth to a
Man upon Credit and then sent a servant to take it from him by Force, and after
bring his Action for the Debt, would any Court of Law or Equity give him his
Demand, without obliging him to restore the Cloth? Then he stated the carrying
off of Goods from Boston, Philadelphia, and the Carolinas, Georgia, Virginia &c.
and the burning of the Towns, &c. and desired that this might be sent with the
rest. . . .

. . . Mr. Fitsherbert, Mr. Oswald and Mr. Stratchey, retired for some time, and
returning Mr. Fitsherbert said that upon consulting together and weighing
every Thing as maturely as possible, Mr. Stratchey and himself had determined
to advise Mr. Oswald, to strike with Us, according to the Terms We had proposed as our Ultimatum respecting the Fishery and the Loyalists.—Accordingly We all sat down and read over the whole Treaty and corrected it and
agreed to meet tomorrow at Mr. Oswalds House, to sign and send the Treaties
which the Secretaries were to copy fair in the mean time.

November 30. Saturday. St. Andrews Day

We met first at Mr. Jays, then at Mr. Oswalds, examined and compared the
Treaties. Mr. Stratchey had left out the limitation of Time, the 12 Months,
that the Refugees were allowed to reside in America, in order to recover
their Estates if they could. Dr. Franklin said this was a Surprize upon Us.
Mr. Jay said so too. We never had consented to leave it out, and they insisted
upon putting it in, which was done.

Mr. Laurens said there ought to be a Stipulation that the British Troops
should carry off no Negroes or other American Property. We all agreed.
Mr. Oswald consented.

Then The Treaties were signed, sealed and delivered, and We all went out
to Passy to dine with Dr. Franklin. . . .

The Finished Treaty

*The treaty, signed on November 30, 1782, by Adams, Franklin, Jay, and
Henry Laurens (recently released from the Tower of London) on the one hand*

The finished treaty, *The Revolutionary Diplomatic Correspondence of the United States*, ed. Wharton. Vol. VI, pp. 96–99.

and Richard Oswald on the other, was termed "provisional." The Americans thought thereby to turn aside charges that they had concluded a separate peace with France. It was a thin fiction, however; and all parties, including France and the leaders of Congress, were under no illusion about the matter. The provisional treaty subsequently became the definitive one without any material change.

The separate article was secret (though not for long), as well it may have been, considering that it was in effect an American invitation to Britain to move against Spain in West Florida.

Articles agreed upon by and between Richard Oswald, esquire, the commissioner of his Britannic majesty for treating of peace with the commissioners of the United States of America, in behalf of his said majesty on the one part, and John Adams, Benjamin Franklin, John Jay, and Henry Laurens, four of the commissioners of the said States for treating of peace with the commissioner of his said majesty, on their behalf, on the other part; to be inserted in, and to constitute the treaty of peace proposed to be concluded between the crown of Great Britain and the said United States. But which treaty is not to be concluded until terms of peace shall be agreed upon between Great Britain and France, and his Britannic majesty shall be ready to conclude such treaty accordingly.

Whereas, reciprocal advantages and mutual convenience are found by experience to form the only permanent foundation of peace and friendship between states, it is agreed to form the articles of the proposed treaty on such principles of liberal equity and reciprocity as that partial advantages (those seeds of discord) being excluded, such a beneficial and satisfactory intercourse between the two countries may be established as to promise and secure to both perpetual peace and harmony.

ARTICLE I. His Britannic majesty acknowledges the said United States, viz., New Hampshire, Massachusetts Bay, Rhode Island, and Providence Plantations, Connecticut, New York, New Jersey, Pennsylvania, Delaware, Maryland, Virginia, North Carolina, South Carolina, and Georgia, to be free, sovereign, and independent States; that he treats with them as such, and, for himself, his heirs and successors, relinquishes all claims to the government, propriety, and territorial rights of the same, and every part thereof; and that all disputes which might arise in future on the subject of the boundaries of the said United States may be prevented, it is hereby agreed and declared that the following are, and shall be, their boundaries, viz:

ARTICLE II. From the northwest angle of Nova Scotia, viz., that angle which is is formed by a line drawn due north from the source of St. Croix River to the

highlands, along the highlands which divide those rivers that empty themselves into the river St. Lawrence from those which fall into the Atlantic Ocean,
to the northwesternmost head of Connecticut River; thence down along the
middle of that river to the 45th degree of north latitude; from thence by a line
due west on said latitude until it strikes the river Iroquois or Cataroquy;
thence along the middle of said river into Lake Ontario; through the middle of
said lake until it strikes the communication by water between that lake and
Lake Erie; thence along the middle of said communication into Lake Erie;
through the middle of said lake until it arrives at the water communication
between that lake and Lake Huron, thence along the middle of said water
communication into the Lake Huron; thence through the middle of said
lake to the water communication between that lake and Lake Superior; thence
through Lake Superior, northward of the Isles Royal and Philippeaux to the
Long Lake; thence through the middle of said Long Lake and the water communication between it and the Lake of the Woods to the said Lake of the
Woods; thence through the said lake to the most northwestern point thereof;
and from thence on a due west course to the river Mississippi; thence by a
line to be drawn along the middle of the said river Mississippi until it shall
intersect the northernmost part of the 31st degree of north latitude; south by a
line to be drawn due east from the determination of the line last mentioned in
the latitude of 31st degree north of the equator, to the middle of the river
Apalachicola or Catahouchi, thence along the middle thereof to its junction
with the Flint River, thence straight to the head of St. Mary's River to the
Atlantic Ocean. East by a line to be drawn along the middle of the river St.
Croix, from its mouth in the Bay of Fundy to its source; and from its source
directly north to the aforesaid highlands which divide the rivers that fall into
the Atlantic Ocean from those which fall into the river St. Lawrence, comprehending all islands within twenty leagues of any part of the shores of the
United States, and lying between lines to be drawn due east from the points
where the aforesaid boundaries, between Nova Scotia on the one part and East
Florida on the other, shall respectively touch the Bay of Fundy and the Atlantic
Ocean; expecting such islands as now are, or heretofore have been, within the
limits of the said province of Nova Scotia.

ARTICLE III. It is agreed that the people of the United States shall continue
to enjoy unmolested the right to take fish of every kind on the Grand Bank and
on all the other banks of Newfoundland; also in the Gulf of St. Lawrence, and
at all other places in the sea where the inhabitants of both countries used at
any time heretofore to fish. And also that the inhabitants of the United States
shall have liberty to take fish of every kind on such part of the coast of Newfoundland as British fishermen shall use (but not to dry or cure the same on
that island), and also on the coasts, bays, and creeks of all other of his
Britannic majesty's dominion in America. And that the American fishermen

shall have liberty to dry and cure fish in any of the unsettled bays, harbors, and creeks of Nova Scotia, Magdalen Islands, and Labrador so long as the same shall remain unsettled; but so soon as the same or either of them shall be settled, it shall not be lawful for the said fishermen to dry or cure fish at such settlement, without a previous agreement for that purpose, with the inhabitants, proprietors, or possessors of the ground.

ARTICLE IV. It is agreed that creditors on either side shall meet with no lawful impediment to the recovery of the full value, in sterling money, of all *bona fide* debts heretofore contracted.

ARTICLE V. It is agreed that the Congress shall earnestly recommend it to the legislatures of the respective States to provide for the restitution of all estates, rights, and properties which have been confiscated, belonging to real British subjects, and also of the estates, rights, and properties of persons resident in districts in the possession of his majesty's arms, and who have not borne arms against the said United States; and that persons of any other description shall have free liberty to go to any part or parts of any of the thirteen United States, and therein to remain twelve months unmolested in their endeavors to obtain the restitution of such of their estates, rights, and properties as may have been confiscated. And that Congress shall also earnestly recommend to the several States a reconsideration and revision of all acts or laws regarding the premises, so as to render the said laws or acts perfectly consistent, not only with justice and equity, but with that spirit of conciliation which on the return of the blessings of peace should universally prevail. And that Congress shall also earnestly recommend to the several States that the estates, rights, and properties of such last-mentioned persons shall be restored to them, they refunding to any persons who may be now in possession, the *bona fide* price (where any has been given) which such persons may have paid on purchasing any of the said lands, rights, and properties since the confiscation. And it is agreed that all persons who have any interest in confiscated lands, either by debts, marriage settlements, or otherwise, shall meet with no lawful impediment in the prosecution of their just rights.

ARTICLE VI. That there shall be no future confiscations made, nor any prosecutions commenced against any person or persons, for or by reason of the part which he or they may have taken in the present war, and that no person shall on that account suffer any future loss or damage, either in his person, liberty, or property, and that those who may be in confinement on such charges at the time of the ratification of the treaty in America, shall be immediately set at liberty and the prosecution so commenced be discontinued.

ARTICLE VII. There shall be a firm and perpetual peace between his Britannic majesty and the said States, and between the subjects of the one and the citizens of the other, wherefore all hostilities, both by sea and land, shall then immediately cease. All prisoners on both sides shall be set at liberty, and his

Britannic majesty shall, with all convenient speed, and without causing any destruction, or carrying away any negroes or other property of the American inhabitants, withdraw all his armies, garrisons, and fleets from the said United States, and from every port, place, and harbor within the same, leaving in all fortifications the American artillery that may be therein. And shall also order and cause all archives, records, deeds, and papers belonging to any of the said States or their citizens, which, in the course of the war, may have fallen into the hands of his officers, to be forthwith restored and delivered to the proper States and persons to whom they belong.

ARTICLE VIII. The navigation of the Mississippi River, from its source to the ocean, shall forever remain free and open to the subjects of Great Britain and the citizens of the United States.

ARTICLE IX. In case it should so happen that any place or territory belonging to Great Britain or the United States should be conquered by the arms of either from the other before the arrival of these articles in America, it is agreed that the same shall be restored without difficulty and without requiring any compensation.

Done at Paris the thirtieth day of November, in the year one thousand seven hundred and eighty-two.

Richard Oswald
John Adams
B. Franklin
John Jay
Henry Laurens

Witness:

Caleb Whitefoord, *Secretary to the British Commission*
W. T. Franklin, *Secretary to the American Commission*

SEPARATE ARTICLE. It is hereby understood and agreed that, in case Great Britain, at the conclusion of the present war, shall recover or be put in possession of West Florida, the line of north boundary between the said Province and the United States shall be a line drawn from the mouth of the river Yazoo, where it unites with the Mississippi, due east to the river Apalachicola.

THREE VIEWS OF THE TREATY

The French Protest

The separate peace made by the American commissioners and Richard Oswald, even though termed "provisional," was deeply resented by the French Government. The official protest reported below by Secretary Livingston clearly indicates as much. French anger and disappointment did not abate as a result of treaty making on their own behalf. The terms of the agreements between Britain on the one hand and France and Spain on the other were altogether disappointing to the Bourbon powers and not at all commensurate, they believed, with their efforts, during the American Revolution.

There had never been any pretense of alliance between Spain and the United States; hence the end of hostilities against Britain meant the resumption of a covert competition for control of the vast American backcountry. French expectations were higher; but after Yorktown, the close cooperation and cordial amity of Franco-American relations quickly weakened. There were several reasons for this, some of which are more fully presented in Part IV of this book; but the initial one was undoubtedly the ill feeling generated by America's separate treaty.

The minister of France, waiting upon Mr. Livingston at twelve o'clock, agreeable to appointment, . . . read to Mr. Livingston a letter of the 19th of December from the Count de Vergennes, in which he informs him that their treaty was not so forward as that of the Americans. Though if his majesty had wished it he could have signed before the American plenipotentiaries, as no essential difference existed between France and Great Britain. But that the King's delicacy induced him to wish that all his allies should be first satisfied, and he had accordingly resolved to continue the war, whatever advantages might be offered him, if Great Britain should bear hard upon any of them. That it still remained to reconcile the interest of Spain and those of Holland. That he had reason to believe with relation to the first that they would soon be fully settled. That the foundation was already laid and that nothing now remained but to

---

Minutes of a verbal communication to the American Government by Luzerne, the minister from France, March 22, 1783, *ibid.,* pp. 330–332.

settle forms. That he was of opinion that it was for the interest of the United States to facilitate a connection with this power, which will be their neighbor.

That it would become the wisdom of Congress to discover moderation with respect to them. That he is persuaded England will see with pleasure divisions introduced between the United States and the court of Madrid, and that it is probable that they will even endeavor to animate them one against the other. That British emissaries have been employed to inspire Spain with apprehensions as to the ambitious views of America. But they will now avail themselves of their intimacy with the American ministers to render them suspicious of Spain, and even to excite their resentments against her. Congress will defeat this design by removing the difficulties which now oppose themselves to a union with his Catholic majesty. That the King wishes so much to see his allies enjoy a solid and durable peace, that in exciting the Americans on one side to discover a more conciliatory spirit, he will spare nothing on the other to remove the difficulties which may be raised by the court of Spain. That he apprehends delays and embarrassments from Holland. That the British administration appear very unfavorable to them.

The minister of France then read to Mr. Livingston another letter from the Count de Vergennes of the 20th of December, 1782, which contained in substance that peace was not yet concluded, though it was anxiously desired by the King. That his majesty's obligations to his allies had not yet permitted him to pronounce with certainty as to the termination of the war. That, expecting peace, prudence required that the allies should act as if the war was to continue. That Congress will judge of the manner in which they can most effectually contribute to distress the common enemy. That in the present state of things it would not be prudent to invite the Americans to form any direct enterprise against the common enemy. That the provisional articles would, when executed at the general peace, put New York into the hands of the Americans, and that Congress could judge better than they could what part it would be expedient for them to take in the then state of things. That, proposing nothing, they leave everything to their discretion. That the minister should, however, inform them that he could not yet determine whether they were at the eve of a peace or if another campaign must be opened. That in the latter case there were two essential objects on which the minister of France should impart to Congress the opinion of his court and the desires of his majesty.

That though if their towns were evacuated the Americans could not take an active part, yet they can compel the enemy to wish for peace by excluding them from all connexion with them and prohibiting under very severe penalties the consumption or importation of British manufactures. That a considerable party among the British wish to form commercial connexion with the United States. That when they shall be convinced that they can reap no benefit therefrom, but by a solid definitive peace conformable to the treaty agreed upon, they will become more tractable and conclude the definitive treaty, which will give force and vigor to the provisional articles and set the seal to the independence of America. That it would also be proper to state to Congress the necessity of providing means to prevent the sending provisions into New York, by which the British armaments are amply supplied with fresh provisions of every kind.

That the King persuades himself that the legislatures of the respective States will concur in measures for this salutary purpose when they shall be informed of the injury occasioned to their ally by the want of the necessary precautions on this subject. That these precautions will not be unnecessary if the enemy are about to abandon New York, without which the enemy will carry with them the means of supplying the places to which they transport their troops.

That he persuades himself that Congress will perceive that they are indebted to the harmony that has subsisted between the King and them for the present happy state of their affairs. But that nothing being yet concluded the present moment is precisely that in which it is of most importance to preserve the same system.

Congressional Reaction: Secretary Livingston to the American Commissioners

Secretary Livingston's sensations of pain, described in the third paragraph of the following letter, were meant to placate the French. Nothing can disguise the "warmest approbation" of Congress and people and the gratitude for the "happy issue" of the negotiations.

Gentlemen: I am now to acknowledge the favor of your joint letter by the *Washington*, together with a copy of the preliminary articles; both were laid before Congress. The articles have met with their warmest approbation, and have been generally seen by the people in the most favorable point of view.

The steadiness manifested in not treating without an express acknowledgment of your independence previous to a treaty is approved, and it is not doubted but it accelerated that declaration. The boundaries are as extensive as we have a right to expect, and we have nothing to complain of with respect to the fisheries. My sentiments as to English debts you have in a former letter. No honest man could wish to withhold them. A little forbearance in British creditors till people have recovered in part from the losses sustained by the war will be necessary to render this article palatable, and indeed to secure

Secretary Livingston to the American Commissioners, Philadelphia, March 25, 1783, *ibid.*, pp. 338–340.

more effectually the debt. The article relative to the loyalists is not quite so accurately expressed as I could wish it to have been. What, for instance, is intended by *real British subjects?* It is clear to me that it will operate nothing in their favor in any State in the Union, but as you made no secret of this to the British commissioners, they will have nothing to charge you with; and indeed, the whole clause seems rather to have been inserted to appease the clamor of these poor wretches than to satisfy their wants. Britain would have discovered more candor and magnanimity in paying to them three months' expense of the war establishment, which would have been an ample compensation for all their losses, and left no germ of dissatisfaction to bud and bloom and ripen into discontents here. Another mad administration may think the non-compliance of the legislatures with the recommendations of Congress on this subject a sufficient cause for giving themselves and us new troubles. You, however, were perfectly right in agreeing in the article—the folly was theirs, who did not either insist upon more or give up this.

But, gentlemen, though the issue of your treaty has been successful, though I am satisfied that we are much indebted to your firmness and perseverance, to your accurate knowledge of our situation and of our wants for this success, yet I feel no little pain at the distrust manifested in the management of it; particularly in signing the treaty without communicating it to the court of Versailles till after the signature, and in concealing the separate article from it even when signed. I have examined, with the most minute attention, all the reasons assigned in your several letters to justify these suspicions. I confess they do not appear to strike me so forcibly as they have done you; and it gives me pain that the character for candor and fidelity to its engagements which should always characterize a great people should have been impeached thereby. The concealment was, in my opinion, absolutely unnecessary; for, had the court of France disapproved the terms you had made after they had been agreed upon, they could not have acted so absurdly as to counteract you at that late day, and thereby put themselves in the power of an enemy who would certainly betray them and perhaps justify you in making terms for yourselves.

The secret article is no otherwise important than as it carries in it the seeds of enmity to the court of Spain, and shows a marked preference for an open enemy. It would, in my opinion, have been much better to have fixed on the same boundaries for West Florida, into whatever hands it fell, without showing any preference, or rendering concealment necessary; since all the arguments in favor of the cession to England would then have operated with equal force, and nothing have been lost by it; for there can be no doubt that, whether Florida shall at the close of the war be ceded to England or to Spain, it will be ceded as it was held by Britain. The separate article is not, I suppose, by this time a secret in Europe; it can hardly be considered as such in America. The treaty was sent out to the General, with this article annexed, by Sir Guy Carleton, without the smallest injunction of secrecy. So that, I dare say, it has been pretty generally read at headquarters. Congress still conceal it here. I feel for the embarrassment explanations on this subject must subject you to, when this secret is known to your allies. . . .

I make no apology for the part I have taken in this business. I am satisfied you will readily acquit me for having discharged what I conceived to be my duty, upon such a view of things as you presented to me. In declaring my sentiments freely, I invite you to treat me with equal candor in your letters, and, in sending original papers, I guard against misrepresentations that might give you pain. Upon the whole, I have the pleasure of assuring you that the services you have rendered your country in bringing this business to a happy issue, are very gratefully received by them, however we may differ in sentiments about the mode of doing it.

I am sorry that the extreme negligence of the different States has prevented, and will probably long prevent, my being able to send you a state of the injury done to real property, and the number of slaves destroyed and carried off by the British troops and their allies, though no pains have been or shall be wanting, on my part, to urge them to it. . . .

Shelburne's Explanation to the House of Lords

When Shelburne made his eloquent apologia for the peace, he was already falling from power, rejected by both Parliament and nation, who considered themselves badly served—even betrayed—by his policies. In personal terms, the speech is a moment of great pathos, the effective end of a long and impressive public career.

Though he was to rise in the peerage to the Marquisate of Lansdowne, Shelburne was never again to hold public office. Shelburne took the long view, looking far into the future to a mighty Anglo-American partnership, but his tragedy lay in his inability to persuade his contemporaries—Americans or Britons—to share his vision.

Professor Harlow detects in the speech the anguish of a man who is coming to terms with his own defeat. Realizing the futility of his cause, he does not do full justice to himself, breaking off almost abruptly and leaving unspoken his great dream of Anglo-American reconciliation.

Shelburne's Explanation to the House of Lords, Feb., 1783, *Parliamentary History*, ed. W. Cobbett, Vol. XXIII, pp. 407–420.

The Earl of Shelburne then rose. The lateness of the hour, my lords, said his lordship, will not suffer me to take the liberty of trespassing so far on your patience, as my feelings would permit me to on the present occassion. I shall not address your passions—that candid province I will leave to those who have shewn such ability for its government to-night. As my conduct has been founded upon integrity—facts, and plain reasoning, will form its best support. I shall necessarily wave the consideration of the critical moment at which I stepped into the administration of the affairs of this country—a moment when, if there be any credit due to the solemn, public declarations of men, who seemed then, and seem now, to have the welfare of the state nearest to their hearts—every hope of renovated lustre was gone, and nothing but dreary despondency remained to the well-wishers of Great Britain. I am now speaking within memory, and consequently within proof. It is not for me to boast of my motives for standing forward at a period so alarming. My circumstances are not so secure as to render my conduct a matter of dubiety, and my own explanation of my feelings would, I flatter myself, fall far short of that credit which sympathy would give me in the minds of men, whose patriotism is not that of words: the ambition of advancing to the service of our country in an hour when even brave men shrink from danger, is honourable, and I shall not be catechized for entertaining such an impulse. I make no merit of my hardi-hood, and when I speak of mine, I wish your lordships to understand me as speaking of the generous enterprize of my noble and honourable colleagues in administration. It was our duty as good citizens, when the state was in danger, that all selfish apprehensions should be banished. I shall not, there-fore, expatiate on my reasons for coming into office, but openly and candidly tell your lordships how I have conducted myself in it. A peace was the declared wish of the nation at that time. How was that to be procured best for the advantage of the country? Certainly by gaining the most accurate knowledge of the relative condition of the powers at war. Here a field of knowledge was required to be beaten, to which no one man, vast and profound as it is possible to picture human capacity, would by any means be supposed equal. Then if one man was inadequate to the whole task, the next question naturally is, what set of men are best qualified as auxiliaries in it? What is the skill re-quired? A knowledge of trade and commerce, with all its relations, and an intimate acquaintance with military affairs, and all its concomitants. Were men of this description consulted previous to, and during the progress of the treaty now before your lordships? I answer, they were. And with this sanction, administration need assume no false brow of bravery, in combat-ting the glittering expressions of that hasty opposition that had been set up to the present terms.

Let us examine them, my lords, let us take the several assertions in their turn, and without wishing to intrude too much on your lordships time, I shall be pardoned for giving a distinct answer to each head of objection. Ministry, in the first place, is blamed for drawing the boundary they have done between the territories of the United States and those of our sovereign in Canada. I wish to examine every part of the treaties on the fair rule of the value of the district ceded—to examine it on the amount of the exports and imports, by which alone we could judge of its importance. The exports of this country to Canada, then, were only 140,000£., has cost this country, on an average, 800,000£. I have the vouchers in my pocket, should your lordships be inclined to examine the fact. But the trade is not given up, it is only divided, and divided for our benefit. I appeal to all men conversant with the nature of that trade, whether its best resources in Canada do not lie in the northward. What, then, is the result of this part of the treaty, so wisely, and with so much sincere love on the part of England clamoured against by noble lords? Why this. You have generously given America, with whom every call under Heaven urges you to stand on the footing of brethren, a share in a trade, the monopoly of which you sordidly preserved to yourselves, and the loss of the enormous sum of 750,000£. Monopolies, some way or other, are ever justly punished. They forbid rivalry, and rivalry is of the very essence of the well-being of trade. This seems to be the æra of protestantism in trade. All Europe appear enlightened, and eager to throw off the vile shackles of oppressive ignorant monopoly; that unmanly and illiberal principle, which is at once ungenerous and deceitful. A few interested Canadian merchants might complain; for merchants would always love monopoly, without taking a moment's time to think whether it was for their interest or not. I avow that monopoly is always unwise; but if there is any nation under heaven, who ought to be the first to reject monopoly, it is the English. Situated as we are between the old world and the new, and between the southern and northern Europe, all that we ought to covet upon earth is free trade, and fair equality. With more industry, with more enterprize, with more capital than any trading nation upon earth, it ought to be our constant cry, let every market be open, let us meet our rivals fairly, and we ask no more. It is a principle on which we have had the wisdom to act with respect to our brethren of Ireland: and, if conciliation be our view, why should we not reach it out also to America? Our generosity is not much, but, little as it is, let us give it with a grace. Indeed, to speak properly, it is not generosity to them, but œconomy to ourselves; and in the boundaries which are established we have saved ourselves the immense sum of 800,000£. a-year, and shewed to the Americans our sincere love and fair intentions, in dividing the little bit of trade which nature had laid at their doors; and telling them that we desired to live with them in communion of benefits, and in the sincerity of friendship. "But the Indians were abandoned to their enemies!" Noble lords have taken great pains to shew the immense value of the Indians; it was not unnatural for noble lords, who had made so lavish a use of these Indians,* to complain of their loss; but those who abhorred their violence would think ministry had done wisely. The Americans knew best how to tame their savage natures. The descendents of the good William Penn would manage them better than all the Mr. Stuarts† with all the Jewsharps, razors, trumpery, and jobs that we could contrive. "But our treaties with them bound us to everlasting protection!" This is one of those assertions which always sounds well, and is calculated to amuse the uninformed mind: but what is the meaning of *in perpetuo* in all treaties? That they shall endure as long as the parties are able to perform the conditions. This is the meaning of perpetual alliances; and in the present treaty with America, the Indian nations were not abandoned to their enemies; they were remitted to the care of neighbours, whose interest it was as much as ours to cultivate friendship with them, and who were certainly the best qualified for softening and humanizing their hearts. But I shall dismiss this subject, though it is blended with others, and proceed to the investigation of the rest of the objections to the treaties of pacification.

"Why have you given America the freedom of fishing in all your creeks and harbours, and especially on the banks of Newfoundland," say the noble objectors to this article? Why? because, in the first place, they could from their locality have exercised a fishery in that quarter for the first season (for there are two), in spite of all our efforts to repel them. In February the first season commences, and that is entirely at their devotion; for our people can never take their stations there so soon. With regard to the other season, let us again revert to what I have said respecting the fur trade; though we have not a monopoly, we have got such superior advantages in the article of drying, curing, and preparing our fish for market, from the exclusive command of the most contiguous shores, that a rivalry can only whet our industry to reap those benefits our preferable situation in this respect presents to us. "But why have you not stipulated a reciprocity of fishing in the American harbours and creeks?" I will tell your lordships:—because we have abundant employment in our own. Would not an American think it sordid in the extreme, nay, consider it bordering on madness, to covet the priviledge of battening our cattle on some of their sterile wilds, when we had our own fertile savannahs to have recourse to? Such would be the opinion entertained of ministry, if it had childishly and avariciously made a stipulation of the nature the objectors think they ought to have. The broad and liberal policy on which the present treaty is formed, is in my opinion much more wise and beneficial than would have been the narrow and wretched plan of bargaining for every little

---

* [A cutting reference to the use of the Indians against the Americans during the war.]

† [A reference to Alexander Stuart, imperial Indian agent.]

particle of advantage which we might have procured, perhaps, by stickling in the negotiation. As to the masts, a noble lord said, we were to have in such abundance at Penobscot, I will oppose a fact to his bare assertion. I have in my pocket a certificate from one of the ablest surveyors in our service, captain Twiss, that there is not a tree there capable of being made into a mast.

But there remains somewhat in these provisional Articles still to be considered, which I have never reflected upon without feelings as pungent as any which the warmest admirers of the virtues of the loyalists can possibly have experienced. I mean the unhappy necessity of our affairs, which induced the extremity of submitting the fate of the property of these brave and worthy men to the discretion of their enemies. I have but one answer to give the House in this particular; it is the answer I gave my own bleeding heart. A part must be wounded, that the whole of the empire may not perish. If better terms could be had, think you, my lords, that I would not have embraced them? You all know my creed. You all know my steadiness. If it were possible to put aside the bitter cup the adversaries of this country presented to me, you know I would have done it; but you called for peace. To make it in the circumstances, which your lordships all know I stood in, was most arduous. In this point, nothing could be more grievous to me. Neither in public nor in private life is it my character to desert my friends. I had but the alternative, either to accept the terms, said Congress, of our recommendation to the states, in favour of the colonists, or continue the war. It is in our power to do no more than recommend. Is there any man who hears me, who will clap his hand on his heart, and step forward and say, I ought to have broken off the treaty? If there be, I am sure he neither knows the state of the country, nor yet has he paid any attention to the wishes of it. But still I do not despond with respect to the loyalists. I rely upon the wisdom, the honour, and the temper of the Congress. Their recommendation was all that in the nature of things we could procure. They were cautious in wording their treaty, lest they should possibly give offence to the new states, whose constitutions had not advanced to those habits of appearence and strength that banishes all suspicions; peremptory language is not the language of a new state. They must soften their applications. In all their measures for money, for men, they have used the word recommendation to the provincial assemblies; and it has always, or at least generally been paid respect to. And, believe me, they do the loyalists the offices not of friends, who surmise doubts on this occassion. But say the worst; and that after all, this estimable set of men are not received and cherished in the bosom of their own country: is England so lost to gratitude, and all the feelings of humanity, as not to afford them an asylum? Who can be so base as to think she will refuse it to them? Surely it cannot be that noble-minded man, who would plunge his country again knee-deep in blood, and saddle it with an expence of 20 millions for the purpose of restoring them.

Without one drop of blood spilt, and without one-fifth of the expence of one year's campaign, happiness and easiness can be given the loyalists in as ample a manner as these blessings were ever in their enjoyment; therefore let the outcry cease on this head. But which of the two stiles of language is the more likely to assist the loyalists: the stile of the Address which declares the confidence of parliament in the good intentions of the Congress, or of the noble lords who declare that recommendation is nothing? It surely requires no great depth of penetration to distinguish between these things. . . .

I have now done, as well as my memory serves me, though the detail of all the objections which have been made to the treaties; and, I trust, your lordships see from the facts to which I have all along referred you, the necessity and the policy of our conduct in this particular. Let me, before I conclude, call to your lordships minds the general state of this country, at the period in which the pacific negociations were set on foot. Were we not at the extremity of distress? Did not the boldest of us cry out for peace? Was not the object of the war accomplished? Was not the independence of America solemnly recognized by Parliament? Could that independence be afterward made a stipulation for the restoration of tranquility? On an entire view of our affairs at that time, is there any honest, sensible man in the kingdom that will not say the powerful confederacy with whom we had then to contend had the most decided superiority over us? Had we scarce one taxable article that was not already taxed to the utmost extent? . . . It is easy for any bungler to pull down the fairest fabric, but is that a reason, my lords, he should censure the skill of the architect who reared it? But I fear I trespass, my lords, on your patience too long. The subject was near my heart, and you will pardon me, if I have been earnest in laying before your lordships our embarassments, our difficulties, our views, and our reasons for what we have done. I submit them to you with confidence, and rely on the nobleness of your natures, that in judging of men who have hazarded so much for their country, you will not be guided by prejudice, nor influenced by party.

4 / THE REESTABLISHMENT OF AN ANGLO-AMERICAN COMMUNITY

INTERPRETATION

CHARLES R. RITCHESON, *Anglo-American Relations 1783–1794*

The emergence of the United States as a dominant world power in the mid-twentieth century has brought in its wake a major revision of views about American civilization, institutions, and relations with other members of the world community. There is a similar process underway presently in England, where the shift in leadership of the western complex of nations to our side of the Atlantic has also brought a probing of implications of the new order. In both countries, the peculiar character and inherent intimacy of the Anglo-American relationship—the analogy of the family is not far from the truth —have meant that an increasing number of historians in Britain and America are preoccupied with the problems of origin and development of the Anglo-American partnership. Although it is too early to gauge the full force of its impact, there is an evident tendency to shift emphasis from purely national considerations to a search for common denominators and an understanding of the "other side." Already, important contributions have been made. They are especially noteworthy in that most touchy of all periods of the common history, the age of the American Revolution.

The purpose of this essay is to invite attention to another critical period in Anglo-American relations, and to make certain suggestions about lines of inquiry and reappraisal which appear to me to promise significant results.

To American historians the dozen years after the Peace of 1783 are of obvious importance: the United States made her debut as an independent power. British historians, however, with eyes fixed on the approaching cataclysm in France, have generally neglected Anglo-American affairs during the closing years of the 18th Century. (So, for that matter, did many British statesmen of the time, and for precisely the same reason.) Lacking any important challenge or correction from British colleagues, American historians have evolved an orthodox treatment of this set piece of our diplomatic history. It may, I think, be stated without too great a risk of oversimplification in these terms: Britain was the villain. Chastised by defeat but vengeful, she was determined to frustrate the legitimate expectations of the new nation. Hence, her unco-operative attitude toward our request for a commercial treaty and her un-

Charles R. Ritcheson, "Anglo-American Relations 1783–1794," *The South Atlantic Quarterly*, LVIII (1959), pp. 364–380. Reprinted by permission of the publisher.

reasonable refusal to allow us the trading privileges we enjoyed as members of the empire. Her retention of the forts in the Old Northwest was provocative and unjustified, threatening our encirclement and providing centers for British intrigue with savage Indians and disloyal westerners.

Admittedly, American citizens owed British merchants a vast sum in prewar debts; but payment was properly suspended until Britain's infraction of the Peace Treaty was rectified. American mistreatment of returning Loyalists—contrary to the Peace—was excusable because of the weakness of the American government and the righteous indignation of her citizens against former enemies. Meantime, payment for slaves "carried off" by withdrawing British forces at the end of the war was a matter of common equity, in our view.

The outbreak of the Anglo-French War in 1793 saw British perfidy and malice toward the United States compounded. The notorious spoliations of our maritime trade under the Orders in Council should have been answered by a firm and manly adherence to the Franco-American alliance of 1778, even at risk of war with England. This honorable end, it is commonly concluded, was frustrated by an Anglophile minority, the Federalists, who were entrenched in political power and who rammed through the Jay Treaty in defiance of the will of the people.

It is tempting for Americans to accept this explanation. It is simple and plausible. It is largely unchallenged. It carries with it the comforting assurance that we were right and they were wrong.

I do not mean to treat every point raised in the brief précis of the orthodox position, but there are certain considerations which have been generally ignored or obscured. They may be able to add a new dimension to our understanding of Anglo-American relations after 1783. They are at least hypotheses worthy of examination.

Two broad questions should be posed at the outset. The first goes to the matter of responsibility for the failure to arrive at a better regulation of Anglo-American relations between 1783 and 1794. The apportionment of blame is surely one of the least rewarding tasks of the historian; yet, as the orthodox school commonly does this to the manifest disparagement of Britain, it is necessary to ask if the balance is as one-sided as it is generally represented. Why should it be ignored or discounted that American violations of the Treaty of 1783 were as provocative to the British as their infractions were to Americans? The notorious and riotous partiality of many citizens of the United States for France after 1793 gave as much offense to Britons as Americans found in spoliations of our maritime commerce. . . .

The second question goes to the common assumption that the triumph or defeat of "democracy" is somehow at issue in Anglo-American differences during our period. The Jeffersonian Republicans are cast in the role of democracy's champions. They and their French friends, after the outbreak of revolution in the country of the latter, are joined in "the cause of mankind against tyrants." The Federalists and their foreign sponsors, the English, are democracy's enemies. The Republicans represent the true interests of the American people; the Federalists, those of "the rich and the well-born."

Leaving aside the exaggerated and anachronistic sense of nationalism implied in such a view, the term "democracy" is surely subject to critical scrutiny. It was rarely a respectable word in the 18th Century. Except in the vocabulary of radicals and visionaries, it was a term of opprobrium. It conjured up pictures not of ballot boxes but of Gordon Riots and Shays's Rebellions; and it was usually prefixed with "mad" or "despotic." Martha Washington referred to "filthy democrats"; and there is every evidence that her husband shared her feelings. Implicit in the word was "demagogue"; and "demon" was not far distant. The eighteenth-century meaning of the word has been obscured by the events of later days: the triumph of the Jeffersonian Republicans, and the advance of the United States (and—it is rarely remarked—of Britain) toward the democratic ideal in the nineteenth and twentieth centuries. Our acceptance today of democracy as the only form of government fit for enlightened and free men has served to produce an almost irresistible identification on the part of orthodox writers with the Jeffersonian Republicans. Thus, the period under discussion is commonly seen not within its own frame of reference, but within that derived from a subsequent period of history and forced upon it. This is unscientific; and it is unjust to Federalists and British alike.

Several matters disrupted Anglo-American relations after 1783. First, there was the weakness of the American government. Rarely mentioned in this connection, and occasionally even denied by orthodox writers, it hamstrung the foreign policy of the new nation and earned the contempt of many Americans and most Europeans. The adoption of the Constitution was a turning point in the miserable tale of impotence, but in 1788 the event remained to be proved. In foreign eyes, the struggle over the new instrument of government and over Hamilton's efforts to put it on a firm financial basis seemed to confirm the widespread belief that Americans could not effect a strong and centralized government.

It is not without irony that Franklin and his colleagues in the negotiation of the Peace of 1783 had used the weakness of the American government as an argument to combat British demands on behalf of the Loyalists. The Americans asserted that Congress could merely recommend, since it could not compel, individual states to do justice to persecuted Loyalists. Hailed as a master stroke of diplomatic maneuver, the appeal to weakness fixed in British minds the persuasion that the government of the United States was powerless at home and abroad.

New evidence pointing to a collapse of the Union accumulated rapidly: the Shays episode, the westerners' dealings with Spain, the correspondence of the Allens of Vermont with Canadian and British officials, the inability to prevent mistreatment of returning Loyalists, the clashing and competitive commercial regulations of the several states, the obstinate and ill-tempered refusal of many of the southern states to allow the recovery of prewar debts owing by American citizens to British merchants, the unsuccessful and disgraceful war against the Indians in the Northwest. In the face of such chaos, is it surprising that British officials doubted that American diplomatists could speak authoritatively for the nation they represented? (Did John Adams, asked the Duke of Dorset in 1783, possess commissions from each of the thirteen States?) American weakness meant to British ministers that representatives of the new nation could not negotiate *pari passu*; they could but supplicate.

The failure of both countries to fulfill the Peace Treaty of 1783 contributed, too, to growing distrust and ill will. There is not a more fruitless exercise in tedium and logical hairsplitting than seeking to assess guilt for "prior infraction." Both parties were delinquent; each had just grievances. The major difference lay in the degree of injury each nation inflicted upon its own cause by its disregard of treaty stipulations. Judged on this basis, there is no doubt that the United States suffered more than Britain. Inferior in terms of relative strength, the United States desired objects which Britain could grant or withhold at pleasure. Among these were the evacuation of the Northwestern posts and access to the British West Indian trade. American violations of the Treaty of 1783, however, strengthened the conviction of the British ministry that the government of the United States was unable, perhaps unwilling, to see to the honorable execution of her pledged word. What use, the British ministers asked themselves, would be a treaty with such a power? No answer was forthcoming until the outbreak of war with France in 1793.

A further disruptive influence in Anglo-American relations came from resurgent mercantilism in Britain after the peace. For a time in 1782 and 1783, it appeared that Shelburne's noble concept of an Anglo-American economic partnership might become reality, but the publication of Lord Sheffield's *Observations* and the brilliant defense of Britain's navigation system by William Eden in the House of Commons aroused every conservative instinct in the war-weary and disgruntled nation. The American Intercourse Bill, inspired by Shelburne and sponsored in the Commons by the younger Pitt after Shelburne's fall, would have allowed Anglo-American trade to return essentially to the prewar footing. The defeat of the bill was smashing. Not many months later, Pitt became prime minister. He admired the doctrines of Adam Smith, and he favored a more liberal trade policy toward the United States; but he was a politician as well as a statesman. He could not stand against the great conservative tide which had set against any infringement of the established mercantile system in favor of former rebels. Pitt thereupon lost interest in American affairs, and turned to more important matters nearer at hand: the rebuilding of his country's European position, badly damaged by the American

War. American policy passed by default to one of the most doctrinaire of mercantilists, Charles Jenkinson, Lord Hawkesbury.

As President of the Privy Council Committee for Trade and Foreign Plantations, Hawkesbury was in a position to defeat all efforts to amend the established mercantile system until 1794. His views were set forth in several reports from his committee, most definitively, perhaps, in that of January, 1791. It recounted that American agents, aided by interested friends within the Empire, especially the West Indian planters, had pressed the British government time and again since the peace for a commercial treaty on terms of "fullest reciprocity." American and British understanding of the term differed fundamentally, however. The Americans took it to mean freedom for their ships to trade within the Empire, particularly to the British West Indies, as they had done before the War. In return, American reasoning ran, the United States would grant "reciprocal" privileges to British vessels in American ports.

The American position, Hawkesbury's report continued, simply did not accord with the realities of the situation. British vessels already enjoyed as much freedom in American ports as other foreign ships. American economic necessity had seen to that. On her side, Britain had admitted the Americans to her home ports on the footing of the most-favored nation. There were even certain small privileges, unrepealed holdovers from colonial days, which only Americans enjoyed. A treaty between the two nations enjoining "reciprocity" was unnecessary; "reciprocity" existed already. What wild stretch of imagination had induced Americans to think "reciprocity" extended to freedom of British colonial ports? Had the United States colonies which she could open reciprocally to the British?

By their secession from the Empire, Hawkesbury reasoned, Americans had excluded themselves from imperial trading privileges. The result had been a veritable silver lining to the dark cloud of disrupted empire: Britain's carrying trade, particularly in the West Indian traffic, had increased in direct proportion to the American loss. To allow a re-establishment of the pre-revolutionary North American–West Indian trade would be folly in the extreme. In the first place, the advance in Britain's carrying trade would be jeopardized by renewed American competition. Further, island dependence on American foodstuffs and supplies would mitigate directly against the mercantilist ideal of a self-sufficient empire. Rather, the remaining North American colonies— Canada, Newfoundland, Nova Scotia—should be cultivated to fill the gap in the imperial economy created by the American secession. Finally, the merchant marine was the great reservoir of trained seamen and ships for the British Navy in time of war. Any encouragement given to American shipping would operate doubly against the "military marine": it would increase American naval potential and, in direct ratio, it would decrease Britain's. In a future war, the West Indian islands themselves might well be lost to the United States.

Grave risks were involved in amending the existing system, Hawkesbury and his committee believed; but there were none in keeping it intact. What could the Americans do? Weak, divided, negligible, they might bluster about discriminations against British ships and merchants, or threaten to cut off supplies to the islands. For Britain, this would, perhaps, prove inconvenient, at least until the North American colonies could be developed as a source of supplies. For America, however, an interruption of trade with Britain would be disastrous. Where else could she dispose of agricultural surpluses save in the West Indies? Where else could she find a market for timber? Did the new nation not require British credit and capital? The Federal government itself was largely dependent for revenue on duties levied on foreign imports. Did not trade with Britain provide the lion's share? In short, hard economic necessity would compel the United States to an acceptance of British policy.

Was the mercantilist argument as stupid as the orthodox school would have us believe? Was British policy as formulated by Hawkesbury and his friends "short-sighted"? Perhaps; but consider what even limited vision would comprehend: increasingly violent revolution in France and a general European conflagration. It is not too unreasonable to suppose that a disruption of the established mercantile system could have had tragic results. With fewer ships and men at his disposal, what might have been Howe's fate on the "Glorious First of June," 1794? What results would have flowed from a reversal at the Battle of the Nile? At Trafalgar? At several important crises in the Anglo-French War, the edge of British naval superiority, upon which hung the fate of the nation, was small indeed. It is conceivable that the conservative mercantilists saved Britain by their obstinate, "short-sighted" defense of the existing system for monopolizing the imperial carrying trade.

A fourth disruptive element in Anglo-American relations consisted of grievances on both sides occasioned by the Anglo-French War. Beginning in 1793, a series of British Orders in Council practically interdicted American trade with France and the French West Indies. Impressment was not yet a serious problem; but search and seizure of our vessels was. Britain's iron-fisted enforcement of the "Rule of '56" caused a mounting wave of resentment in the United States, and bitterness stemming from earlier disputes was exacerbated. As her military position worsened, Britain extended her definition of "contraband" to include many items traditionally considered free goods by the lesser maritime powers. She even prohibited foodstuffs.

Condemnation of Britain's actions by the orthodox school rarely takes into account two mitigating circumstances. First is the provocation offered to the embattled nation by the highly unneutral conduct of certain American citizens. Washington's Neutrality Proclamation notwithstanding, American friends of France seemed bent upon dragging their nation into war at the side of the new Republic. Aid and comfort of the most material sort were tendered to Britain's enemies; and in 1793 and 1794, American ports were bidding fair to become havens of refuge and bases of operations for French privateers and naval forces. Would any nation aspiring to the name of "great" sit supinely by while her maritime lifelines were being cut by belligerent forces enjoying the sanctuary of "neutral" ports?

Secondly, the harshness of Britain's interpretation of contraband may have been unprecedented; but so was the magnitude and the nature of the danger facing her. France was "a nation in arms." It is hard to reject out of hand the British argument that any goods, even foodstuffs, which gave life to or sustained the French nation should be on the prohibited list. The position may be difficult to justify but to writers today, aware of the ultimate development of the concept of total war witnessed in our own century, it is at least understandable. . . .

Unfortunately for Anglo-American friendship, British wartime practices under the Orders in Council bore most heavily upon American shipping. As British pressure grew, the United States could fall back on only one countermeasure short of war, an embargo. Adopted in the spring of 1794, it lasted two months, long enough to demonstrate that it was as hurtful, if not more so, to French and American interests as it was to Britain and her West Indian islands. Founded upon an exaggerated belief in the importance of American trade to the British imperial economy, the embargo and its lame conclusion nonetheless brought home to the British ministry the desirability of safeguarding the source of supplies to the West Indies by reaching an amicable settlement with the United States.

Still another disruptive influence troubled Anglo-American relations toward the end of our period. It came from an increasingly numerous and well-organized party in the United States, the Jeffersonian Republicans. The origin of political parties in the United States has received exhaustive attention. In the case of the Republicans, Charles Beard has illuminated the economic ties which bound several diverse elements—southern planters, westerners, city "mechanics," and artisans—into a common organization. Led by speculative and visionary men such as Jefferson and Madison, they were the "have-nots" and the debtors.

As important in their own right as the other groups are, it is the southern element which has a senior claim on our attention. Possessing already a secure place in the existing political structure, southern planters, large and small, were the active agents in the creation of the new party. What were their motives? Why did they make common cause with those so unlike themselves in social and cultural background? Were they consciously seeking to create a political democracy? Were they striving to realize the noble ideals of their own and of the French Revolution? The motive forces which drive men to action operate on many levels, the two extremes being idealism and material interest. To analyze these forces scientifically, the historian requires the insight and the technique of the psychologist; and even then, the result is likely to demonstrate that more often than not man is moved by a jumble of overlapping desires, some vague, some well defined, all difficult to classify ultimately. It is not my intention to assert that in the case of the southern planters the force of revolutionary idealism was negligible. I do assert, however, that it walked hand in hand with material interest.

Superficially there would appear to be a paradox involved in aristocratic, slave-owning southern planters' acceptance of Jeffersonian Republicanism and the egalitarian doctrines of the French Revolution. If the paradox is not to be resolved on the grounds of purest idealism and selfless devotion to liberal principles, we may well look to more mundane considerations. Did the southern planters have a material interest in joining together in a political party? Charles Beard has demonstrated the affirmative. Had they a common material interest in espousing a pro-French policy after the outbreak of the Franco-British War? To put this question in another (and simpler) way, had they a common material interest in pursuing an anti-English policy?

At this point, the historian is faced with another problem. In mode of living, the planters had for generations copied the pattern afforded by the English country gentry. Many of them referred nostalgically to Britain as "home," and sent their children there to be educated. Plantation economy depended on British markets and credit. Until the American Revolution, Britain had prized the southern colonies over the northern because they fitted more neatly into a mercantilistic scheme of empire. After the Peace of 1783, it was widely assumed both in Britain and in America that the southern planters would favor re-establishing the old order as quickly as possible. Britons and New England Yankees agreed, for instance, that Southerners would fight to the end to prevent passage of an American Navigation Act as a counter to the British system. Most Southerners held that to exclude British shipping from American ports or to hamper their entry by effective discriminations would be to put southern exporters of agricultural produce at the mercy of greedy Yankee shipowners. How is it, then, that the new constitutional government was scarcely functioning before Southerners in Congress began to push for discrimination against British shipping? Why did they force through the embargo in 1794? Why did they feel so deeply British depredations upon our seagoing commerce? To approach the matter from another angle, why did Federalist New England, the center of the American shipping industry, become the champion of peace and conciliation with England? Surely, British offenses bore more heavily upon the northern section of the nation than upon the southern. Would not Madison's speech in favor of discrimination have sounded better in the mouth of, say, Fisher Ames of Massachusetts?

The solution to the problem is far from simple; and it is not the purpose of this essay to explore every facet which must be comprehended in a complete answer. There is, however, a portion of it which the orthodox historians have never adequately appreciated: the intention of southern planters to avoid payment of the prewar debts owing to British creditors.

By 1790, the debts totalled £5 million sterling, including £2 millions for fourteen years' interest. Of this sum, planters in the southern states—Virginia, Maryland, North and South Carolina, and Georgia—owed about £4,190,000, with those in Virginia alone accounting for £2,300,000. (Creditors consisted of 184 trading houses located principally in London and Glasgow; and their agents constituted a well organized and indefatigable pressure group in British politics.) From 1783 on, a great majority of southern debtors caught at every straw to postpone payment of debts, and, pursuing this object, opposed any full and amicable settlement of differences between Britain and America. . . . The review of these several disruptive forces in Anglo-American relations during our period is sufficient, I think, to demonstrate that blame is fairly evenly balanced between the two nations.

To confine ourselves to a discussion of disruptive forces, however—as the orthodox school tends to do—is to avoid a consideration of some importance. It is this: from the first establishment of American independence, many men in England and in the United States thought in terms of a resurgent Anglo-American community. Political ties had been dissolved, but the similarity of cultural and political institutions and complementary economic interests remained. . . .

In England, the Earl of Shelburne stands foremost among those who looked for a new Anglo-American partnership to replace the old one shattered by the American War. His dream, which he sought to forward by the Treaty of Peace of 1783, was of a great co-operative endeavor: Americans moving to settle the vast hinterland of their continent, Britain supplying needed manufactured goods and capital. There were others, however. Not many years after the Peace, even Governor Simcoe, scarcely "pro-American," could speak of the desirability of a "Family Compact"; and George III himself was aware of the many ties of blood and culture which made Anglo-American relations unique in the intercourse among nations.

In the United States, many erstwhile revolutionaries expressed themselves in favor of "making it up" (to use Jay's phrase) with Britain and allowing war-born hatreds to subside. As the weakness of the central government under the Articles of Confederation became apparent, expressions of admiration for the stability and effectiveness of the British constitution were common, especially among the growing number of Americans desiring a reform of their own system. Many of these, including future Federalist leaders, considered themselves, their country, and the liberties for which they had fought as English —not French—derivatives, although they looked to the England of Locke and Shaftesbury, not of North and George III. The violence of the French Revolution taught them to accept even the Britain of George III as the guardian of moral, social, and political order. Concerned with the preservation of their nation and civilization from the insidious and subversive doctrines of a revolution claiming universal sway, the Federalists opened themselves to the Republican charge of "anglophilia" and "monarchomania." It is a calumny from which they suffer to this day.

The idea of an Anglo-American community had another powerful implication. Despite the American secession from the Empire, economic interest bound the two countries together. This was contrary to the expectations of many acute observers before and during the American War.

The truth is that a great deal of flapdoodle had been talked (especially by the followers of the Earl of Chatham) as the American crisis developed in the late 1760's and 1770's. The loss of American trade would follow from the loss of the colonies, it was somberly foretold; and the consequences for the Empire would be dire indeed. The "setting of the British sun" was a favorite figure of speech in these prophecies. Shelburne himself shared the gloomy sentiments; and they doubtless played an important part in his formulation of the liberal peace terms which he hoped would serve as the first step toward a new Anglo-American partnership.

There were at least three reasons why the collapse of the first British Empire did not mean economic calamity for Britain. First, wartime trade between Britain and the rebellious colonies diminished, changed channel, but never ceased. Smuggling and illicit trade, especially in the West Indies, were very common even at the height of hostilities. Secondly, the losses which did occur in the American market were quickly covered and gains registered in an expansion of European and East Indian markets. Thirdly, in an astonishingly short time after the restoration of peace, British merchants and shippers resumed their dominant position in America's foreign trade. Britain, in the first full flush of the Industrial Revolution, could outproduce and undersell any manufacturing rival. Americans, long accustomed to British goods, lacking sufficient shipping, credit, and capital of their own, were generally willing and eager to re-establish the old patterns of Anglo-American trade. By 1788, the postwar glut of the American market (and resultant financial distress to importing merchants) had given way to more stable trading practices. In that year, according to Phineas Bond, the British consul at Philadelphia, total imports of American produce into Great Britain amounted to slightly more than £1 million sterling. British exports to the United States, on the other hand, came well over £2 millions. These figures gain significance when it is remembered that the United States was now excluded from the British West Indian carrying trade, and that British imports into the United States were for domestic consumption, not for re-exportation to the islands. The considerable imbalance of trade indicates the degree to which the United States was dependent on British credit and manufactures. Jefferson, whose heart on more than one occasion overruled his head, and his Republican friends called without ceasing for the substitution of France for Britain as America's major European economic correspondent. The plan was impractical and ignored reality. The year 1789, for instance, was extraordinarily favorable to Franco-American trade because of the severe crop failures in France. Yet that kingdom was able to take off only 25 per cent of America's exports, while Britain engulfed a full 50 per cent. Britain obviously remained the natural European market for American exports.

In addition to Britain's commanding position in America's foreign trade, there was a flood of British capital pouring into the country. Beginning in 1790, for example, there was a growing and significant number of Britons, both private individuals and business houses, investing funds in the public debt of the United States. (Research on this interesting topic has scarcely been begun. Even so, enough data has been accumulated to warrant the general statement that British capital was an important element in the funding of the public debt of the United States.)

The conclusion is obvious: British capital, British credit, and British manufactures were of fundamental importance to the United States. In addition, duties on British imports furnished one of the richest sources of revenue for the new American government. The logic (though not the statesmanship) of the mercantilists was correct. Politically independent the United States might be; but, economically, she remained a client of Great Britain. No other nation on earth could usurp Britain's role. Hamilton's recognition of this fact does not brand him the anglophile his enemies portrayed. Rather, his unflinching acceptance of the framework of the possible and his masterly work within it to achieve a strong, stable, respectable central government, place him in the realm of genius as *Realpolitiker*, political economist, and statesman.

Need existed on the British side, too; but until shortly before the end of our period, it was neither as pressing nor as fundamental as that of the United States. The West Indian possessions required foodstuffs, lumber, and the like, and before the American War these had been supplied by the colonies now comprising the United States. In addition, American shippers had profited greatly from the island carrying trade. As we have seen, however, with the restoration of peace, Hawkesbury and the mercantilists hoped to create anew a self-sufficient empire. To this end, they planned to cultivate the remaining North American colonies as new sources of supply for the islands. As an interim measure, it was reluctantly decided that the islands would have to be supplied from the United States; but the imperial monopoly of the island carrying trade would be secured by excluding American bottoms.

The mercantilists were too sanguine. In the decade from 1783 to 1793, even the remaining North American colonies frequently depended on supplies imported from the United States. Any chance the mercantilists might have had for eventual success was blasted by the outbreak of war with France in 1793. With the vulnerability of the British West Indies underlined by the American embargo, the younger Pitt and his foreign secretary, Lord Grenville, determined, in the face of the most vehement opposition from the mercantilists, to conciliate the United States.

The resurgence of the idea of an Anglo-American community and the recognition of an economic interdependence, both intensified by the British struggle against revolutionary France, provided the background for the Jay Treaty of 1794. The provisions of the Treaty are well known. Subsisting disputes between the two nations were settled or put in the process of arbitration by joint commission; and the United States agreed to a stricter interpretation of neutral duties. More important, however, were the several unique trading privileges extended to the United States by Great Britain. Americans were given access to Britain's East Indian trading preserves, a right withheld even from the remaining North American colonies. Further, trade restrictions between Canada and the United States were eased. The greatest concession of all, however, was permission for American vessels of seventy tons or smaller to enter British West Indian ports with cargoes of supplies from the United States, and to carry away island produce. Certain prohibitions about the re-exportation from the United States of listed West Indian articles and the limit on ship tonnage (suggested in the first instance by Hamilton) were designed to minimize American competition. Even so, the concessions to the United States were in direct contradiction to the established mercantile system. They represented something of a revolution in British imperial and economic thought. Its magnitude may be sensed in the increasingly cold correspondence between Grenville and Hawkesbury during the former's negotiations with Jay in the summer and autumn of 1794. Fighting to the end against allowing American ships into the British West Indies, Hawkesbury agreed with Jay in at least one point: both believed that Grenville's concessions to the Americans would act as a hole in the dike of mercantilistic protection and imperial exclusiveness which would one day broaden into a flood bearing down all restrictions on American trade with the Empire.

Orthodox historians point with awe at the violent reception of the treaty in the United States. Many of them, reasoning that the true voice of the nation was to be found in the popular outcry, not in the views of legally constituted government of the country, accept it as sufficient reason to condemn Jay's work out of hand.

Violence and riot are scarcely constitutional modes of political behavior, but considerations of orderly government quite aside, they are not explanations. They require explanation. Who were these violent men? Why were they violent? Were there material interests to be served in defeating the ratification of the treaty? To what degree did the "patriotic" outburst against

Jay's work cloak less worthy private objects? Such questions require more precise answers than they have received hitherto. When they are answered, it may well be then that the interpretation of the Jay Treaty will not be concerned with Jay's ineptitude and failure to win more concessions for his country. It will ask rather why, in light of American weakness and internal division, he won so much.

The treaty had been long in coming—too long perhaps. In the meantime, there developed in the United States a political party with a "built-in" hostility to Britain. Therein lies the judgment upon Hawkesbury and his mercantilist colleagues who resolutely insisted upon excluding the United States from the West Indian trade. Even so, the treaty was a momentous event in Anglo-American history. It marked British acceptance of the new power as a sovereign equal. It preserved peace at a time when war probably would have brought a dissolution of the American Union. It was a second Declaration of Independence—this time from France, whose efforts to dominate the new nation were inconsistent with American sovereignty and neutrality. The violence of the opposition—conservative in Britain, radical in the United States—subsided. The treaty was ratified. Embodying recognition of a community of interests, it was the triumph of moderation and sanity. It was the first Anglo-American rapprochement.

THE AFTERMATH OF WAR

JOHN JAY, *Letter to Peter van Schaack*

One of the most tragic consequences of the war was the savage and bitter division between Tories and patriots in America. Mistreatment of the wretched minority persisted even after the conclusion of the provisional treaty, and duly figured as a British grievance against the new Republic in the post-war years. Emigration to the northward, to the British West Indies, and to the mother country herself worked toward a solution of the problem; but, more important, was the willingness of Americans like John Jay to be reconciled to former

John Jay to Peter van Schaack, Paris, September 17, 1782, *Jay Correspondence*, Vol. II, ed. H. P. Johnston, New York, 1891, pp. 343–345.

friends who had supported Britain during the struggle. Jay's letter to his old New York friend, Peter van Schaack exudes a spirit of humanity not altogether characteristic of the American attitude immediately after the war. Within a few years, however, it was shared by a considerable number of his fellow citizens who were willing to let bygones be bygones and who looked to friendship with Britain as the natural course for their country's foreign policy.

Doctor Franklin sent me this morning your letter of 11th August last. I thank you for it. Aptitude to change in any thing never made a part of my disposition, and I hope makes no part of my character. In the course of the present troubles I have adhered to certain fixed principles, and faithfully obeyed their dictates, without regarding the consequences of such conduct to my friends, my family, or myself; all of whom, however dreadful the thought, I have ever been ready to sacrifice, if necessary, to the public objects in contest.

Believe me, my heart has nevertheless been, on more than one occasion, afflicted by the execution of what I thought and still think was my duty. I felt very sensibly for you and for others, but as society can regard only the political propriety of men's conduct, and not the moral propriety of their motives to it, I could only lament your unavoidably becoming classed with many whose morality was convenience, and whose politics changed with the aspect of public affairs. My regard for you as a good old friend continued, notwithstanding. God knows that inclination never had a share in any proceedings of mine against you; from such thorns no man could expect to gather grapes, and the only consolation that can grow in their unkindly shade is a consciousness of doing one's duty and the reflection that, as on the one hand I have uniformly preferred the public weal to my friends and connections, so on the other I have never been urged by private resentments to injure a single individual. Your judgment and consequently your conscience differed from mine on a very important question; but though, as an independent American, I considered all who were not for us, and you among the rest, as against us, yet be assured that John Jay did not cease to be a friend to Peter Van Schaack. No one can serve two masters. Either Britain was right and America wrong, or America was right and Britain wrong. They who thought Britain right were bound to support her, and America had a just claim to the services of those who approved her cause. Hence it became our duty to take one side or the other, and no man is to be blamed for preferring the one which his reason recommended as the most just and virtuous.

Several of our countrymen indeed left and took arms against us, not from any such principles, but from the most dishonourable of human motives. Their conduct has been of a piece with their inducements, for they have far outstripped savages in perfidy and cruelty. Against these men every American must set his face and steel his heart. There are others of them, though not many, who, I believe, opposed us because they thought they could not conscientiously go with us. To such of them as have behaved with humanity I wish every species of prosperity that may consist with the good of my country.

You see how naturally I slide into the habit of writing as freely as I used to speak to you. Ah! my friend, if ever I see New York again, I expect to meet with "the shade of many a departed joy"; my heart bleeds to think of it. Where and how are your children? Whenever, as a private friend, it may be in my power to do good to either, tell me; while I have a loaf, you and they may freely partake of it. Don't let this idea hurt you. If your circumstances are easy, I rejoice; if not, let me take off some of their rougher edges. . . .

JOHN ADAMS, *Letter to Secretary Jay*

In the spring of 1785, John Adams was appointed Minister Plenipotentiary to London, his nation's first accredited diplomatic representative to the former mother country. At the same time, Thomas Jefferson was appointed to Paris. The first object of Adams' mission was to secure British surrender of the several posts still occupied in the old Northwest. There were two objects of scarcely secondary importance. The first was to secure compensation for negro slaves alleged to have been abducted by the British in the evacuation of the thirteen states at the end of the war. The second was to negotiate a treaty of amity and commerce with Britain. The American minister soon found that these objects were inextricably bound up with British complaints against the Americans for their own breaches of the peace treaty.

Had Adams' blunt and manly advice been taken, it is possible that the Gordian knot would have been cut; or, at least, the embittering and frustrating trouble over "prior infraction" of the peace would have been avoided. At the bottom, however, was the inability of the Confederation Congress to compel the states to see justice done to British creditors. Adams quite clearly understood that as long as this remained the case,—and it did, as long as the Confederation lasted—there would be no fundamental settlement with Britain.

I have not presented a formal memorial, in the name of our sovereign, concerning the negroes carried off contrary to the treaty, although it has been frequently and constantly insisted upon with the British ministry, for several reasons.

John Adams to Secretary Jay, London, May 25, 1786, Adams, *Works*, Vol. VIII, pp. 394–396.

One was, a desire to confine the first memorial to one point, the frontier posts, that the real motives and intentions of the cabinet might be the more distinctly laid open to congress. Another reason was, the frankness of ministers to own, in conversation, that the negroes must be paid for, as a clear point. Another was, that time might be allowed to you, sir, to transmit me the whole amount and evidence of the claim. And lastly, that I might have the explicit instructions of congress to demand payment for the negroes in money, and especially at what prices they should be stated.

By the answer of Lord Carmarthen to the memorial of the 30th of November, congress will see that the detention of the posts is attempted to be justified by the laws of certain States impeding the course of law for the recovery of old debts, &c. Were another memorial to be now presented relative to the negroes, the same answer would undoubtedly be given, or, more probably, a reference only to that answer. It is my duty to be explicit with my country, and, therefore I hope it will not be taken amiss by any of my fellow citizens, when they are told that it is in vain to expect the evacuation of posts, or payment for the negroes, a treaty of commerce, or restoration of prizes, payment of the Maryland or Rhode Island demand, compensation to the Boston merchants, or any other relief of any kind, until these laws are all repealed. Nor will the ministry ever agree to any explanation concerning the interest during the war, or payments by installments. The old creditors have formed themselves into a society and have frequent meetings, send committees to Mr. Pitt and Lord Carmarthen, and, I am well informed, oppose even a treaty of commerce, upon this ground; and the ministers know them to be so numerous that they could raise a clamor, a consideration which has always had more weight at this Court and in parliament than the interest of America or the British empire.

What, then, is to be done? The States, it may be said, will not repeal their laws. If they do not, then let them give up all expectation from this Court and country, unless you can force them to do as you please by investing congress with full power to regulate trade.

. . . My advice . . . if it is not impertinent to give it, is, that every law of every State which concerns either debts or royalists, which can be impartially construed contrary to the spirit of the treaty of peace, be immediately repealed, and the debtors left to settle with their creditors, or dispute the point of interest at law. I do not believe a jury would give the interest. I beg leave to suggest another thing; if congress are themselves clear that interest during the war was not part of that *bonâ fide* debt which was intended by the contracting parties, they may declare so by a resolution, or the legislatures of the separate States may declare so, and then the courts of justice and the juries will certainly give no interest during the war; but, even in this case, those States which have few debts, and have made no laws against the recovery of them, will think it hard that they should be subjected to dangers by the conduct of such as have many, and have made laws inconsistent with the treaty, both respecting debts and tories. You will give me leave, sir, to suggest another idea; suppose the States should venture to do themselves justice; for example, suppose Maryland should undertake to pay herself for her bank stock and negroes carried off after the treaty, by accepting security for it from her own citizens, who are debtors to British subjects, and giving discharges to those debtors, or engaging to stand between them and the claims of the creditor; suppose the Carolinas, Virginia, and all the other States which had negroes carried off after the peace, should do the same; suppose Massachusetts should make up the losses of the inhabitants of Boston in goods carried off by General Howe, in the same way, at least those of them who were promised compensation by General Howe, for these are undoubtedly creditors of the British government; suppose, further, that each State should undertake, in the same way, to compensate the owners of vessels taken after the commencement of the armistice.

I throw out these hints as possibilities and speculations only, sensible that they might open a door to much altercation; but I will not fail to add, that I think it would be much sounder policy and nobler spirit to repeal at once every law of every State which is in the smallest degree inconsistent with the treaty respecting either debts or tories, and am well persuaded that no inconvenience would be felt from it; neither law suits, nor bankruptcies, nor imprisonments, would be increased by it; on the contrary, the credit and commerce of all the States would be so increased, that the debtors themselves, in general, would find their burthens lighter. . . .

FOREIGN POLICY AND DOMESTIC POLITICS

In 1790, Spain and England very nearly went to war over the Nootka incident. For a time it appeared altogether likely that Britain would mount a blow at Spanish forces along the Mississippi. In such an event, British forces descending from Canada would have to traverse American territory. In September 1790, therefore, President Washington asked his cabinet what his response should be to any British request for permission to march to the Mississippi. The answers from Jefferson and Hamilton are printed below.

Jefferson's brief opinion is redolent of suspicion against Britain and of readiness to go to war to prevent Louisiana and the Floridas from being taken by the British. Hamilton's response is a superb example of political logic and states powerfully the reasons against going to war. An Anglo-Spanish war would in all likelihood directly involve France, bound to Spain by close alliance. Thus the probability arose of American involvement because of the Treaty of 1778. By extension, then, Washington's question touched upon Franco-American relations. Inevitably, the matter became deeply embedded in domestic politics—Hamilton and the Federalists seeing in friendship with Britain the true welfare of their own country; Jefferson and his "Republican" friends looking to France as the natural ally against a malevolent and revenge-seeking Britain.

THOMAS JEFFERSON, Cabinet Paper

I am so deeply impressed with the magnitude of the dangers which will attend our government if Louisiana and the Floridas be added to the British empire, that in my opinion we ought to make ourselves parties in the general war expected to take place, should this be the only means of preventing the calamity.

But I think we should defer this step as long as possible; because war is full of chances which may relieve us from the necessity of interfering; and if necessary, still the later we interfere the better we shall be prepared.

It is often indeed more easy to prevent the capture of a place, than to retake it. Should it be so, in the case in question, the difference between the two operations of preventing, and retaking, will not be so costly, as two, three or four years more of war.

So that I am for preserving neutrality as long, and entering into the war as late, as possible.

If this be the best course, it decides, in a good degree, which should be our conduct, if the British ask leave to march troops thro' our territory, or march them without leave.

It is well enough agreed, in the Law of Nations, that for a Neutral power to give or refuse permission to the troops of either belligerent party to pass through their territory, is no breach of neutrality, provided the same refusal or permission be extended to the other party.

If we give leave of passage then to the British troops, Spain will have no just cause of complaint against us, provided we extend the same leave to her when demanded.

Thomas Jefferson, Cabinet Paper, August 28, 1790, Papers of Thomas Jefferson, Vol. XVII, ed. J. P. Boyd, Princeton, N. J., Princeton Univ. Press, 1950, pp. 129–130.

If we refuse (as indeed we have a right to do) and the troops should pass notwithstanding, of which there can be little doubt, we shall stand committed. For either we must enter immediately into the war, or pocket an acknowledged insult in the face of the world: and one insult pocketed soon produces another.

There is indeed a middle course, which I should be inclined to prefer. That is, to avoid giving any answer. They will proceed notwithstanding. But to do this under our silence, will admit of palliation, and produce apologies, from military necessity; and will leave us free to pass it over without dishonor, or to make it a handle of quarrel hereafter, if we should have use for it as such. —But if we are obliged to give an answer, I think the occasion not such as should induce us to hazard that answer which might commit us to the war at so early a stage of it; and therefore that the passage should be permitted.

If they should pass without having asked leave, I should be for expressing our dissatisfaction to the British court, and keeping alive an altercation on the subject, till events should decide whether it is most expedient to accept their apologies, or profit of the aggression as a cause of war.

ALEXANDER HAMILTON, *Cabinet Paper*

. . . It does not admit of a moment's doubt, as a general rule, that a neutral state, unfettered by any stipulation, is not bound to expose itself to a war, merely to shelter a neighbor from the approaches of its enemy. It remains to examine, if there are any circumstances, in our particular case, capable of forming an exception to that rule.

It is not to be forgotten that we received from France, in our late revolution, essential succor, and from Spain valuable countenance and some direct aid. It is also to be remembered that France is the intimate ally of Spain, and there subsists a connection by treaty between the former power and the United States.

It might thence be alleged that obligations of gratitude towards those powers require that we should run some risk, rather than concur in a thing prejudicial to either of them, and particularly in favor of that very nation against which they assisted us. And the natural impulse of every good heart will second the proposition, till reason has taught it that refinements of this kind are to be indulged with caution in the affairs of nations. . . .

It is necessary . . . to reflect, however painful the reflection, that gratitude is a duty, a sentiment, which between nations can rarely have any solid foun-

Alexander Hamilton, Cabinet Paper, September 15, 1790, Hamilton, *Works*, Vol. IV, ed. H. C. Lodge, New York, 1904, pp. 313–342.

dation. Gratitude is only due to a kindness or service, the predominant object of which is the interest or benefit of the party to whom it is performed. Where the interest or benefit of the party performing is the predominant cause of it, however there may result a debt, in cases in which there is not an immediate adequate and reciprocal advantage, there can be no room for the sentiment of gratitude. Where there is such an advantage, there is then not even a debt. If the motive of the act, instead of being the benefit of the party to whom it was done, should be a compound of the interest of the party doing it and of detriment to some other, of whom he is the enemy and the rival, there is still less room for so noble and refined a sentiment. This analysis will serve as a test of our true situation in regard both to France and Spain.

It is not to be doubted, that the part which the courts of France and Spain took in our quarrel with Great Britain, is to be attributed, not to an attachment to our independence or liberty, but to a desire of diminishing the power of Great Britain by severing the British Empire. . . . This has been accomplished; the advantages of it are mutual; and so far the account is balanced.

In the progress of the war* they lent us money, as necessary to its success, and during our inability to pay they have forborne to press us for it. The money we ought to exert ourselves to pay with interest, and as well for the loan of it, as for the forbearance to urge the repayment of the sums which have become due, we ought always to be ready to make proportionate acknowledgments, and when opportunities shall offer, returns answerable to the nature of the service.

Let it be added to this, that the conduct of France in the manner of affording her aid, bore the marks of a liberal policy. She did not endeavor to extort from us, as the price of it, any disadvantageous or humiliating concessions. In this respect, however, she may have been influenced by an enlightened view of her own interest. She entitled herself to our esteem and good-will. These dispositions towards her ought to be cherished and cultivated; but they are very distinct from a spirit of romantic gratitude, calling for sacrifices of our substantial interests, preferences inconsistent with sound policy, or complaisances incompatible with our safety.

The conduct of Spain towards us presents a picture far less favorable. The direct aid we received from her during the war was inconsiderable in itself, and still more inconsiderable compared with her faculty of aiding us. She refrained from acknowledging our independence; has never acceded to the treaty of commerce made with France,—though a right of doing it was reserved to her,—nor made any other treaty with us; she has maintained possessions within our acknowledged limits without our consent; she perseveringly obstructs our sharing in the navigation of the Mississippi, though it is a privi-

---

* France has made us one loan since the peace.

lege essential to us, and to which we consider ourselves as having an indisputable title. And perhaps it might be added upon good ground, that she has not scrupled to intrigue with leading individuals in the western country, to seduce them from our interests, and to attach them to her own.

Spain therefore must be regarded, upon the whole, as having slender claims to peculiar good-will from us. There is certainly nothing that authorizes her to expect we should expose ourselves to any extraordinary jeopardy for her sake. And to conceive that any considerations relative to France ought to be extended to her, would be to set up a doctrine altogether new in politics. The ally of our ally has no claim, as such, to our friendship. We may have substantial grounds of dissatisfaction against him, and act in consequence of them, even to open hostility, without derogating in any degree from what we owe to our ally.

This is so true, that if a war should really ensue between Great Britain and Spain, and if the latter should persist in excluding us from the Mississippi (taking it for granted our claim to share in its navigation is well founded), there can be no reasonable ground of doubt that we should be at liberty, if we thought it our interest, consistently with our present engagements with France, to join Britain against Spain.

How far it might be expedient to place ourselves in a situation which, in case France should eventually become a party in the war, might entangle us in opposite duties on the score of the stipulated guaranty of her West India possessions, or might have a tendency to embroil us with her, would be a mere question of prudential and liberal calculation, which would have nothing to do with the right of taking side against Spain.

These are truths necessary to be contemplated with freedom, because it is impossible to foresee what events may spring up, or whither our interests may point; and it is very important to distinguish with accuracy how far we are bound, and where we are free. . . .

The conclusion from what has been said is, that there is a right either to refuse or consent, as shall be judged for the interest of the United States; though the right to consent is less questionable than the right to refuse.

The consequences to be expected from refusal or consent present themselves next to consideration. Those of consent shall be first examined.

An increase of the means of annoying us in the same hands is a certain ill consequence of the acquisition of the Floridas and Louisiana by the British. This will result not only from contiguity to a greater part of our territory, but from the increased facility of acquiring an undivided influence over all the Indian tribes inhabiting within the borders of the United States.

Additional danger of the dismemberment of the western country is another ill consequence to be apprehended from that acquisition. This will arise as well from the greater power of annoying us, as from the different policy which it is likely would be pursued by that nation, if in possession of the key to the only outlet for the productions of that country. Instead of shutting, they would probably open, the door to its inhabitants, and by conciliating their good-will on the one hand, and making them sensible, on the other, of their dependence on them for the continuance of so essential an advantage, they might hold out to them the most powerful temptation to a desertion of their connection with the rest of the United States. The avarice and ambition of individuals may be made to co-operate in favor of those views.

A third ill consequence of that acquisition would be, material injury, in time to come, to the commerce of the Atlantic States. By rendering New Orleans the emporium of the products of the western country, Britain would, at a period not very distant, have little occasion for supplies of provisions for their islands from the Atlantic States; and for their European market they would derive from the same source copious supplies of tobacco and other articles now furnished by the Southern States: whence a great diminution of the motives to establish liberal terms of commercial intercourse with the United States collectively.

These consequences are all expressed or implied in the form of the question stated by the President. And as far as our consent can be supposed likely to have influence upon the event, they constitute powerful objections to giving it.

. . . The point of prudence is, to make choice of that course which threatens the fewest or the least, or sometimes the least certain. The consequences of refusal are therefore to be weighed against those of consent.

It seems to be a matter taken for granted by the writers upon the subject, that a refusal ought to be accompanied with a resolution to support it, if necessary, by the sword; or, in other words, to oppose the passage, if attempted to be forced, or to resent the injury, if circumstances should not permit an effectual opposition. This, indeed, is implied in the nature of the thing; for to what purpose refuse, unless it be intended to make good the refusal? or how avoid disgrace, if our territories are suffered to be violated with impunity, after a formal and deliberate prohibition of passage?

There are cases in which a nation may, without ignominy, wink at an infraction of its rights; but this does not appear to be one of them. After having been asked its permission and having refused it, the presumption will be that it has estimated the consequences, calculated its means, and is prepared to assert and uphold its rights. If the contrary of this should turn out to be its conduct, it must bring itself into contempt for inviting insult which it was unable to repel, and manifesting ill-will towards a power which it durst not resist. As, on the one hand, there cannot be conceived to be a greater outrage than to pass through our country, in defiance of our *declared* disapprobation; so, on the other, there cannot be a greater humiliation than to submit to it.

The consequence therefore of refusal, if not effectual, must be absolute disgrace or immediate war. This *appears*, at least, to be the alternative.

Whether a refusal would have the desired effect, is, at best, problematical. The presumption, perhaps, is, that Great Britain will have adverted to the possibility of it; and if, under the uncertainty of what would be our conduct, she should still have resolved on prosecuting the enterprise through our territory, that she will at the same time have resolved either to ask no questions, or to disregard our dissent. It is not unlikely that the reasoning of the British cabinet will have been to this effect: If the United States have no predilection for Spain, or if their views of their own interest are not opposed to the acquisition we meditate, they will not withhold their consent; if either the one or the other be the case, it ought to be determined beforehand, whether their enmity be a greater evil, than the projected acquisition a good; and if we do not choose to renounce the one, we must be prepared to meet the other.

A further ill consequence of the refusal, if ineffectual, not *wholly* destitute of weight, is this, that Great Britain would then think herself under less obligation to keep measures with us, and would feel herself more at liberty to employ every engine in her power to make her acquisition as prejudicial to us as possible; whereas, if no impediment should be thrown in the way by us, more good humor may beget greater moderation, and, in the progress of things, concessions securing us may be made, as the price of our future neutrality. An explicit recognition of our right to navigate the Mississippi to and from the ocean, with the possession of New Orleans, would greatly mitigate the causes of apprehension from the conquest of the Floridas by the British.

The consequences of refusal or consent constitute leading motives to the one or to the other; which now claim a more particular discussion.

It has been seen that the ill effects to be apprehended from the conquest of the Spanish territories in our neighborhood are: an increase of the means whereby we may be hereafter annoyed, and of the danger of the separation of the western country from the rest of the Union; and a future interference with the trade of the Atlantic States, in a manner, too, not conducive to the general weal.

As far as there is a prospect that a refusal would be an impediment to the enterprise, the considerations which have been mentioned afford the strongest inducements to it. But if *that* effect of it be doubtful, the force of these inducements is proportionably diminished; if improbable, it nearly ceases. The prospect in this case would be, that a refusal would aggravate instead of preventing the evil it was intended to obviate. And it must be acknowledged that the success of it is, at least, *very doubtful*.

The consideration that our assent may be construed into want of foresight or want of vigor, though not to be disregarded, would not be sufficient to justify our risking a war in our present situation. The cogent reasons we have to avoid a war are too obvious and intelligible, not to furnish an explanation of and an apology for our conduct in this respect. . . .

Now, it is manifest, that a government scarcely ever had stronger motives to avoid war, than that of the United States at the present juncture. They have much to dread from war; much to expect from peace; something to hope from negotiation, in case of a rupture between Britain and Spain.

We are but just recovering from the effects of a long, arduous, and exhausting war. The people but just begin to realize the sweets of repose. We are vulnerable both by water and land; without either fleet or army. We have a considerable debt in proportion to the resources which the state of things permits the government to command. Measures have been recently entered upon for the restoration of credit, which a war could hardly fail to disconcert, and which, if disturbed, would be fatal to the means of prosecuting it. Our national government is in its infancy. The habits and dispositions of our people are ill-suited to those liberal contributions to the treasury which a war would necessarily exact. There are causes which render war in this country more expensive, and consequently more difficult to be carried on, than in any other. There is a general disinclination to it in all classes. The theories of the speculative, and the feelings of all, are opposed to it. The support of public opinion (perhaps more essential to our government than to any other) could only be looked for in a war evidently resulting from necessity.

These are general reasons against going into war. There are others, of a more particular kind. To the people at large the quarrel would be apt to have the appearance of having originated in a desire of shielding Spain from the arms of Britain. There are several classes of men to whom this idea would not be agreeable, especially if the Dutch were understood to be in conjunction with the British. All those who were not friendly to our late revolution would certainly dislike it. Most of the descendants of the Dutch would be unfriendly to it. And let it not be overlooked, that there is still a considerable proportion of those who were firm friends to the revolution, who retain prepossessions in favor of Englishmen, and prejudices against Spaniards.

In a popular government especially, however prejudices like these may be regretted, they are not to be excluded from political calculations.

It ought also to be taken into the account, that by placing ourselves at this time in a situation to go to war against Great Britain, we embark with the weakest party—with a total uncertainty what accession of strength may be gained—and without making any terms with regard either to succor, indemnity, or compensation.

France is the only weight which can be thrown into the scale, capable of producing an equilibrium. But her accession, however probable, ought not to be deemed absolutely certain. The predominant party there may choose to avoid war as dangerous to their own power. And if even obstacles should not arise from that quarter, it cannot be foreseen to what extent France will be in condition to make efforts. The great body of malcontents, comprehending a large proportion of the most wealthy and formerly the most influential class— the prodigious innovations which have been made—the general and excessive fermentation which has been excited in the minds of the people—the character of the prince, or the nature of the government likely to be instituted, as far as can be judged prior to an experiment—do not prognosticate much order or vigor in the affairs of that country for a considerable period to come.

It is possible, indeed, that the enthusiasm which the transition from slavery to liberty may inspire, may be a substitute for the energy of a good administration, and the spring of great exertions. But the ebullitions of enthusiasm must ever be a precarious reliance. And it is quite as possible that the greatness, and perhaps immaturity, of that transition, may prolong licentiousness and disorder. Calculations of what may happen in France must be unusually fallible, not merely from the yet unsettled state of things in that kingdom, but from the extreme violence of the change which has been wrought in the situation of the people.

These considerations are additional admonitions to avoid, as far as possible, any step that may embroil us with Great Britain. It seems evidently our true policy to cultivate neutrality. This, at least, is the ground on which we ought to stand, until we can see more of the scene, and can have secured the means of changing it with advantage.

We have objects which, in such a conjuncture, are not to be neglected. The western posts, on one side, and the navigation of the Mississippi, on the other, call for a vigilant attention to what is going on. They are both of importance. The securing of the latter may be regarded in its consequences as essential to the unity of the empire.

But it is not impossible, if war takes place, that by a judicious attention to favorable moments, we may accomplish both by negotiation. The moment, however, we became committed on either side, the advantages of our position for negotiation would be gone. They would even be gone in respect to the party with whom we were in co-operation; for, being once in the war, we could not make terms as the condition of entering into it.

Though it may be uncertain how long we shall be permitted to preserve our neutrality, that is not a sufficient reason for departing from it voluntarily. It is possible we may be permitted to persist in it throughout. And if we must renounce it, it is better it should be from necessity than choice; at least till we see a prospect of renouncing with safety and profit. If the government is forced into a war, the cheerful support of the people may be counted upon. If it brings it upon itself, it will have to struggle with their displeasure and reluctance. This difference alone is immense.

The desire of manifesting amity to Spain, from the supposition that our permanent interest is concerned in cementing an intimate connection with France and Spain, ought to have no influence in the case. Admitting the existence of such an interest, it ought not to hurry us into premature hazards. If it should finally induce us to become a party, it will be time enough when France has become such, and after we shall have adjusted the condition upon which we are to engage.

But the reality of such an interest is a thing about which the best and the ablest men of this country are far from being agreed. There are of this number, who, if the United States were at perfect liberty, would prefer an intimate connection between them and Great Britain as most conducive to their security and advantage; and who are of opinion that it will be well to cultivate friendship between that country and this, to the utmost extent which is reconcilable with the faith of existing engagements; while the most general opinion is, that it is our true policy to steer as clear as possible of all foreign connection, other than commercial and in this respect to cultivate intercourse with all the world on the broadest basis of reciprocal privilege.

An attentive consideration of the vicissitudes which have attended the friendships of nations, except in a very few instances, from very peculiar circumstances, gives little countenance to systems which proceed on the supposition of a permanent interest to prefer a particular connection. The position of the United States, detached as they are from Europe, admonishes them to unusual circumspection on that point. The same position, as far as it has relation to the possessions of European Powers in their vicinity, strengthens the admonition.

Let it be supposed that Spain retains her possessions on our right, and persists in the policy she has hitherto pursued, without the slightest symptom of relaxation, of barring the Mississippi against us; where must this end, and at a period not very distant? Infallibly in a war with Spain, or separation of the western country. This country must have an outlet for its commodities. This is essential to its prosperity, and if not procured to it by the United States, must be had at the expense of the connection with them. A war with Spain, when our affairs will have acquired greater consistency and order, will certainly be to be preferred to such an alternative. In an event of this sort, we should naturally seek aid from Great Britain. This would probably involve France on the opposite side, and effect a revolution in the state of our foreign politics.

In regard to the possessions of Great Britain on our left, it is at least problematical whether the acquisition of them will ever be desirable to the United States. It is certain that they are in no shape essential to our prosperity. Except, therefore, the detention of our western posts (an object, too, of far less consequence than the navigation of the Mississippi), there appears no necessary source of future collision with that power.

This view of the subject manifests that we may have a more urgent interest to differ with Spain than with Britain; and that conclusion will become the stronger if it be admitted that when we are able to make good our pretensions, we ought not to leave in the possession of any foreign power the *territories* at the mouth of the Mississippi, which are to be regarded as the key to it. . . .

If the immediate cause of the impending war between Britain and Spain be considered, there cannot be drawn from thence any inducements for our favoring Spain. . . .

Putting, therefore, all considerations of peculiar good-will to Spain or of predilection to any particular connection out of the question, the argument respecting refusal or consent in the case supposed seems to stand thus:

The acquisition of the Spanish territories bordering upon the United States, by Britain, would be dangerous to us. And if there were a good prospect that our refusal would prevent it, without exposing us to a greater evil, we ought to refuse; but if there be a considerable probability that our refusal would be ineffectual, and if being so it would involve us in war or disgrace, and if positive disgrace is worse than war, and war in our present situation worse than the chances of the evils which may befall us from that acquisition, then the conclusion would be that we ought not to refuse. And this appears to be the true conclusion to be drawn from a comprehensive and accurate view of the subject, though first impressions are on the other side.

These reflections also may be allowed to come in aid of it. Good or evil is seldom as great in the reality as in the prospect. The mischiefs we apprehend may not take place. The enterprise, notwithstanding our consent, may fail. The acquisition, if made, may, in the progress of things, be wrested from its possessors. These if pressed hereafter (and we are willing to accept it), may deem it expedient to purchase our neutrality by a cession to us of that part of the territory in question which borders on the Mississippi, accompanied with a guaranty of the navigation of that river. If nothing of this sort should happen, still the war will necessarily have added millions to the debt of Britain, while we shall be recruiting and increasing our resources and our strength. In such a situation she will have motives of no inconsiderable force for not provoking our resentment. And a reasonable confidence ought to be reposed in the fidelity of the inhabitants of the western country in their attachment to the Union, in their real interest to remain a part of it, and in their sense of danger from the attempt to separate, which, *at every hazard*, ought to be resisted by the United States.

It is also to be kept in view that the *same* danger, if not to the *same* extent, will exist, should the territories in question *remain in the hands of Spain*. . . .

The true alternative seems to be to refuse or consent; and, if the first be preferred, to accompany it with an intimation, in terms as free from offence as possible, that dispositions will be made to oppose the passage, if attempted to be forced; and accordingly, as far as practicable, to make and execute such dispositions.

If, on the contrary, consent should be given, it may deserve consideration whether it would not be expedient to accompany it with a candid intimation that the expedition is not agreeable to us, but that thinking it expedient to avoid an occasion of controversy, it has been concluded not to withhold assent. There are, however, objections to this mode. In case of consent, an early and frank *explanation should be given to Spain.* . . .

BRITAIN AND THE POST-WAR PROBLEMS

LORD GRENVILLE, Letter to George Hammond

In 1791, the British ministry dispatched George Hammond to Philadelphia as Minister Plenipotentiary. The instructions given to him indicate the wide range of problems still besetting Anglo-American relations. The delays in extinguishing post-war differences were becoming dangerous: debts and loyalists, and posts and slaves, were caught up in a tangled skein while new issues—the Indian war in the old Northwest, and the attempts of American settlers to take land still occupied by the British—added further complications.

Whitehall, September 2, 1791

In addition to the general Instructions which you will receive, it is necessary that I should signify to you His Majesty's Pleasure relative to the principal points which are likely to come into Discussion upon your arrival in America. You are already apprized of the points in which the Treaty of Peace has not been carried into execution by the respective Parties and the measure adopted by His Majesty of retaining in His hands the Forts to the Southwards of the Lakes cannot certainly be considered as affording even an adequate Compensation for the Losses which this Country has sustained in consequence of the Injustice done to the Loyalists since the year 1783, and of the Obstacles which

Lord Grenville to George Hammond, September 1–2, 1791, and March 17, 1792, *Instructions to the British Ministers to the United States,* ed. Bernard Mayo, Washington, D. C., 1941, pp. 13–19; 25–27.

have been thrown in the way of the recovery of the Debts due to the British Merchants. Whatever Disposition may now prevail in America for removing these and other causes of complaint, it cannot be contended that the American[s] can thereby acquire a right to claim the execution of that Article of the Treaty, by which the Forts were to be ceded to them; both because it cannot be competent to one of the Parties to an Engagement to withhold for any indefinite time the performance of the Stipulations to which it has bound itself, and afterwards, at any moment which may suit its own convenience, to perform those Stipulations and to claim a reciprocal execution of the Treaty; and also because in the present case, it is evident, that no measures that can now be taken can replace the Loyalists and British Creditors in that Situation to which they were entitled by the Articles of the Treaty of Peace. During the interval which has elapsed, many written Evidences must have been destroyed, or lost, many Witnesses must be dead, and many Families dispersed so as to be no longer able to claim that situation to which they were entitled under the Treaty. And in consequence of the nonperformance of those Engagements, Individuals have suffered great and irreparable Losses, and this Country has been subjected to a heavy Expence. On these grounds therefore His Majesty would be fully justified in forming a resolution of maintaining those Posts, and in refusing to enter into any Negotiation upon the Subject: But His sincere desire to remove every occasion of misunderstanding which may arise, has induced Him to direct that you should express His readiness to enter into Negotiation on the Subject, and to consent to such Arrangements as may be found to be of mutual convenience, and not inconsistent with the just claims and Rights of His Subjects. In all your conversations upon the Subject, you will be careful to let it be clearly understood, that it must be an essential and sine quâ non condition of any such Arrangement that every practicable Measure should be adopted by the States for the execution of the Fourth, Fifth, and Sixth Articles of the Treaty of Peace as far as the circumstances of the length of time which has elapsed, render it possible that effect should now be given to those Stipulations. You are to consider this as the first and leading Object of your Mission, and immediately on your arrival in America you are to procure and to transmit to me as accurate a Statement as possible of the Measures which have hitherto been adopted for that purpose since the establishment of the federal Government, and of the points in which such measures are still defective or ineffectual, in order to meet the several cases of complaint, of which you are already informed, or which may come to your knowledge in America. And you will lose no time in stating these Particulars to those with whom you may treat in America, and to the Persons of distinction and weight in the American Government, in order to learn how far they are disposed and by what means, to supply such deficiencies as may still be found to exist. I am not without hopes, from the circumstances of the late Communications which have passed on this Subject, that there exists among those who have the greatest Influence in the Government of America, a real disposition to meet the just Expectations of this Country in that respect. And if you should find this Opinion confirmed by the nature of the Conversations which you will hold with these Persons on your arrival in America, you may assure them of His Majesty's disposition to contribute on His part towards removing the Grounds of future difficulties by some practicable and reasonable Arrangement on the Subject of the Posts. I am unable at the present moment to furnish you with precise Instructions with respect to the nature of such an Arrangement, or to the Ideas which you might throw out for that purpose in the course of the Negotiation, because the Expectation of Lord Dorchester's arrival in England in the course of the present Autumn has occasioned His Majesty's Servants to delay for a few Weeks longer their ultimate decision on points of so much importance to the Government which has been placed under his care, and of the Interests of which he has had so long and particular knowledge. But you are to be careful to let it be understood, that this delay has not arisen from any Disinclination to enter into discussion of this Subject, and to form a satisfactory Arrangement respecting it, and in the expectation of receiving further Instructions from hence, you will express your readiness to enter immediately into the examination of all the different points which may be necessary for the full execution of the Treaty, or at least for such an Arrangement founded upon it, as the circumstances of the present moment will admit, and to receive and transmit for consideration, any reasonable Proposals which may be made to you on those Subjects. But you will represent, that it is absolutely necessary both in point of Justice and from the regard which is due in return for the friendly line of conduct now adopted by His Majesty that no steps should be taken by the American Governments to alter the relative situation of the two Countries, such as it now exists de facto, pending the Negotiation to which your Mission will give rise. And therefore, that every degree of discouragement should be given [by] those Governments as well as [by] His Majesty's officers to any Americans who may under these circumstances attempt to settle themselves within the limits of the Country now occupied by the British. Some recent Circumstances of this nature which have occurred make it particularly necessary that you should urge this point, and I am persuaded that if the American Governments are really desirous to promote a good understanding, it will not be difficult for you to convince them how repugnant it is to such an object to suffer points of so much magnitude to be brought into discussion by the Enterprises of Individuals, instead of being made the Subject of temperate and friendly negotiation between the two Governments. . . .

It will not fail to be an object of your attention to. inform yourself as accurately as possible of the relative Situation of the other Nations of Europe with respect to America, but particularly of France and Spain. If as appears probable the discussions with the latter of those Powers should lead to serious Disputes or to measures of actual Hostility, you are to be particularly careful to use no Expressions which may in any manner commit His Majesty as a Party in those differences. His Majesty's Object in such case would be to interpose his good offices for preventing those differences from leading to an actual Rupture. But if his attempts for that purpose should be ineffectual you will endeavour to maintain with both the contending Parties an uninterrupted and impartial Friendship.

Whitehall, 1st Sept: 1791

You are already informed of the discussions which took place in the last Session of the Congress relative to the American Commerce with Great Britain, and of the intention which was then held out of resuming that subject at their next meeting. This point will form a principal object of your attention, immediately on your arrival in America. You will omit no opportunity of assuring the Members of the Government there, that His Majesty is sincerely disposed not only to maintain a good correspondence and friendship with the United States, but also to promote and facilitate the commercial intercourse between the two Countries, and that he will always be ready to enter into any proper engagements for that purpose. If therefore it should be proposed to you to open a negotiation for a commercial treaty, You are to express His Majesty's readiness to enter into such a negotiation, and to consent to stipulations for the benefit of commerce and navigation, on terms of reciprocal advantage. His Majesty is willing to adopt, as the basis of such a negotiation, the placing the commerce of each country with the other reciprocally, on the terms of the most favored nation. You will observe from the Papers of which you are in possession, that there are several Articles which now pay less duties when imported into this Country from the United States than when imported from other foreign Nations. The establishment of these distinctions in favor of the commerce of the United States, and the circumstance of their having hitherto been continued by this Country, afford the strongest proof of the friendly disposition towards the American Commerce which is entertained here; But His Majesty cannot bind Himself to the continuance of this preference, except in return for stipulations of reciprocal benefit to His Subjects. The same principle of regulating the commerce according to the terms of the most favored nation may be applied to the intercourse between His Majesty's Colonies and the United States, as well as to that which they carry on with His Majesty's European dominions.

On the subject of navigation a distinction has been made by the Congress, in favor of American Shipping by tonnage duties and duties imposed on goods imported in foreign Vessels; and there is reason to believe that some of the persons concerned in the American Government entertain an intention of increasing this distinction in favor of their own navigation. The most natural and convenient principle on this subject is evidently this; that the Vessels of the two Countries respectively should be treated in their respective Ports precisely in the same manner with respect to any distinction of this nature. This principle you will urge to the utmost, and if you should not be able to prevail upon the persons with whom you treat to give effect to it by the stipulations of the treaty You will state your persuasion that measures for that purpose will be adopted by the Parliament of Great Britain, and You will let it be understood that a plan of this nature has already been formed, tho' it will be with the greatest reluctance that His Majesty's Servants will feel themselves obliged to bring it forward.

Whatever other proposals may be brought forward in the course of the negotiation, and whatever means may be suggested for giving effect to the principles above mentioned, must be taken by you ad referendum, and transmitted home for the consideration of His Majesty's Servants, [but you are on no account to conclude anything without previous and express directions from hence]. I do not think it necessary to enter into any further detail either of the arguments to be urged in support of those principles, or of the actual state of the commerce between the two Countries, as you will receive the fullest information on those points from the Report of the Committee of Trade herewith transmitted to you, and which it is hardly necessary for me to observe, is put into your hands for your own information only, and is not to be communicated to any Person in America. You will particularly advert to that part of the Report which points out the liberal and friendly conduct which has been observed by this Country towards the Americans, and contrasts it with the restrictions and disadvantages to which the British Commerce has been subjected by the Laws of Several of the States. And you will observe that even in the maintenance of the present system, Great Britain holds out advantages to America which justly entitle her to a return of reciprocal benefit. It is by no means intended that you should attempt to deny, or even to diminish in argument the advantage which this Country derives from Her commerce with America, but You will state, that this is reciprocal, [that the Commerce is highly beneficial to both Countries, and that the United States have much more to apprehend than Great Britain from any interuption or diminution of it. . . .

Whitehall, March 17th 1792

I have reserved to this Dispatch the Instructions which I have it in command from His Majesty to transmit to you on the important Subject of the Indian War.

The general Language which You have held on this Subject has been in all Respects perfectly proper, but the present Circumstances appear to be favourable for entering more directly and particularly into the Business, and for endeavouring to connect it with the Matter in Discussion between the two Countries with respect to the Frontier Posts on the Lakes, so as, if possible, to come to a satisfactory Arrangement of that long depending Business. If it should appear to you at the time of receiving this Dispatch, that the then existing circumstances continue to afford a prospect of success to such an Interposition on the Part of this Country, you are authorized to make to the American Government, in such Manner and Form as you shall judge most expedient, a Ministerial offer of the good Offices of this Country in restoring Peace between them and the Indians. The general Grounds on which it is intended that You should endeavour to negotiate such an accomodation are to be, the securing to the different Indian Nations, along the British and American Frontiers, their Lands and hunting Grounds, as an independent Country, with respect to which, both His Majesty and the United States shall withdraw all Claims or Possessions whatever, shall agree never to establish any Forts within the Boundaries to be expressed in such Agreement, and shall bind themselves to each other not to acquire or to suffer their Subjects to acquire, by purchase, or otherwise, from the Indians, any Lands or Settlements within the said Boundaries. The time and mode of bringing forward this particular Proposition, whether as part of your original Proposal, or in the course of any subsequent Discussions to which it may lead, must be left to your Discretion, guided by Circumstances on the Spot. But it should, as early as possible, be stated, as the Ground and Foundation of such Interference on our part, as no other Mode of terminating the Business seems to afford so fair a Prospect of a satisfactory Conclusion with a View to the permanent Interests of this Country, in that part of the World.

You are already sufficiently informed on this Subject, to render it unnecessary for me to enter into the Detail of the Arguments by which such a Proposition is to be supported and of the Advantages which it would afford by removing the Ground of difficult and hazardous Discussions between this Country and America, and by securing to the Indians, in the fullest Manner, the unmolested and independent Possession of those Countries which are necessary for their Existence and Support. And you will understand yourself to be distinctly authorized, supposing the course of the Negotiation should lead to such a Step, to offer, that His Majesty will abandon the Posts still occupied by His Troops to the Southward and Westward of the Lakes supposing that the Americans should consent, on their Part, to renounce all claims of theirs to those Posts, and to leave them, in common with the rest of that Country, in the undisturbed and independent Possession of the Indians. It will however be necessary that in that Case, a sufficient Time should be stipulated for the Merchants and others concerned in the Trade to withdraw their Effects from the Posts. This Time should, as far as I am yet informed, not be less than two Years, from the Conclusion of any such Agreement.

By the Vessel which carries out to you these Instructions, Mr. Dundas sends out Orders to Quebec corresponding with them, and His Majesty's Government there will be directed to instruct some Person more particularly versed in the detail of Indian Affairs to repair to Philadelphia, in order to assist you in the Progress of any Negotiation which may be opened on these Grounds and to concert with you the Steps to be taken by the Indian Department in the two Canadas, for disposing the Indians to agree to such Terms as may be proposed on the Ground above stated. Such Person will of course be able to give you distinct Information with respect to the Particulars of any boundary Line which may be proposed. The inclosed Description and Map will shew you the suggestion made on that Subject to Lord Dorchester, by a Deputation of Indians previous to his leaving Canada; this Boundary would I apprehend be sufficient to answer the purpose which this Country has principally in View. I expect however to be able shortly to send You out more particular Information on this Point, and there appears reason to imagine, that you will receive such Intelligence soon enough for your Direction and Guidance in the future Progress of any Negotiation which may be commenced on these Grounds.

You will however bear in mind that it may be a Point of mutual Convenience, that some new Arrangement should be made respecting the Frontier on Lake Champlain to which the Indian Claims are understood not to extend and that it may also be thought right to insert in any Agreement of this Nature with the United States, an Article for securing to the British Creditors, Justice and Protection in the Recovery of their Debts to the utmost Extent which may be found practicable, after the long Delay which has taken place in this respect.

THE DAMPENING OF THE EMBERS

Correspondence between Jefferson and Hammond

The negotiations between George Hammond and Secretary of State, Jefferson, were from the first marked by cold formality and mutual distrust. Jefferson's predilections for France were well known in Britain; and Hammond saw him

Correspondence between Jefferson and Hammond from November 29, 1791 to March 5, 1792, American State Papers, Vol. I, (Foreign Relations), Washington, D. C., 1832, pp. 188–198.

as a stubborn and devious antagonist bent on injuring British interests to the fullest extent. For his part, Jefferson returned dislike with dislike, viewing Hammond as the emissary of a perfidious nation who aimed to keep the Anglo-American quarrel alive and flourishing.

The clash of temperaments was complete, Hammond admitting in his dispatches to London that he much preferred communicating with Hamilton whose openness and candor he admired and trusted.

In the exchange of correspondence between Jefferson and Hammond, the game of "prior infraction" was pushed to its ultimate point. In doing this, neither Jefferson nor Hammond served his cause particularly well since the longer the differences remained outstanding the more dangerous the situation became, especially in view of the revolution which was rapidly unfolding in France.

Jefferson to Hammond, Philadelphia, November 29, 1791

In recalling your attention to the seventh article of the definitive treaty of peace between the United States of America and His Britannic Majesty, wherein it was stipulated, that "His Britannic Majesty should, with all convenient speed, and without causing any destruction, or carrying away any negroes, or other property of the American inhabitants, withdraw all his armies, garrisons, and fleets, from the said United States, and from every post, place, and harbor, within the same," I need not observe to you, that this article still remains in a state of inexecution, nor recapitulate what, on other occasions, has past on this subject. Of all this, I presume, you are fully apprized. We consider the friendly movement lately made by the court of London, in sending a minister to reside with us, as a favorable omen of its disposition to cultivate harmony and good will between the two nations, and we are perfectly persuaded, that these views will be cordially seconded by yourself, in the ministry which you are appointed to exercise between us. Permit me, then, sir, to ask, whether you are instructed to give us explanations of the intentions of your court, as to the execution of the article above quoted?

With respect to the commerce of the two countries, we have supposed that we saw, in several instances, regulations on the part of your government, which, if reciprocally adopted, would materially injure the interests of both nations.

On this subject, too, I must beg the favor of you to say, whether you are authorized to conclude, or to negotiate arrangements with us, which may fix the commerce between the two countries, on principles of reciprocal advantage?

Hammond to Jefferson, Philadelphia, November 30, 1791

I have the honor of acknowledging the receipt of your letter of yesterday. With respect to the non-execution of the seventh article of the definitive treaty of peace, between his Britannic Majesty and the United States of America, which you have recalled to my attention, it is scarcely necessary for me to remark to you, sir, that the King, my master, was induced to suspend the execution of that article, on his part, in consequence of the non-compliance, on the part of the United States, with the engagements contained in the fourth, fifth, and sixth articles of the same treaty. These two objects are, therefore, so materially connected with each other, as not to admit of separation, either in the mode of discussing them, or in any subsequent arrangements, which may result from that discussion.

In stating to you, sir, this indispensable consideration, I must, at the same time, assure you, that, in the confidence of experiencing a similar disposition in the Government of the United States, it is his Majesty's desire to remove every ground and occasion of misunderstanding which may arise between the two countries. And, in conformity to that disposition in his Majesty, I can add, that I am instructed to enter into the discussion of all such measures as may be deemed the most practicable and reasonable, for giving effect to those stipulations of the definitive treaty, the execution of which has hitherto been delayed, as well by the Government of this country as by that of Great Britain.

In answer to your question on the subject of the commerce of Great Britain, and the United States I can also inform you, sir, that the King is sincerely disposed to promote and facilitate the commercial intercourse between the two countries; and that I am authorized to communicate to this Government his Majesty's readiness to enter into a negotiation for establishing that intercourse, upon principles of reciprocal benefit. . . .

Hammond to Jefferson, Philadelphia, December 6, 1791

As I am extremely solicitous to avoid any misapprehension of my letter of the 30th ult. I have now the honor of stating to you, in explanation of that part of it to which you have adverted in yours of yesterday, that, although (as I formerly mentioned in my first conversations with you, after my arrival in this country) I am not as yet empowered to *conclude* any definitive arrangement, with respect to the commercial intercourse between the two countries, I still meant it to be understood, that I am fully authorized to enter into a negotiation, for that purpose, and into the discussion of such principles as may appear best calculated to promote that object, on a basis of reciprocal advantage.

I am farther authorized to receive any propositions which this government may be pleased to make to me upon this subject.

Jefferson to Hammond, Philadelphia, December 13, 1791

I have laid before the President of the United States, the letters of November 30th, and December 6th, with which you honored me; and in consequence thereof, and, particularly, of that part of your letter of Dec. 6, where you say that you are fully authorized to enter into a negotiation, for the purpose of arranging the commercial intercourse between the two countries, I have the honor to inform you, that I am ready to receive a communication of your full powers for that purpose, at any time you shall think proper, and to proceed immediately to their object.

Hammond to Jefferson, Philadelphia, December 14, 1791

In answer to your letter of yesterday, I can only repeat what I have before stated, in my first conversations with you after my arrival, and, subsequently, in my letter of the sixth of this month, viz: that I have no special commission, empowering me to *conclude* any *definitive* arrangement, upon the subject of the commercial intercourse between Great Britain and the United States; but that I conceive myself fully competent to enter into a negotiation with this Government, for that purpose, in the discussion of the principles which may serve as the basis, and constitute the stipulations, of any such definitive arrangement.

This opinion of my competency is founded upon my instructions, inasmuch as they are to regulate my personal conduct, and upon the conviction that the letter of credence from his Majesty, investing me with a general *plenipotentiary* character, which I had the honor of presenting to the President of the United States, and his consequent recognition of me in that character, are authorities decidedly adequate to the commencement of a preliminary negotiation.

Jefferson to Hammond, Philadelphia, December 15, 1791

I am to acknowledge the honor of your letter of November 30th, and to express the satisfaction with which we learn, that you are instructed to discuss with us the measures, which reason and practicability may dictate, for giving effect to the stipulations of our treaty, yet remaining to be executed. I can assure you, on the part of the United States, of every disposition to lessen difficulties, by passing over whatever is of smaller concern, and insisting on those matters only, which either justice to individuals or public policy render indispensable; and in order to simplify our discussions, by defining precisely their objects, I have the honor to propose that we shall begin by specifying, on each side, the particular acts which each considers to have been done by the other, in contravention of the treaty. I shall set the example.

The provisional and definitive treaties, in their 7th article, stipulated that his "Britannic Majesty should, with all convenient speed, and without causing any destruction, or *carrying away any negroes, or other property,* of the American inhabitants, *withdraw all his armies, garrisons, and fleets, from the said United States,* and from every port, place, and harbor, within the same."

But the British garrisons were not withdrawn with all convenient speed, nor have ever yet been withdrawn from Michillimackinac, on Lake Michigan; Detroit, on the strait of Lakes Erie and Huron; Fort Erie, on Lake Erie; Niagara, Oswego, on Lake Ontario; Oswegatchie, on the river St. Lawrence; Point Au-fer, and Dutchman's Point, on Lake Champlain.

2d. The British officers have undertaken to exercise a jurisdiction over the country and inhabitants in the vicinities of those forts; and

3d. They have excluded the citizens of the United States from navigating, even on our side of the middle line of the rivers and lakes established as a boundary between the two nations.

By these proceedings, we have been intercepted entirely from the commerce of furs with the Indian nations to the northward—a commerce which had ever been of great importance to the United States, not only for its intrinsic value, but as it was the means of cherishing peace with those Indians, and of super-seding the necessity of that expensive warfare we have been obliged to carry on with them, during the time that these posts have been in other hands.

On withdrawing the troops from New York, 1st. A large embarkation of negroes, of the property of the inhabitants of the United States, took place before the commissioners on our part, for inspecting and superintending embarkations, had arrived there, and without any account ever rendered thereof. 2d. Near three thousand others were publicly carried away by the avowed order of the British commanding officer, and under the view, and against the remonstrances of our commissioners. 3d. A very great number were carried off in private vessels, if not by the express permission, yet certainly without opposition on the part of the commanding officer, who alone had the means of preventing it, and without admitting the inspection of the American commissioners; and 4th. Of other species of property carried away, the commanding officer permitted no examination at all. In support of these facts, I have the honor to enclose you documents, a list of which will be sub-joined, and in addition to them, I beg leave to refer to a roll signed by the joint commissioners, and delivered to your commanding officer for transmission to his court, containing a description of the. negroes publicly carried away by his order as before mentioned, with a copy of which you have doubtless been furnished.

A difference of opinion too having arisen as to the river intended by the plenipotentiaries to be the boundary between us and the dominions of Great Britain, and by them called the St. Croix, which name, it seems, is given to two different rivers, the ascertaining of this point becomes a matter of present urgency: it has heretofore been the subject of application from us to the Government of Great Britain.

There are other smaller matters between the two nations, which remain to be adjusted, but I think it would be better to refer these for settlement through the ordinary channel of our ministers, than to embarrass the present important discussions with them: they can never be obstacles to friendship and harmony.

Permit me now, sir, to ask from you a specification of the particular acts, which, being considered by his Britannic Majesty as a non-compliance on our part with the engagement contained in the 4th, 5th, and 6th articles of the treaty, induced him to suspend the execution of the 7th, and render a separate discussion of them inadmissible.

[Supporting documents follow.]

Hammond to Jefferson, Philadelphia, March 5, 1792

In conformity to the mode which you have pursued and suggested, I have now the honor of submitting to you an abstract of such particular acts of the United States as appear to me infractions, on their part, of the definitive treaty of peace, concluded between the King, my master, and the United States. The necessity of collecting from distant parts of this continent the requisite materials, of combining and arranging them, has occasioned a much longer delay in presenting to you this abstract than I at first apprehended. I trust, however, that it will be found so comprehensive as to include every cause of complaint, resulting from the treaty, and so fully substantiated as to require no subsequent elucidations to prove and to confirm the facts which I shall specify.

Many of the legislative acts and judicial determinations, which I shall adduce as violations of the treaty, having been common to a majority of the States, I have thought it expedient, in order to avoid repetitions, not to discuss the tendency and extent of their operation in the several States distinctly and separately, but to reduce the infractions under general heads, and to throw into the form of an appendix references to justify and explain the documents by which they are authenticated.

Although I have employed every exertion in my power to acquire the most accurate and general information upon the respective points comprehended in this abstract, it is still possible, that many materials may have been out of my reach, or that, in the extensive collection of laws and of other documents which I have been obliged to peruse and digest, many objects may have escaped my notice. It is possible, that acts of the States, of which I have complained, as militating against the treaty of peace, may have been repealed or modified by succeeding Legislatures; and that decisions of the State courts, which I have alleged as violations of the treaty, may have been rectified by subsequent determinations. I am not conscious of any errors or misrepresentations of this nature; but if any such should exist in the abstract, I desire you, sir, to be persuaded, that they have been totally unintentional on my part, and that I shall be extremely solicitous to have them explained and corrected.

Immediately after the ratification of the definitive treaty of peace, the Congress of the United States, by a proclamation, announcing that event, and by a resolve, dated 14th Jan. 1784, required and enjoined all bodies of magistracy, legislative, executive, and judiciary, to carry into effect the definitive articles, and every clause and sentence thereof, sincerely, strictly, and completely; and earnestly recommended to the Legislatures of the respective States to provide for the restitution of all estates, rights, and properties, confiscated, belonging to real British subjects, and of estates, rights, and properties, of persons resident in districts in possession of his Majesty's arms, between the 30th Nov. 1782, and 14th Jan. 1784, who had not borne arms against the United States; and that persons of any other description should have liberty to go to any part of the United States, to remain twelve months, unmolested in their endeavors to obtain the restitution of their estates, rights, and properties, confiscated. It was also recommended to the several States to reconsider and revise all laws regarding the premises, so as to render them perfectly consistent with justice and that spirit of conciliation, which, on the return of the blessings of peace, should universally prevail; and it was farther recommended, that the estates, rights, and properties, of such last mentioned persons should be restored to them, they refunding the bona fide price, paid on purchasing any of the said lands, rights, and properties, since the confiscation.

In consequence of the little attention which had been manifested to this proclamation and recommendation, and of the answer given, (20th Feb. 1786) by the Marquis of Carmarthen, to the requisitions of Mr. Adams, respecting the posts and territories, ceded by the treaty of peace to the United States, the Congress transmitted, in April, 1787, a circular letter to the Governors of the respective States, recommending it to the different Legislatures to repeal such acts, or parts of acts, as were repugnant to the treaty of peace between his Britannic Majesty and the United States, or any article thereof, and that the courts of law and equity should be directed and required, in all causes and questions cognizable by them respectively, and arising from, or touching the said treaty, to decide and adjudge according to the tenor, true intent, and meaning, of the same, any thing in the said acts or parts of acts to the contrary thereof in any wise notwithstanding.

In this circular letter, after enforcing in the most energetic manner the regard due to solemn national compacts, and the impropriety of the individual States attempting to contravene, or even discuss stipulations, which had been sanctioned by their General Government, the Congress further declare, "they have deliberately and dispassionately examined and considered the several facts and matters urged by Great Britain as infractions of the treaty of peace, on the part of America; and regret, that, in some of the States, too little attention appears to have been paid to the public faith, pledged by the treaty."

It is observable that Congress, neither in this proclamation nor recommendation, take any notice of the fourth article of the treaty of peace, by which it was *agreed* that creditors on either side should meet with no lawful impediment to the recovery of the full value, in sterling money, of all bona fide debts, theretofore contracted; nor does either the proclamation or recommendation extend to the stipulations in the close of the fifth article, whereby it was *agreed* that all persons who have any interests in confiscated lands, either by debts, marriage settlements, or otherwise, should meet with no lawful impediment in the prosecution of their just rights.

This omission of these essential points can only be ascribed to the conviction that Congress entertained, that it was totally unnecessary to specify them, as they were stipulations positive and obligatory upon the individual States, and that no local regulation was competent either to confirm or invalidate them. It does not, however, appear that this proclamation and recommendation had any general and extensive effect upon the Legislatures of the respective States, as, in consequence thereof, even the formality of a municipal adoption of the treaty, either in the nature of a repeal of existing laws, repugnant to the treaty of peace, or of a declaratory law, establishing the treaty of peace as the supreme law of the land, seems to have been confined to a small portion of the several States.

Having thus stated the measures pursued by Congress to give validity and effect to the engagements contained in the treaty of peace, it is now expedient to specify in detail the particular acts which Great Britain considers as infractions of the treaty on the part of the United States; and it will tend to simplify the discussion, to make the following arrangement:

I. To define what Congress has enforced or omitted.

II. To advert to the conduct observed by the individual States generally, in respect to the treaty of peace—

In not repealing laws that existed antecedently to the pacification;

In enacting laws, subsequent to the peace, in contravention of the treaty;

And in the decisions of the State courts upon questions affecting the rights of British subjects.

As to the first of these points, it cannot be presumed that the commissioners, who negotiated the treaty of peace, would engage in behalf of Congress to make recommendations to the Legislatures of the respective States, which they did not expect to be effectual, or enter into direct stipulations, which they had not the power to enforce. And yet the laws were not repealed which Congress recommended to be repealed, nor were the stipulations enforced which Congress was absolutely pledged to fulfil. It does not appear that any of the State Legislatures repealed their confiscation laws, or provided for the restitution of all estates, rights, and properties, of real British subjects, which had been confiscated, and of persons resident in districts in the possession of his Majesty's arms, who had not borne arms against the United States; that persons of other descriptions were at liberty to remain twelve months in the United States, unmolested in their endeavors to obtain the restoration of their confiscated estates, rights, and properties; that the acts of the several States which respected confiscations, were in many of the States reconsidered or revised; nor, finally, have British creditors been countenanced or supported, either by the respective Legislatures, or by the State courts, in their endeavors to recover the full value of debts, contracted antecedently to the treaty of peace. On the contrary, in some of the States, the confiscation laws have been acted upon since the peace, and new legislative regulations have been established to carry them into effect. In many of the States, the subjects of the crown, in endeavoring to obtain the restitution of their forfeited estates and property, upon refunding the price to the purchasers, have been treated with indignity, menaced, exposed to personal danger, and in some instances imprisoned. Prosecutions have been commenced against his Majesty's subjects for the part which they had taken in the late war. In many of the States, laws have actually passed, delaying the legal investigation of just claims, and abridging the demands of British merchants. Local regulations, in respect to the tender of property, in discharge of just debts, have prevailed to such an extent, as to amount to a prohibition of suits. Paper money, emitted by particular States, has been made, at its nominal value, legal tender and payment for all debts, for the recovery of which actions were commenced at the time when money of that description was greatly depreciated. Creditors, too, in some of the States, were exposed to the necessity of taking real or personal property, at a valuation made by a partial, prejudiced, or interested neighborhood, while, in other States, when the question of alienage has been under discussion, the courts of law and equity have determined, that a subject of Great Britain, residing within the King's dominions, at and after the declaration of independence, was not competent to acquire or hold real property within the United States. In many of the State courts, decisions have taken place, reducing the amount of British debts, in violation of the terms of the original contracts, and some of those courts have positively refused to take cognizance of suits instituted for the recovery of British debts. These facts will be more fully illustrated under the next head of arrangement.

II. To advert to the conduct observed by the individual States, generally, in respect to the treaty of peace.

1st. In not repealing the laws that existed antecedently to the pacification. . . . [Substantiating details follow. Ed.]

2d. In enacting laws subsequent to the peace in contravention of the treaty.

In stating the particular acts that relate to this head of arrangement, it will be proper to place them in three classes.

1. Such as relate to the estates of the loyalists.

2. Such as respect their persons; and lastly,

3. Such as obstruct the recovery of debts due to the subjects of the crown. . . . [Substantiating details follow. Ed.]

From the foregoing detail, it is evident, that the recommendations of Congress to the respective State Legislatures have, in some of the States, been totally disregarded, and in none have produced that complete and extensive effect, which Great Britain, from the stipulations of the treaty, was perfectly justifiable in expecting and requiring; that, since the peace, many of the States have passed laws in direct contravention of the definitive treaty, and essentially injurious to the estates, rights, and properties, of British subjects, in whose favor precise distinctions were clearly defined and expressed in the treaty; that, although some of the States may have repealed their exceptionable laws partially or generally, yet, in a majority of the States, they still exist in full force and validity; and that, in some of the State courts, actions have been commenced and prosecuted with success, against individuals, for the part they had taken in the war, which actions were, in their origin, positive contraventions of the 6th article of the treaty, and, in their consequences, materially detrimental to the rights and property of many subjects of the crown of Great Britain. In consequence of the violation of the treaty in these particulars, great numbers of his Majesty's subjects have been reduced to a state of penury and distress, and the nation of Great Britain has been involved in the payment to them of no less a sum than four millions sterling, as a partial compensation for the losses they had sustained.

It is further manifest, that the stipulation of the fourth article of the treaty, which provides for the recovery of the debts due to the subjects of the two countries respectively, has been not only evaded in many of the States, but that municipal regulations have been established in them, in avowed contravention of it, and that, in many instances, the means and prospect of obtaining redress are nearly as remote as ever; since, in one State, in which a sum far exceeding one million sterling, is still due to British creditors, the supreme federal court has thought proper to suspend, for many months, the final judgment on an action of debt brought by a British creditor; and, since, in the same State, the county courts (which alone can take cognizance of debts of a limited amount) have uniformly rejected all suits instituted for the recovery of sums due to the subjects of the crown of Great Britain.

The delay which has arisen in the administration of justice, has, with equal propriety, been stated as equivalent to an infraction of the treaty: for, by the effect of that delay, many descriptions of his Majesty's subjects have been exposed, not only to material inconvenience, but, in various cases, to the ruin and absolute loss of their property. . . .

Such is the nature of the specific facts which the King, my master, has considered as infractions of the treaty on the part of the United States, and, in consequence of which, his Majesty has deemed it expedient to suspend the full execution, on his part, of the 7th article of that treaty. On this head, also, it is necessary to premise the following evident distinction: that the King has contented himself with a mere suspension of that article of the treaty; whereas, the United States have not only withheld from subjects of the crown that re-dress to which they were entitled, under the terms of the treaty, but, also, many of the States have, subsequent to the peace, passed new legislative regulations, in violation of the treaty, and imposing additional hardships on individuals, whom the national faith of the United States was pledged, under precise and solemn stipulations, to ensure and protect from future injury.

On the grounds, therefore, of the irreparable injury which many classes of his subjects have sustained, and of the heavy expense to which the British nation has been subjected by the non-performance of their engagements, on the part of the United States, the measure that the King has adopted (of delaying his compliance with the 7th article of the treaty) is perfectly justifiable. Nevertheless, his Majesty's sincere desire to remove every occasion of mis-understanding, has induced him to direct me to express his readiness to enter into a negotiation with respect to those articles of the treaty, which have not been executed by the two countries, respectively, and to consent to such arrangements upon the subject, as, after due examination, may now be found to be of mutual convenience, and not inconsistent with the just claims and rights of his subjects.

[Supporting appendices follow. Ed.]

Treaty of Amity, Commerce, and Navigation

The Jay Treaty of 1794 may be taken as the completion of the American struggle for independence. Jay, Chief Justice of the Supreme Court, a friend

---

Treaty of Amity, Commerce, and Navigation between His Britannic Majesty and the United States of America, November 19, 1794, *ibid.,* pp. 520–525.

of Alexander Hamilton, and a leading Federalist, wished ardently for the firm establishment of Anglo-American amity. By 1794, the situation was exceedingly explosive. There were, of course, the long-subsisting differences over both the treaty of peace and the Indian war. In addition, there were the even more volatile issues: the French Revolution and the war between Britain and France. The United States trying to pursue its course as a neutral power found maritime trade suffering from both belligerents. Irritation against Britain far outstripped that against France, however, since British maritime power and Anglo-American trade were so much greater.

Jay's mission partook indeed of the nature of a last-ditch effort to save the peace with Britain. That he went to London at all was no small triumph for the Federalists—no little chagrin to the Republicans. The treaty which he negotiated with Secretary of State Lord Grenville, succeeded finally in settling the relations of the two nations on a peaceable and firm basis. The alternative to the treaty would almost certainly have been renewed war with Britain; and in view of political pressures building up inside the new republic, very probably the collapse of the United States as then constituted.

His Britannic Majesty and the United States of America being desirous, by a treaty of amity, commerce, and navigation, to terminate their differences in such a manner, as, without reference to the merits of their respective complaints and pretensions, may be the best calculated to produce mutual satisfaction and good understanding; and also to regulate the commerce and navigation between their respective countries, territories, and people, in such a manner as to render the same reciprocally beneficial and satisfactory . . . have, respectively, named their plenipotentiaries, and given them full powers to treat of, and conclude the said treaty . . .

ART. 1. There shall be a firm, inviolable and universal peace and a true and sincere friendship, between his Britannic Majesty, his heirs and successors, and the United States of America; and between their respective countries, territories, cities, towns, and people, of every degree, without exception of persons or places.

ART. 2. His Majesty will withdraw all his troops and garrisons from all posts and places within the boundary lines assigned by the treaty of peace to the United States. This evacuation shall take place on or before the first day of June, one thousand seven hundred and ninety-six. . . .

ART. 3. It is agreed that it shall at all times be free to His Majesty's subjects, and to the citizens of the United States, and also to the Indians dwelling on either side of the said boundary line, freely to pass and repass, by land, or inland navigation, into the respective territories and countries of the two parties, on the continent of America, (the country within the limits of the Hudson's Bay Company only excepted) and to navigate all the lakes, rivers, and waters thereof, and freely to carry on trade and commerce with each other. But, it is understood that this article does not extend to the admission of vessels of the United States into the seaports, harbors, bays, or creeks, of His Majesty's said territories; nor into such parts of the rivers in His Majesty's said territories as are between the mouth thereof and the highest port of entry from the sea, except in small vessels trading bona fide between Montreal and Quebec, under such regulations as shall be established to prevent the possibility of any frauds in this respect. Nor to the admission of British vessels from the sea into the rivers of the United States, beyond the highest ports of entry for foreign vessels from the sea. The river Mississippi shall, however, according to the treaty of peace, be entirely open to both parties; and it is further agreed that all the ports and places on its eastern side, to whichsoever of the parties belonging, may freely be resorted to and used by both parties, in as ample a manner as any of the Atlantic ports or places of the United States, or any of the ports or places of His Majesty in Great Britain.

All goods and merchandise whose importation into His Majesty's said territories in America shall not be entirely prohibited, may freely, for the purposes of commerce, be carried into the same in the manner aforesaid, by the citizens of the United States, and such goods and merchandise shall be subject to no higher or other duties than would be payable by His Majesty's subjects on the importation of the same from Europe into the said territories. And in like manner, all goods and merchandise whose importation into the United States shall not be wholly prohibited, may freely, for the purposes of commerce, be carried into the same, in the manner aforesaid, by His Majesty's subjects, and such goods and merchandise shall be subject to no higher or other duties than would be payable by the citizens of the United States on the importation of the same in American vessels into the Atlantic ports of the said States. And all goods not prohibited to be exported from the said territories respectively, may, in like manner, be carried out of the same by the two parties, respectively, paying duty as aforesaid.

No duty of entry shall ever be levied by either party on peltries brought by land, or inland navigation, into the said territories, respectively, nor shall the Indians passing or repassing with their own proper goods and effects, of whatever nature, pay for the same any impost or duty whatever. But goods in bales, or other large packages, unusual among Indians, shall not be considered as goods belonging bona fide to Indians.

No higher or other tolls or rates of ferriage than what are or shall be payable by natives, shall be demanded on either side; and no duties shall be payable on any goods which shall merely be carried over any of the portages or carrying places on either side, for the purpose of being immediately reimbarked and carried to some other place or places. But as, by this stipulation, it is only meant to secure to each party a free passage across the portages on both sides, it is agreed that this exemption from duty shall extend only to such goods as are carried in the usual and direct road across the portage, and are not attempted to be in any manner sold or exchanged during their passage across same; and proper regulations may be established to prevent the possibility of any frauds in this respect.

As this article is intended to render in a great degree, the local advantages of each party common to both, and thereby to promote a disposition favorable to friendship and good neighborhood, it is agreed that the respective Governments will mutually promote this amicable intercourse, by causing speedy and impartial justice to be done, and necessary protection to be extended to all who may be concerned therein.

ART. 4. Whereas it is uncertain whether the river Mississippi extends so far to the northward as to be intersected by a line to be drawn due west from the Lake of the Woods, in the manner mentioned in the treaty of peace between His Majesty and the United States, it is agreed that measures shall be taken in concert between His Majesty's Government in America and the Government of the United States for making a joint survey of the said river, from one degree of latitude below the falls of St. Anthony, to the principal source or sources of the said river, and also of the parts adjacent thereto; and that if, on the result of such survey, it should appear that the said river would not be intersected by such a line as is above mentioned, the two parties will thereupon proceed, by amicable negotiation, to regulate the boundary line in that quarter, as well as all other points to be adjusted between the said parties, according to justice and mutual convenience, and in conformity to the intent of the said treaty.

ART. 5. Whereas doubts have arisen what river was truly intended under the name of the river St. Croix, mentioned in the said treaty of peace, and forming a part of the boundary therein described, that question shall be referred to the final decision of commissioners, to be appointed in the following manner, viz:

One commissioner shall be named by His Majesty, and one by the President of the United States, by and with the advice and consent of the Senate thereof, and the said two commissioners shall agree on the choice of a third; or, if they cannot so agree, they shall each propose one person, and of the two names so proposed, one shall be drawn by lot in the presence of the two original commissioners. . . .

ART. 6. Whereas it is alleged by divers British merchants, and others, His Majesty's subjects, that debts to a considerable amount, which were bona fide contracted before the peace, still remain owing to them by citizens or inhabitants of the United States, and that, by the operation of various lawful impediments since the peace, not only the full recovery of the said debts has been delayed, but also the value and security thereof have been in several instances impaired and lessened, so that, by the ordinary course of judicial proceedings, the British creditors cannot now obtain, and actually have and receive full and adequate compensation for such losses and damages which they have thereby sustained, it is agreed that, in all such cases, where full compensation for such losses and damages cannot, for whatever reason, be actually obtained, had, and received, by the said creditors, in the ordinary course of justice, the United States will make full and complete compensation for the same to the said creditors; but it is distinctly understood that this provision is to extend to such losses only as have been occasioned by the lawful impediments aforesaid, and is not to extend to losses occasioned by such insolvency of the debtors, or other causes, as would equally have operated to produce such loss, if the said impediments had not existed, nor to such losses or damages as have been occasioned by the manifest delay or negligence, or wilful omission, of the claimant.

For the purpose of ascertaining the amount of any such losses and damages, five commissioners shall be appointed, and authorized to meet and act in manner following, viz. Two of them shall be appointed by His Majesty, two of them by the President of the United States, by and with the advice and consent of the Senate thereof, and the fifth by the unanimous voice of the other four; and if they should not agree in such choice, then the commissioners named by the two parties shall respectively propose one person and of the two names so proposed one shall be drawn by lot, in the presence of the four original commissioners. . . .

ART. 7. Whereas complaints have been made by divers merchants and other citizens of the United States, that, during the course of the war in which His Majesty is now engaged, they have sustained considerable losses and damage, by reason of irregular or illegal captures or condemnations of their vessels and other property, under color of authority or commissions from His Majesty; and that, from various circumstances belonging to the said cases, adequate compensation for the losses and damages so sustained cannot now be actually obtained, had, and received, by the ordinary course of judicial proceedings; it is agreed that, in all such cases where adequate compensation cannot, for whatever reason, be now actually obtained, had, and received, by the said merchants and others, in the ordinary course of justice, full and complete compensation for the same will be made by the British Government to the said complainants. But it is distinctly understood that this provision is not to extend to such losses or damages as have been occasioned by the manifest delay or negligence, or wilful omission, of the claimant.

That, for the purpose of ascertaining the amount of any such losses and damages, five commissioners shall be appointed, and authorized to act in London, exactly in the manner directed with respect to those mentioned in the preceding article. . . .

And whereas certain merchants and others, His Majesty's subjects, complain that, in the course of the war, they have sustained loss and damage, by reason of the capture of their vessels and merchandise, taken within the limits and jurisdiction of the States, and brought into the ports of the same, or taken by vessels originally armed in ports of the said States, it is agreed that, in all such cases, where restitution shall not have been made agreeably to the tenor of the letter from Mr. Jefferson to Mr. Hammond, dated at Philadelphia, September 5, 1793, a copy of which is annexed to this treaty, the complaints of the parties shall be, and hereby are, referred to the commissioners to be appointed by virtue of this article, who are hereby authorized and required to proceed, in the like manner, relative to these as to the other cases committed to them; and the United States undertake to pay to the complainants or claimants, in specie, without deduction, the amount of such sums as shall be awarded to them respectively by the said commissioners. . . .

Art. 9. It is agreed that British subjects, who now hold lands in the territories of the United States, and American citizens, who now hold lands in the dominions of His Majesty, shall continue to hold them according to the nature and tenure of their respective estates and titles therein; and may grant, sell, or devise, the same, to whom they please, in like manner as if they were natives; and that neither they, nor their heirs or assigns, shall, so far as may respect the said lands, and the legal remedies incident thereto, be regarded as aliens.

Art. 10. Neither the debts due from individuals of the one nation to individuals of the other, nor shares, nor moneys which they may have in the public funds, or in the public or private banks, shall ever, in any event of war or national differences, be sequestered or confiscated; it being unjust and impolitic that debts and engagements contracted and made by individuals, having confidence in each other and in their respective Governments, should ever be destroyed or impaired by national authority, on account of national differences and discontents.

Art. 11. It is agreed, between His Majesty and the United States of America, that there shall be a reciprocal and entirely perfect liberty of navigation and commerce between their respective people, in the manner, under the limitations, and on the conditions, specified in the following articles:

Art. 12. His Majesty consents that it shall and may be lawful, during the time hereinafter limited, for the citizens of the United States to carry to any of His Majesty's islands and ports in the West Indies, from the United States, in their own vessels, not being above the burthen of seventy tons, any goods or merchandises, being of the growth, manufacture, or produce, of the said States, which it is or may be lawful to carry to the said islands or ports, from the said States, in British vessels; and that the said American vessels shall be subject there to no other or higher tonnage duties or charges than shall be payable by British vessels in the ports of the United States; and that the cargoes of the said American vessels shall be subject there to no other or higher duties or charges than shall be payable on the like articles if imported there from the said States in British vessels.

And His Majesty also consents that it shall be lawful for the said American citizens to purchase, load, and carry away, in their said vessels, to the United States, from the said islands and ports, all such articles, being of the growth, manufacture, or produce, of the said islands, as may now by law be carried from thence to the said States in British vessels, and subject only to the same duties and charges, on exportation, to which British vessels and their cargoes are, or shall be, subject, in similar circumstances.

Provided always, That the said American vessels do carry and land their cargoes in the United States only; it being expressly agreed and declared that, during the continuance of this article, the United States will prohibit and restrain the carrying [of] any molasses, sugar, coffee, cocoa, or cotton, in American vessels, either from His Majesty's islands, or from the United States, to any part of the world, except the United States, reasonable sea stores excepted. *Provided also,* That it shall and may be lawful, during the same period, for British vessels to import from the said islands into the United States, and to export from the United States to the said islands, all articles whatever, being of the growth, produce, or manufacture, of the said islands, or of the United States, respectively, which now may, by the laws of the said States, be so imported and exported. And that the cargoes of the said British vessels shall be subject to no other or higher duties, or charges, than shall be payable on the same articles if so imported or exported in American vessels.

It is agreed that this article, and every matter and thing therein contained, shall continue to be in force during the continuance of the war in which His Majesty is now engaged; and also for two years from and after the day of the signature of the preliminary or other articles of peace by which the same may be terminated.

And it is further agreed that, at the expiration of the said term, the two contracting parties will endeavor further to regulate their commerce in this respect, according to the situation in which His Majesty may then find himself, with respect to the West Indies, and with a view to such arrangements as may best conduce to the mutual advantage and extension of commerce. And the said parties will then also renew their discussions, and endeavor to agree whether, in any, and what, cases neutral vessels shall protect enemy's property; and in what cases provisions and other articles, not generally contraband, may become such. But, in the mean time, their conduct towards each other in these respects shall be regulated by the articles hereinafter inserted on those subjects.

ART. 13. His Majesty consents that the vessels belonging to the citizens of the United States of America shall be admitted, and hospitably received, in all the seaports and harbors of the British territories in the East Indies; and that the citizens of the said United States may freely carry on a trade between the said territories and the said United States in all articles of which the importation or exportation, respectively, to or from the said territories, shall not be entirely prohibited. . . . The citizens of the United States may also touch for refreshment at the island of St. Helena, but subject in all respects to such regulations as the British Government may from time to time establish there.

ART. 14. There shall be, between all the dominions of His Majesty in Europe, and the territories of the United States, a reciprocal and perfect liberty of commerce and navigation. . . .

ART. 15. It is agreed that no other or higher duties shall be paid by the ships or merchandise of the one party in the ports of the other, than such as are paid by the like vessels or merchandise of all other nations. . . .

But the British Government reserves to itself the right of imposing on American vessels, entering into the British ports in Europe, a tonnage duty equal to that which shall be payable by British vessels in the ports of America; and also such duty as may be adequate to countervail the difference of duty now payable on the importation of European and Asiatic goods, when imported into the United States in British or in American vessels.

The two parties agree to treat for the more exact equalization of the duties on the respective navigation of their subjects and people, in such manner as may be most beneficial to the two countries. The arrangements for this purpose shall be made at the same time with those mentioned at the conclusion of the twelfth article of this treaty, and are to be considered as a part thereof. In the interval, it is agreed that the United States will not impose any new or additional tonnage duties on British vessels, nor increase the now subsisting difference between the duties payable on the importation of any articles in British or in American vessels.

ART. 16. It shall be free for the two contracting parties, respectively, to appoint consuls for the protection of trade, to reside in the dominions and territories aforesaid. . . .

[Articles 17 through 26 deal with matters arising chiefly from the state of hostilities among the European powers and the position of the United States as a neutral. Article 27 regulated the extradition of criminals. Ed.]

ART. 28. It is agreed that the first ten articles of this treaty shall be permanent, and that the subsequent articles, except the twelfth, shall be limited in their duration to twelve years, to be computed from the day on which the ratifications of this treaty shall be exchanged, but subject to this condition, that, whereas the said twelfth article will expire, by the limitation therein contained, at the end of two years from the signing of the preliminary or other articles of peace which shall terminate the present war in which His Majesty is engaged, it is agreed that proper measures shall, by concert, be taken, for bringing the subject of that article into amicable treaty and discussion, so early before the expiration of the said term, as that new arrangements on that head may, by that time, be perfected, and ready to take place. But, if it should, unfortunately, happen, that His Majesty and the United States should not be able to agree on such new arrangements, in that case all the articles of this treaty, except the first ten, shall then cease and expire together.

Lastly. This treaty, when the same shall have been ratified by His Majesty, and by the President of the United States, by and with the advice and consent of their Senate, and the respective ratifications mutually exchanged, shall be binding and obligatory on His Majesty and on the said States, and shall be by them respectively executed and observed, with punctuality and the most sincere regard to good faith. And whereas it will be expedient, in order the better to facilitate intercourse, and obviate difficulties, that other articles be proposed and added to this treaty, which articles, from want of time and other circumstances, cannot now be perfected, it is agreed that the said parties will, from time to time, readily treat of and concerning such articles, and will sincerely endeavor so to form them as that they may conduce to mutual convenience, and tend to promote mutual satisfaction and friendship; and that the said articles, after having been duly ratified, shall be added to, and make a part of, this treaty.

JOHN JAY, *Letter to Secretary Randolph*

In view of the enormous furor in the United States which greeted Jay's treaty, his own explanation of his work is particularly important. The riots and emotional outbursts from the Jeffersonian Republicans notwithstanding, it is impossible not to conclude that his treaty saved the peace and very probably the independence of the United States.

The long expected treaty accompanies this letter. . . .

My opinion of the treaty is apparent from my having signed it. I have no reason to believe or conjecture that one more favorable to us is attainable.

John Jay to Secretary Randolph, London, November 19, 1794, *ibid.*, pp. 503–504.

Perhaps it is not very much to be regretted that all our differences are merged in this treaty, without having been decided; disagreeable imputations are thereby avoided, and the door of conciliation is fairly and widely opened, by the *essential* justice done, and the conveniences granted to each other by the parties.

The term limited for the evacuation of the posts could not be restricted to a more early day; that point has been pressed. The reasons which caused an inflexible adherence to that term, I am persuaded, were these, viz: That the traders have spread through the Indian nations goods to a great amount; that the returns for those goods cannot be drawn into Canada at an earlier period; that the impression which the surrender of all the posts to American garrisons will make on the minds of the Indians cannot be foreseen. On a former occasion it was intimated to them (not very delicately) that they had been forsaken, and given up to the United States; that the protection promised on our part, however sincere, and however, in other respects, competent, cannot entirely prevent those embarrassments which, without our fault, may be occasioned by the war; that, for these reasons, the traders ought to have time to conclude their adventures, which were calculated on the existing state of things; they will afterwards calculate on the new state of things: but that, in the mean time, the care of Government should not be withdrawn from them.

The third article will, I presume, appear to you in a favorable light; a number of reasons which, in my judgment, are solid, support it. I think they will, on consideration, become obvious. It was proposed and urged that the commercial intercourse opened by this article ought to be exempted from all duties whatever on either side. The inconveniences which we should experience from such a measure were stated and examined; it was finally agreed to subject it to native duties. In this compromise, which I consider as being exactly right, that difficulty terminated; but for this compromise the whole article would have failed, and every expectation of an amicable settlement been frustrated. A continuance of trade with the Indians was a decided ultimatum; much time and paper, and many conferences were employed in producing this article; that part of it which respects the ports and places on the eastern side of the Mississippi, if considered in connexion with the—article in the treaty of peace, and with the article in this treaty which directs a survey of that river to be made, will, I think, appear unexceptionable.

In discussing the question about the river St. Croix, before the commissioners, I apprehend the old French claims will be revived; we must adhere to Mitchell's map. The Vice President perfectly understands this business.

The 6th article was a *sine qua non*, and is intended as well as calculated to afford that justice and equity which judicial proceedings may, on trial, be found incapable of affording. That the commissioners may do exactly what is right, they are to determine according to the merits of the several cases, having a due regard to all the circumstances, and as justice and equity shall appear to them to require.

It is very much to be regretted that a more summary method than the one indicated in the seventh article could not have been devised and agreed upon for settling the capture cases; every other plan was perplexed with difficulties, which frustrated it. Permit me to hint the expediency of aiding the claimants, by employing a gentleman, at the public expense, to oversee and manage the causes of such of them as cannot conveniently have agents of their own here; and whether, in some cases, pecuniary assistance might not be proper. I do not consider myself at liberty to make such an appointment, nor to enter into any such pecuniary engagements. It would, probably, be more easy to find a proper person on your side of the water than on this. Here there are few fit for the business, and willing to undertake it, who (having many affairs of their own to attend to) would not be tempted to consider the business of the claimants in a secondary light; several objections to giving him a fixed salary are obvious; in my opinion a moderate commission on the sums to be recovered and received, would be a more eligible method of compensating him for his services. Our consul here talks, and, I believe, in earnest, of returning to America, or I should expect much advantage from his zeal and endeavors to serve such of the claimants as might commit their business to his management.

You will find in the 8th article, a stipulation which, in effect, refers the manner of paying the commissioners very much to our election. I prefer paying them jointly; the objection to it is, that the English pay high. I have always doubted the policy of being penny-wise.

The Lord Chancellor has prepared an article respecting the mutual admission of evidence, &c. which we have not had time fully to consider and decide upon; it contains a clause to abolish alienism between the two countries. His lordship's conduct and conversation indicate the most friendly disposition towards us; a copy of his article shall be sent, and I wish to receive precise instructions on that head.

The credit of some of the States having, to my knowledge, suffered by appearances of their being favorable to the idea of sequestrating British debts on certain occasions, the 10th article will be useful. Persons wishing to invest their property in our funds and banks, have frequently applied to me to be informed whether they might do it without risk of confiscation or sequestration; my answer has been uniform, viz: that, in my opinion, such measures would be improper, and therefore, that, in my opinion, they would not be adopted; some pressed me for assurances, but I have declined giving any.

The 12th article, admitting our vessels of seventy tons and under, into the British Islands in the West Indies, affords occasion for several explanatory remarks. It became connected with a proposed stipulation for the abolition of all alien duties, of every kind, between the two countries. This proposition was pressed, but strong objections opposed my agreeing to it; a satisfactory statement of the negotiation on this point would be prolix; at present, I cannot form a very concise one, for that would not require less time: the selection and arrangement necessary in making abridgments, cannot be hastily performed. The duration of this article is short, but if we meet the disposition of this country to good humor and cordiality, I am much inclined to believe it will be renewed; the duration of the treaty is connected with the renewal of that article, and an opportunity will then offer for discussing and settling many important matters.

The article which opens the British ports in the East Indies to our vessels and cargoes, needs no comment. It is a manifestation and proof of good will towards us.

The questions about the cases in which alone provisions become contraband, and the question whether, and how far, neutral ships protect enemy's property, have been the subjects of much trouble, and many fruitless discussions. That Britain, at this period, and involved in war, should not admit principles which would impeach the propriety of her conduct in seizing provisions bound to France, and enemy's property on board of neutral vessels, does not appear to me extraordinary. The articles, as they now stand, secure compensation for seizures, and leave us at liberty to decide whether they were made in such cases as to be warranted by the *existing* law of nations; as to the principles we contend for, you will find them saved in the conclusion of the 12th article, from which it will appear that we still adhere to them. . . .

I must draw this letter to a conclusion; Lord Grenville is anxious to dismiss the packet as soon as possible. . . .

It is desirable that I should have the earliest advice of the ratification; and be enabled to finish whatever may be expected of me, in season to return in one of the first spring vessels. My health is not competent to a winter's voyage, or I should be the bearer of the treaty. This climate does not agree with me, and the less so on account of the application and confinement to which it was necessary for me to submit.

It will give you pleasure to hear that great reserve and delicacy has been observed respecting our concerns with France. The stipulation in favor of existing treaties was agreed to without hesitation; not an expectation, nor even a wish has been expressed that our conduct towards France should be otherwise than fair and friendly. In a word, I do not know how the negotiation could have been conducted, on their part, with more delicacy, friendliness, and propriety, than it has been from first to last.